LUCERNE VALLEY

A Wild West Town of Character(s)

2nd Edition

Cover photo captions from left to right:
Baldridge Cabin in Cove; Oil Derrick South of Rabbit Dry Lake; Homestead Bakery;
Turner family at Willow Well; Crane at Texas Granite Quarry; Teacher Olga Johnson Rosenau;
Lucerne Valley School House; Junie Gobar's Manure Spreader; Box S Ranch;
Virginia Hemphill's Cabin Techatticup

This book is only a sketch of a little town called Lucerne Valley –pictures of school houses, old business fronts, and landmarks. All towns are a compilation or the sum of these parts, but the heart and reason for the town is the people: those who first decided to come here. What were their goals, and motivations, their character, their personality? Do these early pioneers still have family here, or was their presence fleeting? What did they add to or take from this small dot on the map of California?

Secondary, but no less important, is the setting of this place we call the Crossroads of the High Desert. What attracted the early residents? Was it the climate, the views, the opportunities or lack thereof? What drew people back then and what brings them here now?

What makes this town stand out to those who choose to make it their home? Why do some live 50, 60, even 90 years in this little valley nestled at 3,000 feet between the towering, tree covered San Bernardino Mountains to the south and the rocky Granite and Ord Mountains to the North?

There are still a few old timers here to share their stories, as well as the written tales of some hardy, early independent settlers from as early as the 1800s. We hope these stories will reveal some of the treasures that make up this little jewel of a town called Lucerne Valley.

Again, this is only a sketch, to fully appreciate all the facets of this little jewel in the desert, you must spend time here; mingle with the local characters and color. Sit and watch the sun set over Strawberry Peak, while the quail and mockingbirds settle in for the night. Experience each season as it comes, the spring winds that knock remnants of last year's leaves from the trees, making room the new buds to emerge. The hot heat of summer, tempered with the scant monsoon rains that scent the air with creosote. Savor the fruits of your labor on the porch each fall evening as perfect balmy weather slowly slips into the chilly but mild desert winters full of sunshine. Come, take the time to enjoy the treasures and the beauty of this little place we call home. ~Editor

ACKNOWLEDGEMENTS

This is by no means a complete or comprehensive list of those who contributed. There were so many past and present historians whose stories we have used and local residents who made themselves available for us to pick their brains, along with those who provided pictures and advice. We are going to try to name as many of them as possible here in no certain order, but we apologize now for those we may have neglected to include.

Doris Althouse	Don Fife	Jan Lembright	Allen Redden
Cindy Anderson	Frank Francis	Gary Lister	Clifford Reed
Kathryn Anema	June Francis	Gail Little	Linda Reed
Gertie Baldridge	Julian Gobar	Pat Lugo	Valerie Rice
Louis Basura	Virginia Hemphill-	Bill Mann	Bob Riddle
Chuck Bell	Gobar	Bob McDougall	Linda Riddle
Michelle Boren	Linda Gommel	Gert McDougall	Franz Rishell
Art Bristol	James Goulding	Rugh McLoy	Lee Risler
Jeff Bristol	Cindy Granados	Max McNeely	Jessica Risler
Phillp Brown	Bob Halleck	Janet Miller	Gary Schlenz
Donna Bytheway	Francis Hankin	Billy Mitchell	Debbie Schultz
Harriet Calfee	Kathy Hert	Julie Mitchell	Allan Stanfield
Evelyn Carpenter	Scott Hert	Dave Mount	Roberta Stanfield
Gregg Carpenter	Lynn Dee Hilton	Laura Mount	Carol Tevis
Donna Chandler	Sharon Hoffman	Pattie Muldoon	Karen Thomas
Carolyn Clark	Karen Horst	Ralph Muldoon	Tom Thompson
Sam Clark	John Hudson	Peggy Oliver	Floyd Tidwell
Shirley Clemmons	Fran Jones	Ethel Owen	Georgia Turner
Ron Core	Don Judkins	Charlie Parsons	Pam Turner
Ruth Core	Pat Judkins	Sandy Partin	Barbara Veale
Tom Core	Tonya Judkins	Robert Penn	Scott Wallace
Martha Coutant	Wayne Judkins	Sue Powell	Cliff Walker
Stanley Coutant	Harold Keesee	Dave Phillips	Rev. Richard Wood
Lorraine Cross	Carol LaCroix	Marion Phillips	Gloria Wood
Bob Delperdang	Denise LaCroix	Chuck Rader	Felix Wu
Sara Delperdang	Barbara LaGrange	David Rader	
Donaldson Family	Cindy Lazenby	Martha Rader	
Sally Emerson	Bill Lembright	Millie Rader	

TABLE OF CONTENTS

Chapter 1 – The Early Days

Chapter 2 – Looking for Gold and More

Chapter 3 – Cowpunchers and Clodhoppers

Chapter 4 – Going to school

Chapter 5 – Characters

Chapter 6 – Fighting Fire and Outlaws

Chapter 7 – Need a Job?

Chapter 8 – What the Hicks do for Kicks

Chapter 9 – Let's Go To Church

Chapter 10 – Last Thoughts

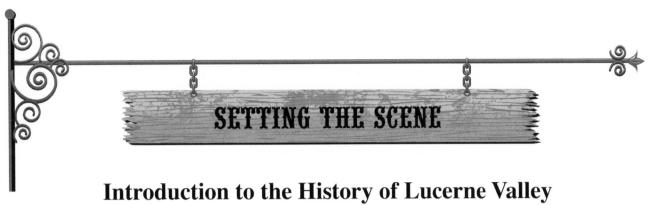

SETTING THE SCENE

Introduction to the History of Lucerne Valley
by Bill Lembright

In 1981, my wife, Jan, and I moved from Reche Canyon, south of Colton to Lucerne Valley to help the Gommels and friends operate Lucerne Valley Market, which at that time was in the former Leo's Market building in the Lucerne Valley Shopping Center, across the parking lot from the liquor store. My personal preference at the time was for green grasses and trees which are not abundant in the desert, but we were convinced God wanted us in Lucerne Valley, so we came anyway.

Sign designed and painted by the late Pete Leibrick. Photo courtesy of Bill Lembright.

Soon, Orville Green, the energetic president of the Lucerne Valley Museum Association talked us into becoming members. Orville led us on several field trips. One notable one was to the Deep Tank petroglyph site. When Orville passed on, Gil Tegelberg, another local historian and famous cactus grower, showed us more historic sites, including the ancient King Clone creosote ring. My aversion to the "boring dry desert" was transforming into an excitement for points of historical and geographical significance waiting to be discovered. In the mountains, points of interest are often hidden by forests, or are in advanced stages of decay accelerated by mold or collapsed under the weight of snow. In the desert, structures are not nearly as susceptible to water and snow damage, tending to last MUCH longer; plus, they're not hidden by trees.

Then we met Chuck Rader, who for a couple of years took us ALL over Lucerne Valley and Johnson Valley. Chuck had a unique driving style. He drove slowly while on pavement and WAY too fast for our 2 wheel drive minivan on dirt and rocky roads or sand. Chuck gave us an overview of Lucerne Valley's interesting past. He taught us to pour over topographic maps and find targets to explore. We pretty much became addicted to exploring the area and have never stopped.

We talked with many of the town's pioneers and increased our knowledge of local history. Often we were told tales difficult to believe. Three people told us of hidden Confederate Army uniforms and silver coins hidden with them. We spent four days off searching for these and other treasures. We discover our targets only part of the time. And I go NUTS over unsolved mysteries!

As an example, several years ago, Barbara Veale told us that while in high school, her class was driven in a school bus all the way to Deep Creek Hot Springs. I've hiked there a few times and know you can't even start to drive there even in a Jeep! When questioned, Barbara insisted it was so and that the bus had traveled on paved road most of the way there from Hesperia. We tried to confirm such a road had existed, but all the old timers we asked said such a road had never existed. SO, Jan and I HAD to investigate. We drove south on Lake Arrowhead Rd., then left on SH173 to the end of pavement where the Pacific Crest

The once paved road from Hesperia to Deep Creek Hot Springs. Photo courtesy of Bill Lembright.

Trail to Deep Creek Hot Springs crosses the road. As we hiked the trail we found lots of old asphalt even with yellow lines painted on it. When the trail reached the creek we saw concrete footings from an old bridge. After hopping on rocks across the creek, we found a section of an old asphalt paved road with yellow lines. The road headed north toward Hesperia and was buried further on by the emergency over-flow earth dam below Lake Silverwood. The pavement also started up Deep Creek but had been removed by heavy equipment or floods. Barbara's story was TRUE!

Years ago a customer dropped us off at a site alongside an old road on the north face of the San Bernardinos. It was an abandoned mine tunnel with an old moonshine still inside that had been destroyed by government agents during the Prohibition years of the 1920s. Over the years I lost the photos I had taken. To retake those photos for this book, it took us three days to rediscover the site as the forest has a way with hiding things and my "photographic" memory seems to have lost its edge.

Another site called "The halfway cabin" by Big Bear historian Tom Core, took four days to discover. The story goes that as the miners fled the 16 foot snowfall and the bitter cold during the Holcomb Valley gold rush they built a cabin on the mountain slopes halfway between Big Bear and Lucerne Valley, in which to overnight. Because of my insatiable curiosity, I searched for ANY written records or clues. Years after first hearing about it, I heard a truck driver who thought he spotted something like a brown cabin hiding in the trees way up the mountain. On our third attempt hiking in, we discovered the cabin in disrepair, but REALLY there! Confirming history through discovery and documentation excites me.

Tracking history is a challenge and so has been the creation of this book. Years ago, I asked a couple of members of our local writers club, Writer's Ink, to consider writing a book on the History of Lucerne Valley. They respectfully declined. A few years later Arcadia Publishing Company asked for someone to volunteer to write one of their short photo and history books on Lucerne Valley. Millie Rader volunteered and I thanked and encouraged her. But then it became apparent that Arcadia's short book format did not allow enough space for the mass of information being gathered on Lucerne Valley history; so, a much larger project was launched and Millie pled for volunteers. NOW I felt on the spot for having pushed Mille to proceed earlier, so Jan and I, who are NOT writers volunteered along with a handful of others, hoping this would be a short-term effort. NOT!

Idealistically, one would think an author could brainstorm the chapters and ask others in the know to write what they remember, then gather those essays, proof read and organize them, then send it all off to a publisher. But, that's not how it works. Almost everyone says, "I would love to, but I'm not a writer." So, we found ourselves setting up interviews, trying to iron out contradictions of details from different contributors, and trying not to offend anyone by saying something that could put their family history in a bad light. The whole task became so burdensome, that we learned to start and finish each meeting by asking God to help and steer us, which is a darned good idea but not something I had expected.

We know that when this book is read by many, that some will speak up and say that they know of errors and omissions. Then we'll wish we had known that before going to print; but, if we wait much longer so as not to omit something or make mistakes, there's a good chance we'll lose momentum and burn out. So we've decided to "sin boldly" and "do something even if we're wrong!" I also hope that writing this book was God's idea and not ours alone. There are so many interesting true stories in this book I haven't taken the time to read, that I'm planning on buying a copy and reading it myself.

Map Use Instructions

Reading Junie Gobar's *Raising The Dust* and Virginia Hemphill-Gobar's *Range One East* left many of us readers wanting to know the location of historic sites and events described in those two classics. So, we researched site locations and have included them on a street map of the business and residential core of Lucerne Valley and on a regional map covering more distant sites. Some sites are well known and documented; others are more debated and we chose what we considered the most likely location based on a variety of clues.

If the site of a photo is on one of the two maps, there is a location number on the lower right below the photo. The first digit is the number of the chapter where the first photo of a map site appears followed by a dash and then the numerical sequence of photo sites in each chapter. An example would be 3-5, which would signify chapter 3, site 5.

Some sites reappear throughout the book since many significant events occurred there. The original photo site number will appear on all those photos of the same geographical site. For example, a photo of Box S is labeled 1-4 because it is the fourth photo in chapter one that is labeled on a map. In every subsequent chapter, all photos at that location are still labeled 1-4.

Not only do we hope you will find this book worthwhile, we hope you will take many tootles and discover the location of the sites where this history occurred.

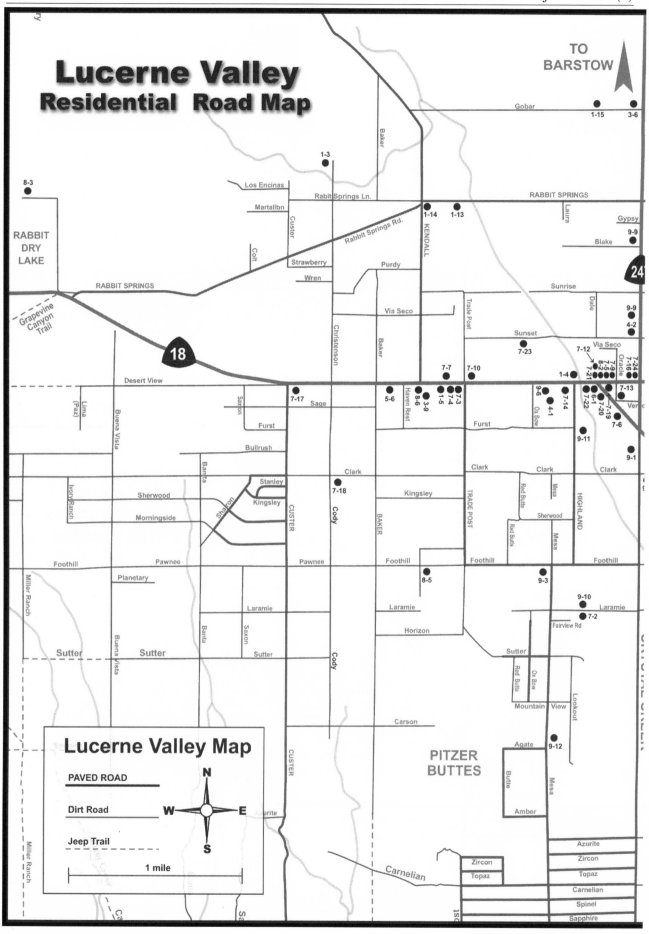

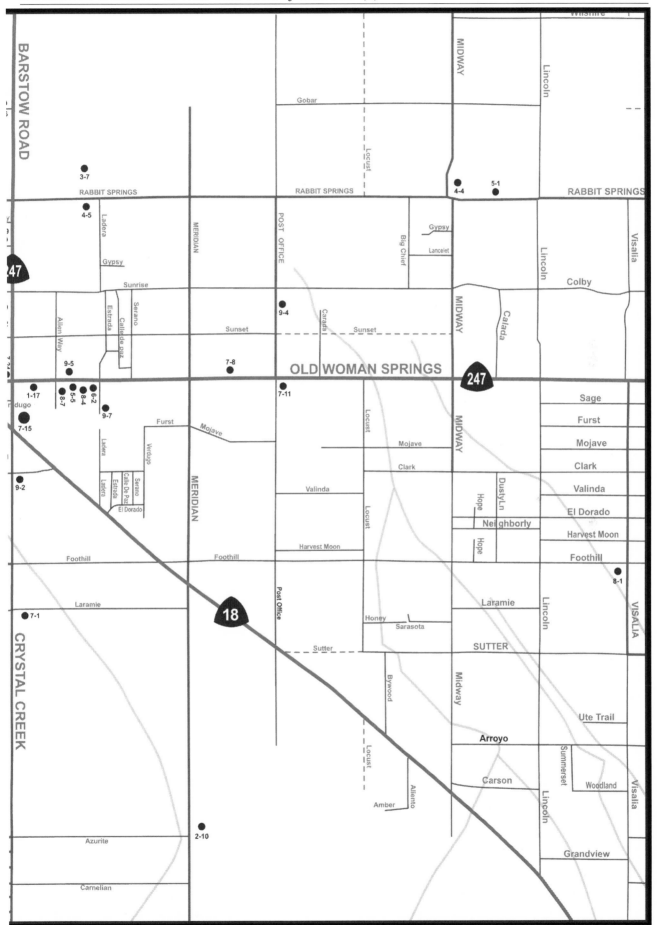

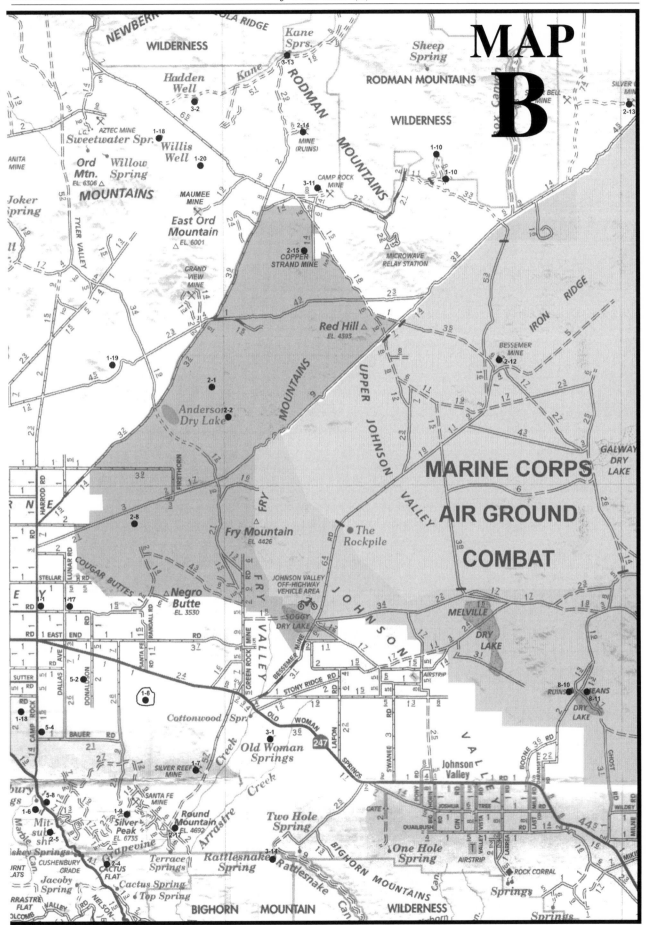

Dedication

We would like to dedicate this book to our God - Father, Son, and Holy Spirit, without whom we likely would have given up on this effort long ago. We're not positive whether this undertaking was His idea or not; but, we hope so.

This undertaking became a much larger project than we ever imagined it would, and there were many times we felt like giving up, but we would ask God for His help and then soldier on. We are elated and thankful to complete it and very appreciative of His help from start to finish.

Why a Second Edition?

The Lucerne Valley Economic Development Association (LVEDA) group that put the first edition of this book together were volunteers who had never put a book together. They worked for six years gathering stories, interviewing the families of early pioneers, and writing more stories. Some of the work had multiple editors and some did not.

After the final story was written this group was tired and ready to get this book on the shelves. Without taking the time to do one final edit they put the book out for sale. It was a few months before they realized that many mistakes had been included and they had to make the hard decision to pull the book from publication and do some very tedious editing.

One bright spot in all of this is that they were able to include one more historical account and some pictures they found after the first edition had been published.

They wish to thank the readers who were very gracious in helping to locate and correct many of the typos, misspelling and names that were wrong.

There may still be further corrections needed, but they hope that you will be able to read and enjoy this work despite its imperfections.

CHAPTER I

The Early Days

Early Settlers

By Millie Rader

It's tough to find the history of early people who only wrote on rocks! But we had a few early pioneers who took the time to record the adventures and hardships of living the early primitive life in this valley.

The first inhabitants of what we now call Lucerne Valley came from many different regions. We have included stories researched by a variety of local writers. Please know, this is not a complete picture of our early settlers; it's not even a snapshot.

The first Native Americans

Lucerne Valley from Grapevine Canyon Rd. 2.5 miles above railroad crossing. Photo courtesy of Bill Lembright.

left signs of their existence at different sites in the valley including on pottery, arrowheads, and potshards. The most notable evidence are the writings left on dark volcanic basalt described in Bill Lembright's article on the petroglyphs, included in this chapter.

In March of 2016, three of our history book team: Cyndie Granados, Lorraine Cross and I traveled to the Dorothy Ramon Learning Center in Banning, California to visit with Cahuilla-Serrano Tribal Elder, Ernest Siva. When we arrived, we found a group of women dissecting a Yucca stalk. They kindly directed us to where Mr. Siva was waiting for us. Later the ladies brought us samples of Yucca heart, the light green, almost white center of the Yucca stalk. It had a fresh, sweet taste.

We enjoyed our visit with Mr. Siva, and though he did not know much of Lucerne Valley's early history, he did share the history of the Yuhaviatam or People of the Pines. His band of indigenous people, are part of the Serrano Tribe that roamed the San Bernardino Mountain area, traveling down into the desert in the fall to harvest pinion nuts and mesquite beans.

According the San Manuel website, www.sanmanuel-nsn.gov/Culture/History, the Yuhaviatam

One of Lucerne Valley's oldest standing houses on Camp Rock Rd. owned by late Pat and Debbie Lane. Photo courtesy of Bill Lembright. B 1-1

were an independent and self-sustaining community. Everything the land provided was held sacred. The first Spanish settlers used "Serrano," the Spanish term for highlander, to identify people of the San Bernardino Mountains. There is also record in other High Desert histories of Vanyume, Paiute and Chemehuevi Tribes who lived peacefully in the area, and moved around with the seasons.

There are traces of Spanish history in the furnace located in the foothills, between the mines of Specialty Minerals and Omya, but we did not find any written history on this group. The area around San Bernardino has history of Spanish missionaries and settlers in the 1800s. They may have sent prospectors over the hill and into our valley. This section also includes interesting reading on the first permanent European settlers as well as others who used our valley for protection.

Photo courtesy of Lucerne Valley Museum Assoc. B 1-2

This 1913 photo shows Carrie Lenter and Clarian Martin Steele standing in front of an old adobe hut built in 1862 at Box Springs Ranch on Highway 18, below Cushenbury Springs. At that time, this hut was known as the oldest structure in the valley. This picture was printed in the January 1958 edition of the *Lucerne Valley Leader* newspaper, with the caption stating the photo was courtesy of Frances Hanken, long time resident and valley historian.

This home was built in the early 1950s by Teresa Farabee pictured here, and her husband Oby with help from various relatives. They purchased the property on Christianson Road, north of Rabbit Springs Road shortly after he retired. She would come to visit on the weekends by bus until she retired from Fullerton Broadcasting in 1954. She then moved to Lucerne Valley fulltime. The first portion

Teresa Farabee. Photo courtesy of Doris Althouse. B 1-3

of the small house was built with wood and had wood siding. They added the front porch later and gave it a stucco finish. Teresa lived to be 102 and lived in this house, on her own, well into her nineties. Teresa's daughter-in-law, Doris Althouse, still lives in the house today.

Quick History of Lucerne Valley

By Ethel Owen

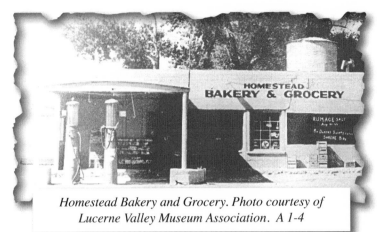

Homestead Bakery and Grocery. Photo courtesy of Lucerne Valley Museum Association. A 1-4

In the early days, natural springs in what is now Lucerne Valley provided good camping grounds for Indians on their way into the San Bernardino Mountains to gather pinion nuts. The Indians resented white pioneers settling in the territory and committed some violent acts against them. Instead of discouraging the settlers, it caused them to marshal forces and attack the Indians. (Piute, Chemehuevi and Serrano) In February 1867, a decisive battle at Chimney Rock caused the Indians to retreat and leave the territory to the white pioneers. (Chimney Rock is at the north edge of Rabbit Dry Lake. A historical marker is beside the highway at the east end of the lake. A quite complete story of the Chimney Rock Massacre is available at the Lucerne Valley Branch of the County Library.)

In July, 1873 five men; L.D.Wilson, John E. McFee, W.S. Manning, W.P. Morrison and (?)Holmes located the springs known as Rabbit Springs. They laid claim to the springs and the 100 surrounding acres (20 acres each) according to a recorded document.

In 1884, Peter Davidson operated a Way Station at Rabbit Springs. Travelers could get fresh water, exchange news, rest and/or sleep over. "Uncle Pete" died in 1906. His grave is at Kendall and Rabbit Springs Roads.

In 1886 W.W. Brown brought his family to this valley, which was without a name at the time. Brown had the water rights at the Box S. (The Box S Ranch was where the drainage ditch now crosses Highway 18 at Highland Road) The family stayed at "Uncle Pete's" until an old abandoned house could be moved onto the Box S property.

In 1896 Al Swarthout acquired the Box S, intending to raise cattle. There was plenty of water but not much forage. Swarthout and a friend found a place about 15 miles to the east, which had even more water and lots of forage. After one year, he gave up the Box S and moved to Old Woman Springs Ranch. (It is said the Indians used to leave their old people camped there while the young ones went into the mountains after pinion nuts.)

In 1897 James Goulding came to the Box S with his wife, Anna, and two small children, Mamie and George. Three more children, Minnie, Jim, and Nellie were born in Lucerne Valley. "Dad" Goulding proved the fertility of our soil with his apple orchard, vegetable garden and alfalfa fields. He also raised cows, horses and other animals. He dug a well which proved to be artesian. In 1905 a friend suggested to Goulding that this valley should have a name. Because of his success in growing alfalfa (also known as lucerne) he christened this place Lucerne Valley. Dad Goulding is generally acknowledged as the founder of Lucerne Valley.

In 1907 Goulding legally established Lucerne Valley School District. Hanna Brown, a cousin whose family lived near Oro Grande, came to live with the Gouldings so the requirement of six students could be met. The school building was a former cook shack on wheels, 8 by 18 feet. With wheels removed, and one end inside painted black for a blackboard, the school opened September 9 on the Box S Ranch. Meantime, more families were settling all over Lucerne Valley. In 1910, Goulding donated property for a new school where the Baptist Church now stands. (At the time of this publishing that church now houses Foursquare Crossroads Chapel.)

In 1912, people in the east end of the valley thought the school should be closer to them, so they formed a new school district to be known as Midway. In 1915 still another school district, Rodman, was formed in North Valley. In 1916 windstorm and fire destroyed both Lucerne Valley and Midway schools. All the students attended Rodman school until the other two were rebuilt, which took a couple of years, because of war-time problems. In 1920 Rodman school lapsed and joined with Midway, which by then was in its present form.

In 1941 Lucerne School was condemned as unsafe and all students went to Midway. The building and grounds were purchased by the Community Church which eventually became the Baptist Church (now the present Foursquares Crossroads Chapel) and used until 1952, when the building burned to the ground during a terrific windstorm.

In 1951, construction was begun on the new Lucerne Valley Elementary school at its present site. Lucerne Valley's Library history began with 140 books in the front room of the Box S ranch house, in 1912. Most of them were for school use but some could be borrowed by local residents.

In 1915 the library was at Midway School and was made a branch of the county library.

In 1916 a storm damaged some of the books and the library was moved to the Boom Ranch, on Wilshire, northeast of Midway. After being closed during World War I, both Midway School and the library re-opened in September, 1918. The library continued as a combination school-public library until March, 1928 when it became a Community Branch of the

Oberlin's Rock House located on Highway 18 between Trade Post and Kendall. Photo courtesy of Bill Lembright. A 1-5

County Library System. When the Lucerne School building was condemned for school use, the library moved in. When the church bought the building, the library was moved into a smaller room. Later it was moved into a small, narrow trailer behind the present China House. Ethel Windschanz Clafton, the librarian, said that looking out the little, port-hole-shaped windows during a strong wind made her feel like she was on a sinking ship.

The library moved again to the building which is now occupied by the Sheriff's office. Mrs. Vera Russell (John's mother) was one of the librarians at that location. It then moved to the Lucerne Valley Shopping Center into a new building generously provided by John Russell with very low rent. It is now the home of Quality Treasures. From there the library moved into its beautiful new permanent home west of the Community Center, for which ground was broken March 17, 1988.

Lucerne Valley Post Office was established in 1912 at the ranch of John and Rosa Koehly, who came here in 1909. It was at the southeast corner of Rabbit Springs Road and Post Office Road. (Have you wondered about that road name?) Rosa Koehly was first Postmaster. Some days only 8¢ worth of stamps were canceled, so that was the Postmaster's salary. In 1935 the Post Office (P.O.) moved to a one-room building on the highway, west of the Box S Ranch, with Ed Smith as Postmaster. (Ed Smith was also a licensed electrician and Scoutmaster of Lucerne Valley's first Boy Scout Troop 71 from

1928 to 1933. Some of those Scouts are still living here, among them Harold Reed and Dick Owen.)

Later the P.O. moved again, and shared the Clark Building with John Hutson's and Irving Seeberg's Hardware store. (The Clark building is now occupied by the China House.) Flora Ann Clark was Postmaster. The P.O. moved again to "the triangle" on Verdugo Road at Oracle Road (now renamed Oracle by the county street-sign makers) Early Postmasters there were Vern Ely and Ray Bonin. The Post Office is now in its permanent location on Highland Avenue south of Highway 18.

A Volunteer Fire Department was first organized during World War II, along with Fire Watchers, Sky Watchers, Plane Watchers, Civil Defense, etc. In the early 1950s, a firehouse was built with donated material (cinder block) and volunteer labor. It was located about where the Sinclair and Valero Gas Stations are now. They had a unique system. People would phone Dick's Center Store to report fires. Dick Grobaty would then press a button on his wall, which was wired to the siren on top of the firehouse. That was how the volunteer firemen were summoned. The building was

Homestead Bakery today. Photo courtesy of Lucerne Valley Museum Association. A 1-4

torn down after a short period and the present County Fire District was formed in 1962-63. At that time it still operated with volunteer firemen and one paid chief.

Some of the descendants of the early settlers still live here. William Russell (John's father) filed on his land at Lucerne Springs in 1911. John came here to live in 1949, and has been building houses and commercial buildings ever since. Also in 1911 Theodore P. Owen filed on 640 acres two miles north of Midway School. His son, Dick, has come and gone but has lived here steadily since 1950.

Athene Sieswerda was another very early settler. She was the first to have pistachio trees here. Her son, Joe Sherman, lives here now. Orlando and Mildred Jacobs came here in 1928. There were about 250 people in Lucerne Valley then. At the Jacobs home in North Valley, Jake baked 60 or 70 loaves of bread, sweet rolls, cakes and pies on Saturdays and sold them through Max Lewis's grocery store. Later he rented from Goulding the building now empty and established Homestead Bakery and Grocery (at the end of Highland.) At the same time Mildred ran the Jackrabbit Cafe, located on land now occupied by Valero. In 1936, Jake and Mildred moved their house onto land they bought from Southern Pacific RR, se corner Barstow Rd. and Old Woman Springs Rd. The Jacobs donated 10 acres of their land which is now Pioneer Park. As Jake's health failed, Mildred gave up the cafe and ran the Homestead Bakery. She still found time to clear and plant for the Park along with other citizens. The Jacobs had two daughters, Shirley Ann and Millie Lou. Millie Lou lives in Maryland and Shirley Ann (Mrs. Bob Fuller) lives in Apple Valley.

Ethel Owen came in 1946 as Ethel Johnston and built Lucerne Valley's first Beauty Shop. Ethel and Dick Owen were married in 1950 in the old Community Church and their daughter, Lilli Ann, born in 1952 was dedicated there shortly before it burned down.

The foregoing was prepared by Ethel Owen on March 25, 1988, from material obtained from L.V. Library and from her own memory. She apologizes for any inaccuracies of dates or facts and/or omissions. There is much to be added that could not be contained in these pages.

Geologist's View of Lucerne Valley History

Excerpts from "Mineral Wealth of Lucerne Valley" by Don Fife.
Edited by Bill Lembright.

Modern Period

Before William Holcomb's discovery of gold on May 4, 1860, small-scale gold mining was in progress in the mountains around Lucerne Valley. After Holcomb's strike, thousands of prospectors and miners swarmed over the north slopes of the San Bernardino Mountains. Mining in this area has continued to the present.

In 1860 John Cushenbury founded "Cushenbury City" near Cushenbury Springs. His silver strike in this area was found to be in "base-ore" and not economic to mine at the time.

In 1863 John G. Nichols, former judge and mayor of Los Angeles ... built the first wagon road up Cushenbury Canyon. Highway 18 follows Nichol's route up to Johnson

Cushenbury Springs ranch house, August 1900.
Photo courtesy of Lucerne Valley Museum Association. B 1-6

Grade where the highway then follows the general route pioneered by Lucky Baldwin to his Gold Mountain mines in 1874. The present highway is basically the improved version of these mining roads made by the builders of Big Bear Dam in 1880 to handle freight wagons hauling cement and supplies for building the dam.

Peter Davidson, the first permanent resident of Lucerne Valley, was one of almost 2,000 prospectors and miners in Holcomb Valley in the 1870s. He later turned to running cattle at "Cushenbury Station" (presumably at the springs below the canyon.) About 1877 he moved to his Way Station where his commemorative monument stands today near Rabbit Springs.

During the 1880s attention turned to gold and silver strikes in southeast Lucerne Valley. The Silver Reef Mine in the Blackhawk landslide was found to contain enormous amounts of low-grade silver ore with just enough high-grade lenses to excite the miners. These silver ores probably led to Bill McHaney's famous 1890's story of Lucerne Valley's Lost Ruby Silver Ledge and the murder of two prospectors at Rabbit Springs.

Silver Reef Mine. Courtesy of Lucerne Valley Leader. B 1-7

The miners did not know that they were digging in a massive landslide. Many of the mining shafts were sunk on high-grade outcrops only to find the ore non-existent once the shaft penetrated to the desert sand or granite schist below the landslide. It was not until 1928 that geologists Woodford and Harris of Pomona College unlocked the mystery of the dead-end silver lodes when they discovered that the area was a massive landslide.

Pioneer Ranchers

In 1893 Albert Swarthout homesteaded the Box-S Ranch a mile south of Peter Davidson's Way Station. Four years later Swarthout had moved on to Old Woman Springs, and later became a prominent San Bernardino County cattleman. Old Woman Springs was so named because the local Indians were said to leave their elderly there to die when they were too old to travel with

Blackhawk Landslide. Photo courtesy of Lucerne Valley Museum Association. B 1-8

the tribe. Indians dug caves into the soft clay gouge there. Metates and other Indian artifacts have been found intact in the area.

James Goulding, a silver miner from Colorado, who was affectionately known as "Dad" in later years, did more than a little prospecting around Lucerne Valley. Like most serious miners he did not

Al Swarthout and family at Box S. Photo courtesy of Lucerne Valley Museum Association. A 1-4

talk much about his mines. In 1898 Dad found some rich ore, but there was no mill to process it. So he built an arrastra at the Box S Ranch for crushing the ore. He processed about 100 pounds of ore an hour. This ground up gold ore was amalgamated with mercury and the amalgam was sold. According to Goulding, the richest of this hand–cobbed (hand-picked) ore ran up to $200 per ton. He acquired the Box S homestead and proceeded to build a thriving ranch, which pioneered the development of Lucerne Valley.

Perhaps Goulding's greatest achievement was the fact that he discovered artesian water when he drilled a well on his property. His ranch prospered due to irrigation. Goulding located his well along the Helendale fault near the place where the moisture from Rabbit Springs died out. The site was known to Indians in prehistoric times because their midden deposits were frequently encountered while digging around the Box S Ranch property. The Helendale fault is a 70-mile-long fault that acts as a subterranean dam or groundwater barrier along its northwest trend between Helendale on the Mojave River and Cushenbury Canyon. Had Goulding drilled a few hundred feet east of his famous artesian discovery well, he would have been east of the Helendale fault and groundwater barrier, and he would not have encountered artesian water.

Mining

At the same time Lucerne Valley gained its first permanent residents involved in mining, the biggest local gold strike was being developed on Blackhawk Mountain. Algernon P. Del Mar, later to become an internationally known British mining engineer, was overseeing the development of the gold discoveries of prospectors Cook and Leach. Del Mar supervised three different phases of mining on Blackhawk Mountain between 1880 and 1940. A series of mining operations produced more than 10,000 ounces of gold from workings high on the mountain where the Blackhawk landslide

Blackhawk Goldmine Pilot Mill Photo courtesy of Del Mar. B 1-9

of 15,000 years ago exposed the bedrock. Mining ceased on Blackhawk Mountain in the 1940s by President Roosevelt's Executive Order 208-L which closed all gold mining operations in the nation during World War II.

When gold mining ceased during the war, the diverse geology and mineralization around Lucerne Valley attracted the attention of government geologists involved in the war effort. Minor amounts of copper, zinc, and lead were mined from the San Bernardino, Rodman, and Ord mountains. Access in the area from near Blackhawk Mountain to Rattlesnake Canyon was restricted because thorium, a radioactive mineral, had been secretly discovered. The Manhattan Project was in need of related uranium isotopes to build the first atomic bomb; however, thorium never proved useful.

Tungsten was discovered and mined near the Rose Mine. Tungsten almost won World War I for the Germans because they knew the secret of hardening steel with it and thereby making munitions and armament several times more efficient than standard arms products. The demand for tungsten continued into the mid-1950s. West Ord Mountain in north Lucerne Valley became the source of additional tungsten.

The most important metallic mineral deposits discovered in Lucerne Valley during the wartime exploration were the large iron ore bodies in the northeast part of the valley at the Bessemer and Morris load mines. However, significant production from those deposits was not realized until World War II was over. These deposits were mined intermittently for several years into the 1950s and still contain substantial iron ore reserves for society's future needs. Northwest of the Kaiser Steel Bessemer iron mine, along the base of the Rodman Mountains, U.S. Steel found significantly larger reserves of deeply buried iron ore in the mid-1950s. The mining economics have never been quite right to open the deposit, but it has been blocked out by core drilling and is an available source of iron ore.

During the late 1950s a geologist with Kaiser Steel Company discovered that a local miner was drilling, blasting, and shipping iron ore owned by Kaiser to a nearby plant for processing. As it turned out, the property had been illegally "leased" to the unsuspecting miner. After the unintentional trespass was discovered, it became apparent to Kaiser officials that this small-scale mining operation was efficient and cost effective. The local miner has been the mining contractor for Kaiser Steel in the area ever since.

During World War II Lucerne Dry Lake and many of the surrounding areas were used for military maneuvers and aerial bombing practice. Millions of target bombs and rounds of shellfire impacted the Valley. The desert was full of bomb fragments and scrap metal. In 1945, scrap dealers converged on the valley. Bomb targets were bulldozed up on the dry lakes and in adjoining areas. Within 3 to 4 years the area was picked clean.

Each bomb or shell impact left a small crater, which filled with water after every rain. On the alluvial fan soil surrounding the dry lake, the impact crater formed a trap for seeds to grow, producing beautiful "flower pots" after the first cloudburst of the season. By the early 1950s, these had become clumps of sagebrush surrounded by mounds of sand.

Other Mining Activities

Granite: During the 1930s, blue granite was discovered lying at a shallow depth beneath the yellow-brown decomposed granite of the Cougar Butte area. This "Texas" quarry, as it was known, and other quarries in the area produced high quality granite dimension stone for tombstones and building facings throughout the Pacific southwest. These quarries have been operated intermittently from the 1940s to the present time.

Limestone and Cement: At the turn of the century, the interest in commercial limestone moved to Oro Grande and the Victorville area. By 1920 two cement plants were operating along the Mojave River north of Victorville.

The first commercial white limestone-dolomite mining operations in north Lucerne Valley were started during the 1940s at Peterman Hill. The material was mainly a magnesium (dolomite) marble. It was used as building stone, as granules for white roofing rock, and was tried as a filler extender in putty, rubber, and paint. By the late 1940s the ore was basically mined out.

Other limestone deposits in the area were mined and hauled to the Thorne railroad siding in Apple Valley and shipped to Kennedy Minerals in Los Angeles. There the ore was ground for use as a filler extender and white pigment in putty and paint, and in refining sugar and glass. This production led to more extensive bulk testing for use as a local source of high-grade steel flux limestone for Kaiser's Fontana Steel Mill.

By the early 1950s Kaiser Steel had optioned all Minerals Materials Company's claims in Cushenbury Canyon and were planning a railroad line and cement plant for Lucerne Valley. The Lucerne Valley limestone rush was on. Many small gold miners suddenly found the limestone surrounding their gold prospects got far more attention than their gold. Some miners who were trying to revive gold mines in the Furnace Canyon area, found themselves engulfed by limestone miners. Many of these early limestone operators produced white roofing granules from various quarries in the area from upper Rattlesnake Canyon to Furnace Canyon.

In 1952 Lucerne Valley miners began to feel the demand for local aggregate materials. Ed Fife, Gene Fife, and Joe Sheldon started mining sand and gravel on the lower Crystal Creek fan south of Highway 18 and east of the present location of Meridian Road. This operation was named Lucerne Valley Mining and Minerals Company and consisted of a modern screening plant, three dump trucks, and two ready-mix trucks.

During 1953 to 1957, Kaiser spent nearly $20 million to bring a railhead to Lucerne Valley to serve the first large limestone quarry and the cement plant to be constructed. With the arrival of the railroad, limestone deposits in Furnace Canyon came into production. In the mid-1960s, an additional limestone operation was opened at Terrace Spring near the mouth of Arrastra Canyon above Old Woman Springs.

Clay: During the 1960s, the State Department of Water Resources investigated all the dry lakes within about 30 miles of the proposed Cedar Springs Dam (that created Lake Silverwood) for high quality, low plastic clay for the core of the dam. The only suitable deposit found was east of Deadman's Point at the small dry lake north of Highway 18. This quarry now intermittently supplies clay to the brick and tile industry of southern California.

During the 1970s deposits of feldspathic-quartzite were discovered between the Ord and Rodman Mountains. This material is an important ceramic raw material for bathroom and kitchen fixtures. The deposit has been operated by Industrial Mineral Company, which operates a small grinding facility at the Thorne railroad siding in Apple Valley.

Economic Importance of Limestone Mining

The Lucerne Valley limestone district is one of the largest, if not the largest, limestone producing district in the United States. It is estimated that up to three million tons of limestone are quarried from this district each year for use in cement, steel flux, whiting, filler extenders, pharmaceutical products, and the chemical industry. Whereas the bulk of the tonnage is used in the cement and white pigment-filler extender markets related to the construction industries, there is a diverse market for food, pharmaceutical, and chemical-grade limestone. High-grade limestone from the deposit is used to manufacture explosives, rubber, sugar, glass, white paper, and Styrofoam. Finely ground limestone is used as a filler in antacid preparations, in chewing gum, as a preservative in fruit juice, and as a leavening agent in bread. It is also used in ice cream, cereal, frozen milk products, and as a dusting agent to prevent hard candy from sticking.

Products made of Lucerne Valley Ore are traded all over the world. It is estimated that the local gross annual sales from Lucerne Valley limestone quarries and the cement industry are on the order of $180 to $220 million each year.

Gold Mining Renewal

With the rise in the price of precious metals in the late 1970s and vastly improved techniques of processing gold and silver, Lucerne Valley and the surrounding mountains again have their share of gold seekers. New geologic information and models of ore accumulation are being used in Lucerne Valley to prospect for the yellow metal. New gold mines are starting up. Perhaps Lucerne Valley will experience another gold rush!

Petroglyphs And Rock Alignments in the Rodman Mountains

Compiled by Bill Lembright

Our first human settlers were the Native Americans who were attracted to sources of water, hunting grounds, plant food, and lava flows which served as canvases for their art and communications medium. Between Lucerne Valley and Newberry Springs there is an eight-mile long lava flow whose vertical edges served these natives well. Three of these sites are close to each other east of the Pitkin Cinder Cone (site of the cinder mine) in the Rodman Mountains.

In the 1950s Ellis Estabrook prospected for uranium by aircraft around the Rodman Mountains and noticed a lot of rock alignments from the air. Later, he used a Jeep where there were no roads, constantly dodging bushes, to find the rocks from the ground. The roads there today may very well be the result of Ellis's Jeep tracks.

David Whitley in *A Guide to Rock Art Sites* writes that the Surprise Tank site has about 900 petroglyphs crammed into its small area, making it one of the largest sites in the region. At its

Snake petroglyph. Photo courtesy of Bill Lembright. B 1-10

lower end, are several flat grinding rocks. In the middle there appears to be a snake shaman's cave, possibly to reduce the risk of snake bites and/or to assist in healing from such.

Just north of Surprise Tank, is a small chain-link fenced area protecting what is nicknamed the Rams Horn Rock Alignment. Farther north is a larger fenced area protecting a boomerang shaped rock alignment 56-feet-long made up of hundreds of small stones. This is nicknamed The Boomerang.

A little further northeast of the two-track road is an exposed wall of lava that drops off into a wash, which for hundreds of yards features petroglyphs. This is nicknamed the Oxbow site.

Two miles north is another famous center of petroglyphs and rock alignments named Howe's Deep Tank site. Here, a generous display of petroglyphs graces the face of a usually dry waterfall that flows over the edge of a lava flow. Above the waterfall are numerous small rock circles that some believe were used in ceremonial purification rites of Indian virgins before marriage. Possibly the virgin was placed in a hole surrounded with heated soil and

Big Horn Sheep petroglyph. Photo courtesy of Bill Lembright. B 1-10

ringed with stones. After three days the maiden was supposedly considered purified.

Our Native predecessors left intricate records behind for us to puzzle over.

Last Battle at Chimney Rock

Compiled by Cindy Lazenby

Chimney Rock in Lucerne Valley was the site of the last Indian fight in Southern California. However, there were many important events leading up to the historic fight. Indians had used the mountain areas of San Bernardino, for many years, to supply food for their families. When the white man began cutting down trees and building sawmills, the Indians felt their hunting grounds were being ruined. This began a campaign to rid the area of the white man.

In 1863 the Indians killed a Spaniard named Polito at the mouth of the Little Sand Canyon. As they fled, the Indians stole a mule from Sam Pine and a short time later, they shot a horse and mule belonging to W. F. Holcomb and Pete Smith. Around the same time, the Indians shot and wounded Dr. Smith in Cajon Pass. Bill Holcomb formed a posse and followed the Indians, but he had to give up the chase for lack of provisions. Meanwhile in Cajon Pass, S. P. Waite shot at an object a blue jay was darting after. It was not until the next morning, that he realized he had shot and killed an Indian.

Lucerne Valley Leader, May 16, 1968. B 1-11

In 1866 J. W. Gillette, Ed Parrish, and Nephi Bemis started a roundup of some stray cattle at the Dunlap Ranch. Gillette's mule was worn out, so he was sent back to get Pratt Whiteside to take his place. Gillette stayed with the herd and a while later, the horses of Parrish and Bemis came back; the Parrish horse had blood on the saddle. Gillette went back to the ranch house to inform Mr. Dunlap of the discovery and to gather more men and arms.

The body of Bemis was found about sundown. The searchers found evidence that he had been killed by Chemehuevi Indians. The bodies of Whiteside and Parrish were found the next morning; Par-

Chimney Rock Plaque.
Photo courtesy of Bill Lembright.

rish still had a stone in his hand he had been using to defend himself. The Indians had taken the clothing from all three bodies, along with Whiteside's riding rig and pistol. The Indians returned to the desert that evening, after eating Whiteside's horse.

In the winter of 1867 the Indians returned to the mountains and looted some houses in Little Bear Valley. From there they went to the home of Bill Kane and stole the horses, supplies and guns of George Lish and John Dewitt. The next morning, Frank Talmadge, Jonathan Richardson, George Armstrong, and Bill Kane started after the Indians. The men went back to Kane's home and found it burned to the ground and all items the Indians could not carry had been destroyed.

The families of the men were protected at the mill, and help from San Bernardino was on the way, so the men continued to track the Indians through new fallen snow. At Willow Canyon they saw eight Indians. Talmage and Kane gave chase on their horses, with Richardson and Armstrong following on foot with the pack animal.

The Indians hid behind a log and Kane was on top of them but didn't realize it. They shot Kane's horse, which threw him off. Talmage arrived in time to prevent the Indians from killing Kane; he killed one Indian and the others scattered. The men returned to the mill to get more ammunition and more men to help fight the Indians.

The next day Talmage, Kane, Richardson and Armstrong were joined by William Caley, A.J. Currey, "Noisy" Tom Enrufty, Henry Law, George Lish, Tom Welty, Frank Blair, and Joab

Chimney Rock. Photo courtesy of Bill Lembright. B 1-11

Roar. In some thick timber at the top of the first ridge past the mill, the posse met up with about sixty Indians. The Indians opened fire with guns and bows and arrows. After several hundred shots were fired, the Indians took their wounded and headed for the desert. The posse let them go and returned to the mill with their wounded. Tom Welty had been shot in the shoulder and Bill Kane in the leg. One Indian had been killed.

More men and supplies arrived from San Bernardino. The posse split up with some going through the mountains and the others going through Cajon Pass. They met at the Dunlap ranch on the Mojave River. This posse consisted of W.F. Holcomb, Jack Martin, John St. John, Samuel Bemis, Edwin Bemis, Bill Bemis, Harrison Bemis, Bart Smithson, John McGarr, Johnathan Richardson, Frank Blair,

Indian Cave near Chimney Rock. Photo courtesy of Bill Lembright. B 1-12

George Armstrong, George Birdwell, Joseph Mecham, Jack Ayres, George Miller and an unknown man. The posse located the Indians on a rocky mountain northwest of Rabbit Springs. A few men went home and the next day David Wixom, 'Noisy' Tom Enrufty, Sam Button, a preacher named Stout, Stout's son, and son-in-law (Griffith) joined the posse.

That night the men divided into two parties; St. John led the party who went north of the mountain and Stout was leader of the party of men who took the wagon road. The north party arrived late, and at daylight the south

party was already in place. The south party saw no Indians, fired some shots to let the north party know where they were, and started back down to the wagons. The noise woke the Indians who only saw the south party and they began to try and cut the men off from the wagons. The north party began to climb the rocks and were unseen by the Indians until they were upon them. The arrows and bullets began to fly and Richardson was struck in the breast with an arrow. He fell into the arms of George Miller who tried to remove the arrow but could not get the tip out. Miller went to get help, but met St. John who told him to guard the rocks the Indians were escaping through. St. John then went to get the other men.

The Indians yelled like coyotes during the battle and all escaped except two squaws, a fourteen year old boy, a ten year old girl, and a baby. The Indians were surprised and scattered when they thought they were trapped. The men took the prisoners and Richardson back to the wagons. Holcomb, Button, Armstrong, and Blair took Richardson to San Bernardino for medical attention. The next day, Martin, Miller, Bill Bemis, and Ed Bemis went back to the battle scene to pick up the Indian's trail. When they found the trail, they discovered that the Indians had gotten together --and determined there were about 150-200 Indians. They heard a shot but turned around because it was almost sundown and they had a six-mile walk back to camp, with no water. The next morning all the men, except three, who stayed in camp, picked up the trail. They discovered from the tracks that the Indians had been close to them on both sides of the canyon; had they gone any farther the evening before, they would have all been killed.

They followed the tracks traveling in a half circle until 3:00 in the afternoon and decided to return to camp, which was closer to them than when they had left that morning. They met Stout's son who had two extra horses, a canteen of water, and lunch for his father and brother-in-law. These three decided to follow the Indians against the advice of St. John and Martin. When the other men at camp heard gunshots, Miller looked through a field glass and saw Stout's son coming on a baldfaced horse across the dry lake. The men hurried to help and arrived just in time to save the two men. Stout's horse had been shot and his son-in-law had a broken arm. The Indians had lain in wait in the rocks and opened fire on them as they came through a small pass. The posse exchanged fire with the Indians, who again scattered. The men took Stout's wounded son-in-law back to camp and the posse then decided to take him to San Bernardino for medical treatment. It was decided there would not be enough men left to fight the Indians so they all went back home. This ended  a thirty-two day campaign against the Indians and it stopped the mountain raiding parties.

Note: I originally wrote this paper in 1989 for a college history class at Victor Valley College. I retain all rights to this paper. If someone wants to reprint or use any information in this article, contact me at cindylazenby@gmail.com for permission.

Many newspaper and magazine articles were written about this event; however, I wanted to base this paper on eyewitness accounts of the events. I spent considerable time researching old documents and microfilm archives at the California Room of the San Bernardino City Library. I went through the accounts and tried to put the stories of J. W. Gillette, the eyewitness at the Dunlap Ranch incident, together with the letter from George Miller, and the interview Miller gave in 1937 of his Chimney Rock battle in the proper time sequence.

The article by William Talmage gives much information; however, he was not an eyewitness and was only retelling stories of his father, Frank Talmage. I only used his information on the speculated reasons the Indians began the attacks.

Romance Gone Sour
Willie Boy's Grave and Story

By Bill Lembright. Photo courtesy of Lucerne Valley Museum Association.

Let me begin with a quick summary of Willie Boy's story, of which there are at least two basic versions. The *Digital-Desert* reports that Chemehuevi elder, Mary Lou Brown, wrote that Willie Boy was a talented young runner admired by the tribe in Twentynine Palms, CA. He had fallen in love with his distant cousin, Carlota Mike, and persuaded her to elope with him. Her father, William Mike, tracked them down and brought them back. Shortly afterward, Willie Boy shot and killed William, and escaped with Carlota into the desert. He left Carlota hidden in a wash with his coat and water skin. She died, either shot by the posse by mistake, or from exposure. According to Chemehuevi tradition, Willie Boy escaped, but has not been seen again.

Willie Boy.

A more dramatic version of the story comes from an LA Times article by Cecilia Rasmussen: In 1900, 19-year-old Willie Boy was living in Victorville, CA with his sister and her family. He became a quiet, hardworking cowpuncher with a good, sober reputation. He worked ranches from Morongo Valley to Joshua Tree before moving to Twentynine Palms. There, in 1909, he fell in love with his 16-year-old distant cousin, Carlota. Carlota's father, William, was a shaman and spiritual leader who refused to let his daughter marry a relative; plus, he didn't like Willie Boy. Despite that, Carlota ran off with him and relatives brought them back. A few months later, Carlota moved with her family to Banning to pick fruit at the Gilman Ranch. Willie Boy followed and confronted William with a gun and William ended up dead.

The two lovers ran and eluded a posse for 200 miles on foot in 100-degree heat. Food was running low, so Willie Boy left Carlota and ran for more supplies. One of the trackers far ahead of the posse mistook Carlota for Willie Boy and shot and killed her. He kept mum about his mistake and let everyone conclude Willie Boy killed her. Willie Boy returned and spotted the posse near Carlota, not knowing she was dead, and tried to protect her by luring them north to Ruby Mountain. Willie Boy avoided killing the men, but killed three of their horses and wounded another. They yelled at Willie Boy and accused him of killing Carlota. After that Willie Boy, stopped shooting at them and finally shot himself. After that, reporters trumped up an extensive tale of an Indian outlaw attempting to assassinate the President of the United States in an effort to increase circulation for their newspapers.

Those stories prompted novelist Harry Lawton to write *Willie Boy: A Desert Manhunt*, which in turn led to the production of the famous movie *Tell Them Willie Boy Was Here*. I suspect the truth lies between the account given by the Chemehuevi tribe and the story by Cecilia Rasmussen.

Over my years of exploring the desert, one of the most difficult sites to locate was Willie Boy's grave. We had seasoned desert-rat guides make attempts to help, but to no avail. So one day my wife, Jan, and I stopped in at an old convenience store on Reche Road in Landers and asked a clerk who we might seek out for answers to local desert mysteries.

She said, "Go to the Castle Inn Bar when it opens at 10 am, and within five minutes a motley group of old geezers will wander in. One of them can probably answer your questions." So, I carried our topography maps into the bar and spread them on a table; and, as on cue, in straggled several thirsty geezers. I explained our mission to the barkeep who announced it to his clientele. They pushed forward one chap, who they claimed knew "everything."

He looked at the maps and said, "Now understand, I ain't very good reading maps. But I'll tell you what I remember. If you walk south from the petroglyphs to Morongo Red's old cabin below the spring, then keep hiking south and upwards, you will possibly find it surrounded by a chain link fence."

That was about as detailed a set of clues as we often get, so we thanked them all and headed for the petroglyphs, which weren't all that easy to find.

We figured out where to turn at each fork of the creek in Yaranka Canyon based on our memory of what the old story teller related. Jan and I argued at MANY points along the way. I am very patient as long as she agrees with me. We finally made our way to what must have been Morongo Red's cabin, now totally vandalized, then up around the literal jungle at Crazy Calf Spring, and to our surprise, there was a cow, which we chose to leave behind as we continued our quest.

At this point the going got tougher. As is often the case, Jan became irritated (that's when I nicknamed her "Grumpy") as the climb became steeper with rock scrambling. Plus, we were running low on water… the perfect setting for a movie! At a dry waterfall, where we saw mountain lion

Willie Boy.

tracks, Jan said she could go no farther; so, I suggested she rest in the shade of the huge boulders until I returned. However, she didn't relish encountering the lion in my absence and mysteriously became motivated to carry on. I continued to insist that it was probably "just around the next bend," and then the next, and then the next. It was hot and I was concerned. Then up ahead in a wash was the one and only tree since the spring, miles back. Unfortunately, the tree was dead and had no leaves; but even its partial shade felt good.

Then I surprised Jan by saying, "We'd better turn back. We're searching for a needle in a haystack."

As we rested I looked at a distant ridge and saw a small section of chain link fencing. "Jan, look at that mirage up ahead!" So onward we trudged and were rewarded with Willie Boy's grave, commemorative plaque and all! Suddenly the legend became reality to us. The trip back was downhill and we were upbeat because of our find. Before we knew it, we passed the spring with its resident cow, then Red's cabin, the petroglyphs, and finally our Safari minivan full of ice cold beer and sodas! We were THANKFUL!

Portrait of James Goulding (2/23/1861-10/6/1959) by Virginia Hemphill. Photo courtesy of Lucerne Valley Museum Association.

Father of Lucerne Valley
James Goulding

Written by Virginia Hemphill
First published in the Desert Grapevine newspaper July 1946.
Condensed by Jan Lembright August 18, 2017

The first time we saw Dad Goulding he was scooping duck eggs out of the reservoir at Box S Ranch with a long-handled dipper. That was 16 years ago. The other day when we went to see him, his first act was to show us a lot of very young baby ducks. While we watched the busy little things scurry about, the giant cottonwoods dappled the earth and the warm grey walls of the old house. The late morning sun made patches of gold where it shone through the leafy canopy and it fell like a benediction on the head of this quiet man who looked on with amused enjoyment. The thoughtful consideration he gives to the simple things might be a fair gauge by which to measure any man.

Where to begin the story of a life that was 85 years in the making? A man is born, marries, fathers children, and achieves some material success. This is the usual pattern, if there is no one thing that sets him apart from the common herd. Environment tends to dwarf or enhance certain personalities, we know, but there are men who by their inner being alone influence an entire community. In a setting such as this, Dad Goulding steals the show. There are, to be sure, a few dissenting boos from the gallery but he would not consciously hear these, knowing, perhaps that failing is human nature whereby some of us would rather be here for a moment than be right for a lifetime. But no man worth his salt is too passive and if Dad sometimes exchanges the egg scoop for a baton with which to beat time, politically speaking, he at least knows the score. That it took him a lifetime to learn it does not interest us much, but the fact that he has become something within himself in the process does matter to us, because Dad Goulding's 50 years in the desert country make sense to a far reaching degree.

James Goulding was born in February 1861 in Colorado and lived there for the first 30 years of his life. He was married there. The first child was born in a Colorado mining settlement, for he was a mining man; owning silver mines in 1892 when the bottom dropped out of that market and left men flat broke. Dad stood it as long as there was hope, then one day he asked Mrs. Goulding if she didn't think it time they moved on to California where she had

First Artesian well in the Valley dug at Box S by James Goulding. Photo courtesy of Lucerne Valley Museum Association. A 1-4

often expressed a desire to live. She answered, that as he was making the living, he should decide. They came to California by easy stages, landing in Chino to stay awhile till the fog drove them to the desert country. Asked how they made the trip, Dad said simply, " If I drove through any town today in the rig I brought my family to this country in, every small boy would trail us." He added that, even though

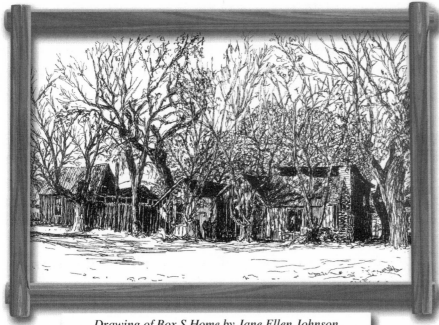

it was bitter cold when they left Colorado, the little family was comfortable in their covered wagon and they had plenty to eat.

From Chino, Dad went to the region about the Salton Sea, which at that time supplied salt to this part of the country, but conditions were so terrible there that even his clear vision failed to see how it would profit him to brave them at the possible expense of losing a member of his family. In 1897 the Gouldings came to Lucerne Valley

Drawing of Box S Home by Jane Ellen Johnson.
Photo courtesy of Loren Johnson. A 1-4

and lived on the land we know as Box S Ranch. Swarthout had been there shortly before and had dug a surface well but had soon moved to Old Woman Springs.

By then Uncle Peter Davidson had been nearly 20 years at Rabbit Springs Way Station and had what business the traffic brought through the road that went by his place. He did not think much of the newcomers and, though they were a mile apart, Uncle Pete felt that he was being crowded out since

some of the freight wagons were beating a new trail past Goulding's site where they got water and hot meals besides.

Uncle Pete spoke out of turn, as the saying goes, but what really railed the old man was that the gentle Goulding, kind by nature held no ill feelings against anyone and never quarreled.

Dad says that no one ever knew where Uncle Pete came from nor what his life was before he homesteaded here on the desert. In the 26

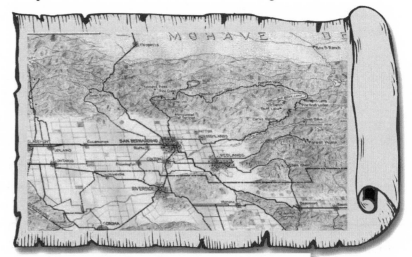

1915 Map. Photo courtesy of Lucerne Valley Museum Association.

years he lived here, though he made one or two good friends who lived up on the flats at Big Bear and at the mines, he never confided in anyone. He did however, give Goulding certain instructions he wanted carried out at his death. Uncle Pete was then in his eighties and in bad health. Dad says he always thought that the old Scot had been disappointed in life, possibly in love, that his harsh manner was only surface; and tells the following to prove this point. Once when Uncle Pete was ill and had no wood Goulding brought a load and was putting it at the door when Uncle Pete poked his head out and demanded what the hell Goulding was doing. When told, he slammed the door only to open it a moment later and ordered Goulding inside, handed him a bottle, adding that it was "good for the vitals." That was the nearest they ever got to friendship.

Box S, Early photo from 1985 LV phone book. A 1-4

When Uncle Pete died, Goulding sent word to the coroner who brought the coffin. The roads those days were poor, and by the time the coroner got here, they had to get the body in the earth as soon as possible, but it was done decently. Goulding's mother read from the Bible and the few adults and children sang a couple of hymns. Uncle Pete's adobe house remained closed until the Gobar brothers came and "followed the cat in" as Junie expressed it. They occupied the house while their own homestead was being built.

How did a man make a living in those days? From the first, Dad Goulding kept the wolves away from the door by working mining assessments for owners who were unable to do so and when he worked he got about $10 a day. When he saved enough to care for his family, he went about the real task he had set for himself and thereby earned the gratitude of all who have come to the valley to find a place in the sun. Being a geologist of ability and having faith himself, he actually spent about six years in proving his calculations.

Goulding would spend weeks at a time camping in the desert, digging test holes by hand; Dad would chuckle and say "Not like Junie Gobar who can locate water with a crooked stick." Not until he was convinced that there was adequate water for a large community did Goulding homestead Box S and produce the first flowing well here. The county then paid him five dollars a month to provide watering troughs for the public.

Box S ranch in 1896, homestead of A.R. Swarthout. Photo courtesy of Lucerne Valley Museum. A 1-4

Dad began to experiment with alfalfa, fruit trees and gardening of every kind. He learned the hard way and he is still learning, he is a living well of information to those who come after.

Dad Goulding was the first to organize a school and donated ground for the first school building. He is always in favor of improvement but seems to have an uncanny sense that prompts him to stop short of that "little too much." He also gave the land for the cemetery. The "Old Seeker of the Peace" (Dr. Henrietta Sweet) one who for years had tried vainly to shout Goulding down, from a safe seat in the gallery, always spoke of the cemetery as "Old Man Goulding's." Once she was ill and a visitor listened patiently to a long-winded account of the latest run-in she had with "the old man." Finally, the visitor jokingly suggested that if the Seeker should die now, Dad might not have her in his cemetery. Caught off guard, the old lady sputtered, then shouted "He could or he could go straight to hell." When Dad heard this for the first time the other day he grinned, then seriously remarked that "The old lady was a trying person." This could be the understatement of a lifetime.

This mule drawn wagon was hauling lumber from Victor (Victorville) to Lucerne Valley. The photo was taken by William Russell Sr. in 1912. Photo courtesy of Lucerne Valley Leader.

Dad was married twice. The first Mrs. Goulding, the mother of his 6 children, died in 1915, and the second in 1935. Both are buried in the cemetery here. His son James Jr. (Jim) was the first white child to be born in the valley. Jim and his sister Nellie, live at Box S with their father. Jim operates the ranch and Nellie carries the mail. The Goulding's live in the old house by preference, and we suspect they would not be so happy elsewhere. The house has never been painted: the weather-seasoned boards have grown old gracefully. The room has different floor levels, having been added from time to time to the small cabin of the 1897 days. It is home in the truest sense.

James Goulding 1956, 95th birthday. Photo courtesy of Lucerne Valley Leader Newspaper.

Now in his 86th year, Dad rests a great deal in his favorite old chair, receives callers, scoops the duck eggs from the reservoir and collects the rent from Mildred and Jake. Jake says that in the nearly 20 years they have rented his store building from Goulding, there never has been "the scratch of a pen" between them. Dad reads without glasses, he believes in the Bible, and in the future of Lucerne Valley. He has great respect for accuracy, in fact, he insists upon it. Dad's sense of humor is all right too.

(Editor's note: James Goulding lived to the ripe old age of 98. He is buried in the "Pioneer" section of "Old Man Goulding's Cemetery," the Lucerne Valley Memorial Park. Copy editors found words and style that they felt should be changed. But a writer in 1946, spoke much different than a writer today, so we chose to leave the wording as Virginia wrote it.)

The first Lucerne Valley Day Celebration was held July 4, 1914. This photo shows many

Photo from the Lucerne Valley phone book.

of the early pioneers including Rosa Koehly, Junie Gobar, Jim and Nellie Goulding, the Rices, Bunns, Lees, Browns, Webers, Wilfirths and Garretts. The picture was a prized possession of "Dad" James Goulding, who was not in the photo, because Harold Gobar had driven him to Victor for ice for the celebration in his California Tourister, and the old car decided it had had enough and broke down while there and he missed the party. They did send the ice back with Mr. Gamby, a local homesteader, who had been to Victor for supplies. Gamby drove his team of four burros back after dark. The ice was on time and ample for ice cream and lemonade, as told by Junie Gobar in his book *Raising the Dust*.

First Way Station - Peter Davidson's Cabin

Compiled by Millie Rader

Peter Davidson was the first permanent resident of Lucerne Valley, according to *Raising the Dust,* the first published book of Lucerne Valley history, by Julian Smith Gobar and Virginia Hemphill-Gobar, and verified in *Mineral Wealth of Lucerne Valley,* by geologist and historian Don Fife. He started out as one of the 2,000 prospectors in Holcomb Valley in the 1870s. In about 1877 he started a Way Station at Rabbit Springs, providing water for horses, a warm meal, and the floor of the cabin or soft grass under a tree to rest for the night. He built the four-room house, pictured here, out of adobe and rough sawn 1x20 inch boards. Davidson died January 7, 1906. The

Peter Davidson, Jack Rabbit Way Station July 14, 1928 Photo courtesy of Cindy (Hoffman) Anderson. B 1-13

house was then used by Charlie Martin and Albert Swarthout as a cattle station. It was also used by Julian, Harold, and Dave Gobar, who camped in it while developing their homestead in 1911.

Peter Davidson, Jack Rabbit Way Station July 14, 1928. Photo courtesy of Allen Stanfield. B 1-14

This photo was taken by LA Times staff photographer, Julian Robinson on November 21, 1946. Robinson had come into the Jackrabbit Café, where Bonnie Stanfield worked, and asked for directions to Peter Davidson's grave. Stanfield's children, Allen and Alice, were sitting there doing their homework, and Robinson asked if he could borrow them for the photo, which was published that week in the *Times*. The grave was then located on Davidson's former property at Rabbit Springs. It has since been moved to its present location at the corner of Kendall and Rabbit Springs Roads.

Well Driller, Alfalfa Farmer and Dairyman – Julian Gobar

August 22, 1892 - June 2, 1965. Compiled by Millie Rader.
Photos courtesy of Al Gobar.

Julian (Junie) Gobar was the first to write a book about Lucerne Valley. He is probably second only to James Goulding for his early contributions to the valley. He perfected the technique for growing alfalfa, drilled wells, operated a dairy, and built the Rabbit Dry Lake dike for what is now State Route (Highway) 18. He also helped to bring electricity to the valley and provided a hand to anyone in need.

Most of the information in this account comes from his own book, written with the help of his wife, Virginia Hemphill Gobar, titled *Raising the Dust*. His book draws from memories stirred up by an old journal he kept when he was just a young man fresh out of high school and new to the valley.

Some of the information here has also been gleaned from newspaper clippings in either the early *San Bernardino County Sun* or *The Desert Grapevine*.

Also included are facts and stories from first-hand accounts of his son, Dr. Alfred (Al) Gobar, who Chuck Bell and I had the pleasure of interviewing early in the process of writing this book.

Al was born in 1932, in the little house that still stands on Gobar Road, not far off Barstow Road. He lived in the valley as a young boy, but moved away with his mother when his par-ents separated. Growing up he spent many summers working with his father on the Gobar Ranch in Lucerne Valley learn-ing what he calls the value of hard work. Al grew up to be a world renowned economist, mentioned is several *Who's Who* books. Al's older brother, Kenny, stayed and worked with their dad, living most of his life in Lucerne Valley.

Original Gobar Ranch house, west of Barstow Road. B 1-15

Junie's father, Dr. Frank Joseph Gobar, first came to Lucerne Valley in 1911 to stake out the land that his family would homestead and where Junie would live most of his life. According to *The Desert Grapevine*, Dr. Gobar was a man of clear vision and great strength of character. Though he was actively engaged in the practice of medicine in Fullerton, California, with a lot of help from his sons, he was able to create the Gobar Ranch which became the finest in the valley. Dr. Gobar and his wife, Nellie, finally came to live permanently on the ranch in 1939. He always said he felt it a great privilege to be able to spend his last years in the peace and quiet of the desert. He passed away on April 19, 1946.

Junie first came to the valley June 29, 1912, with his brothers, Harold and Dave. It was the day after he had graduated from high school. They came to live and "prove up" the homesteads in a settlement that was then known only as "Box S." They came in a one-cylinder car called "The Cal-ifornia Tourist." Their story of driving that car up over the Cajon Pass the first time is an adventure in itself. It was just a deeply rutted wagon road and they had to dig themselves out after repeatedly getting high centered. They had to ford Cajon Creek many times. It was running 16 inches deep in places. The trip took two days to get to Victor (Victorville).

The three brothers took up residence at the abandoned Rabbit Springs Way Station as Peter Davidson's cabin was still in fair condition. Though it seemed to be locked, they found a cat door cut in the back door and looking through it discovered the front door held shut by a board. With a stick they knocked it down and thus they "followed the cat in."

Young Junie Gobar on the homestead with his dog and mule.

Junie wrote that James Goulding was not too happy to have them staying at the springs, but nobody ran them off and they used the place as headquarters until they had their own homes built.

According to Junie, his father believed in "all for one and one for all." This meant that though they had each homesteaded a piece of land they would all work the land for the benefit of the entire family. The oldest brother, George, attended Berkeley and later became a lawyer. He did not at any time enter the desert projects, though he visited frequently and looked after the legal matters. Their sisters Charlotte, and Eunice, also visited but never participated in the land improvements.

In the first five years the boys concentrated on developing the 157 acre claim at Lakeview. There they drilled their first deep well for irrigation and planted fifteen acres of alfalfa. They also planted shade and fruit trees, all while still living at Rabbit Springs. This took five years because they had to earn money to support themselves by clearing land and drilling wells for others while developing their own claim.

When Junie came of age he filed on the 160 acres North of Lakeview. The road out to his property was later named Gobar Road. To prove up home-

Spreading manure.

steaded land, one had to raise an irrigated crop. To do this he dug a ditch from the Lakeview well to water his crops. This was legal because he had earned an interest in the well. This became the Gobar Ranch, and Junie then moved from Rabbit Springs to his new ranch. He was living there in 1917, when he married his first wife, Hilda Millbanke, the mother of his two sons. His brothers Dave, and Rowland, also lived there for a time.

Well Drilling

Junie doesn't say how old he was when he started drilling wells, but it was probably pretty early on. He said money was tight, and he did many things to make ends meet: clearing land for absentee owners, raising cattle and selling a little alfalfa. He began to drill wells with a Case drilling rig that was too heavy to make it profitable moving from site to site. A man named Mr. Angel who lived on the west side of the Mojave River had a lighter rig but didn't want to sell it because he still needed

Junie and Red servicing a well.

to dig a domestic well at his ranch house. Junie made him a deal to dig his well in trade for the rig. Expenses in welling drilling were heavy, but he was able to make a living even though payments were slow. When not drilling, he worked at Gobar Ranch helping with planting and irrigating more alfalfa, or doing whatever needed to be done around the valley. Once Junie started drilling wells he never quit until he finally retired in August, 1957.

Money was scarce back then but those who were putting down roots seemed to be able to live without much cash. When the California Power Company offered him a job in 1928 as a troubleshooter and bill collector, Junie jumped at it. He created most of the roads required to run the big power lines from the Colorado River through Lucerne Valley. His son, Al, remembers driving those roads with his dad one day doing 30 miles an hour around a curve when his dad rolled the truck. It had landed on its wheels and after they got out and dusted themselves off, Junie looked at the road and said, "Well I guess I had better straighten that curve a bit." Then they climbed back into the truck and continued on their way.

Building the road across Rabbit Dry Lake

When the boys came to the Valley in 1912, the road from Victor (Victorville) was just several trails through Rabbit Dry Lake in the summer. In winter, travelers went around the full or muddy lake either by a north or south road. But not long after the boys arrived, the Improvement Association was organized with James Goulding as its chairman. The first item on the agenda was a road over the dry lake bed. After five meetings filled with nothing but arguments, Goulding appointed a committee to look over the proposed routes and bring a report to the next meeting. The committee went one

better and contacted the County Board of Supervisors asking if they would help. They responded that there were no funds to create the road, but if local residents created it, the County would maintain it. They also offered up an old Fresno scraper that was rusting away at Cedar Springs. By this time the Gobars had acquired a Rumley tractor. Using their equipment, they did the work of plowing the roadbed straight across

Junie helping bring electricity to Lucerne Valley.

the lake bed, then back-furrowed, to establish the line and to loosen the dirt so the Fresno scraper could load more easily.

They built up the dike and then graded the road from Box S to Deadman's Point. There were always five or six men working on the project at any given time. They would stay on the job for a week at a time and then take turns going home to tend to their own homesteads. Junie does not say how many days it took to build the dike or grade the roads, but he did say that the dike did not solve all of their problems. The first rainstorm after the road was built filled the lake bed and waves promptly washed away parts of the dike. The county repaired the damage, but then another storm would come and wash it out again. This went on for 20 years until the population had increased enough to

Rumley disking the dry lake.

put pressure on the government. The county finally turned the road over to the state, which came in and built a new dike on the original foundation that had been built with the cooperation, frustration and hard work of the early pioneers.

Dairy

Parts of the Gobar Dairy still stand today. The cold room made of adobe, with thick walls originally filled with hay for insulation, can still be seen from Barstow Road. We don't have the dates of when the dairy came into existence, but it was closed down sometime in the 1940s. We do know from the June 2, 1935 *San Bernardino County Sun* newspaper statement "The dairy of Julian Gobar, a modern establishment supplies milk to the Bear Valley Region," that the dairy existed at that time.

According to *Raising the Dust*, Junie purchased what was known then as the Oasis Ranch at the corner of Rabbit Springs and Barstow Roads in 1934. He lived there until 1941. No mention is made of why he moved from there or where he moved to, most likely he moved back to his original homestead. He did record that the years 1940 to 1941 were not exactly good years for the Gobars, especially Junie. His brother Kenny went into the navy. Junie's wife, Hilda, left the valley for good taking their son, Al, age 9 with her. By 1941 his brother Rowland, tired of working 7 days a week with the dairy, ended up shutting that down as well. After they sold the cows their hired hands moved to Victorville for jobs and Julian rented out their cottages. In 1945 Julian was kicked by a cow which took a long time to heal.

We know that Virginia Hemphill Gobar helped him compile the book and published it after his death in 1969, but there is no mention in the book about his marriage to Virginia. We do know that at the time *Raising the Dust* was written they lived in St George, Utah. Son, Al, told us that Junie had to move away from Lucerne Valley to get some rest because whenever a local resident had a problem they always went to Junie for help.

Junie passed away June 2, 1965, and is buried in the Lucerne Valley Memorial Park.

Bringing Power to Lucerne Valley

Info taken from Junie Gobar's Raising the Dust page 237-245
Compiled by Millie Rader

Electricity came to Apple Valley in 1917. About that same time a mining speculator named Hume bought Gold Mountain, the Lucky Baldwin holdings near Baldwin Lake, near what is now known as Big Bear, California. Hume had no intention of operating the mine, but planned to sell it and felt he

Photo courtesy of Millie Rader.

would have a better chance, and make more money, if he could get electricity up there. He worked a deal with Nevada-California Power Company to build a line from the Apple Valley substation to Gold Mountain. He would install the poles and the electric company would run the wire.

Hume hired old prospectors who knew the desert, as well as every canyon in the mountains. These old guys planted power poles from Apple Valley to High Road in Lucerne Valley. Then, they cut diagonally across the desert and through, what is now, the Gem Track between Mesa and Crystal Creek Roads. They continued, on the diagonal, right through

what is now Specialty Minerals Inc. and up over the steep slope just southwest of the Mitsubishi Cement Corporation quarry to Gold Mountain. If you stand on Trade Post Road between Emerald and Carnelian, you can see a faint outline of the old power line road to what used to be Sky-High Ranch Road at Highway 18.

Though there are a few fences along the way, the old power line road is still passable and fun on a mountain bike, if riding downhill. This writer (rider) and her husband have done just that. Using Google Earth, the old line can be followed with the eye to Gold Mountain.

With power so close, Lucerne Valley residents decided they were tired of pumping water to their fields and orchards with unreliable gas engines, and they began to plot a way to bring electricity into town. They formed a committee and then went to the power company office in Riverside to try to make it happen. The company required them to draw a map of all Lucerne Valley's potential users. Junie Gobar drew a map on the back of wrapping paper, which according to Junie in his

Junie Gobar helping to bring electricity to Lucerne Valley. Photo courtesy of Al Gobar.

book, was still on file with Edison in the late sixties. After the company had accepted the map, the Committee was told that a line to Lucerne Valley would cost $12,341.75. That pretty much took the wind out of their sales, but they never gave up and though it took the residents 11 years to raise the capitol, they finally brought power to the valley in 1928.

Gertie's Chicken Coops Keep 1890s Alive

Written by Pat Judkins, September 1988.
Photo courtesy of Lucerne Valley
Museum Association.

Gertie get yer gun. B 1-16

Ben Wilson, and his wife, Dorrie, bought their cove property from Lucerne Valley pioneer Gertrude Baldridge in 1973. Gertie's home, the garage in which she housed her old Cadillac, a separate sewing house, her mother's home, chicken coops and other buildings still stand keeping 1898-1920 architecture alive in our community.

Wilson's information shows Gertie as being a very hard worker. She hauled her own water from nearby hills and built her own buildings. She lifted all the rocks used in her beautiful stone walls and did her own cement work.

"Apparently, she was a very strong lady," said Ben. "She did have some help from her husband and a young boy named Jack, but most of the work was done by Gertrude herself." The Baldridge's never had children of their own, but Jack became like a son to them, eventually building his own home near Gertie's and looking after her after her husband, John, passed away.

Junie Gobar's book *Raising the Dust,* tells of the romance of John and Gertie Baldridge.

Her own desert art was depicted in her cement work. Walls of her buildings show cacti, hills, clouds, tortoises, and rabbits. She also poured cement stepping stones in which she embedded leaves from different trees and flowers. She signed her initials by these impressions in many of these stones. She had a large cellar, where she stored food canned from her date and other fruit trees and from her large vegetable garden. According to Junie, "Nearly all the furniture in her home was the work of her capable hands." He also writes that the Baldridges and Jacobs were the first people to take up land in the cove. He also makes note of the fact that Gertie was the first president of the "Birthday Club," which in 1926, developed into the Federated Women's Club, the valley's first organization.

According to Virginia Hemphill in *The Desert Grapevine* newspaper, Gertie and John named their place "Bluebird Springs Ranch" after the two springs they developed in the mountains on their land. What we now know as simply "The Cove," was originally named "Sunset Cove." Hemphill said that since John was a retired tree surgeon, they grew every sort of tree that will live here. They raised rabbits and chickens, and had a nice paying crop of black currants that netted Gertie several hundred dollars a year.

Gertie's first kitchen. B 1-16

Gertie's mother, Mrs. Joseph, built her home in the 1890s and in the early 1900s Gertie and her sister and brother-in-law, Bill and Harriet Logan, homesteaded on this property. The Logan Ranch still stands down the street and is in better shape. It was not built until the 1930s.

According to Ben, the Baldridge's were old Pasadena people. Gertie's mother owned a hotel there in the 1800s. She only lived in Lucerne Valley for a short time and then returned to Pasadena. Gertie lived here until 1976, when she moved to a rest home, where she passed away in 1978.

The Baldridge homestead was ¼ sections, or 160 acres, and Gertie made good use of it. Much like the Winchester House in San Jose, California, Gertie kept adding on rooms as needed. She even built two fireplaces in one room.

A Strong-Willed Woman
Dr. Henrietta E. Sweet

Compiled by Millie Rader. Photo courtesy of Lucerne Valley Museum Association.

Dr. Henrietta Sweet, 1910

Dr. Henrietta Sweet was a woman ahead of her time. According to the March 13, 1910 *Los Angeles Herald*, Dr. Sweet is listed as the president of the E.G. Lewis Chapter of the American Women's League. She believed that health was a woman's first duty and that she should be instructed in how to remedy defects and overcome weaknesses often considered incurable. She was also head of the "Reconstructive Body Building" classes there. She believed that a sound, vigorous body and a well-balanced mentality would insure power and self-mastery to every woman, regardless of age or environment. She was a graduate physician and studied medicine in four schools. Her motto was "Causa remota rese cessat," remove the cause and the effect ceases. The article also stated that she had worked out this problem in her own life and had evolved from being an invalid without the power to walk, into a splendid expression of healthy womanhood. Before moving to California, she had also demonstrated her theory in her private sanitarium near Philadelphia, as well as in her general practice. The article said that she had a fine, magnetic personality and a marked ability to inspire others. She was an ardent believer in optimism and right thinking and that the tonic effect of happiness should be expressed in health; that knowledge is power and that a perfect mental balance depends upon physical harmony.

The *San Bernardino County Sun* mentioned her in an article covering the Victorville Businessmen's Association meeting on July 16, 1914. It said, "The only woman member, Dr. Henrietta E. Sweet, who started the *Victor Valley Herald* one year ago, having disposed of her interest in that lively little weekly, tendered her resignation, as she considered she was no longer eligible for membership. She was overwhelmed with surprise when the members refused to accept it and drafted a set of resolutions thanking her for the help and co-operation she had given the valley and tendered her life membership in the organization."

Dr. Sweet is also mentioned in Junie Gobar's book *Raising the Dust*. The author writes about Dr. Sweet's frequent run-ins with James "Dad" Goulding," the man considered to be the founder of Lucerne Valley." What can be inferred from different accounts within that book is that pioneer Dad Goulding, who had been in the valley since 1897 and had started the first school and donated many pieces of property for the town's use, was pretty much in charge of what transpired in these parts. Then Dr. Sweet, a highly educated and accomplished woman with plenty of management experience of her own moved to town. This probably happened shortly after Dr. Sweet applied for and received a land patent on the south side of Rabbit Springs Road, just east of Midway (School) Park on April 15, 1925. According to Gobar, there were more than a few heated discussions between these two outspoken, hard-headed individuals. One can only imagine the sparks that must have flown, as Goulding, the elder, being a gentleman set in his ways, came up against this newcomer, a woman, who should have known her place. New ideas and "outsider" ways of doing things probably grated hard upon this self-appointed guardian of the valley.

There may have been many reasons that compelled Dr. Sweet to live in Lucerne Valley. But it was known that she recognized the desert atmosphere to be a healthy place to live and to bring patients who were suffering ailments aggravated by humidity. Her doctoring skills are noted in a historical account written by Veda Mae (Priester) Hoffman. Veda's family had lived in the valley since before World War I, and she writes that her husband, Jack Hoffman, had been plagued with asthma during a childhood spent in orphanages in the state of Washington and later in Los Angeles. In 1932 at age 22, he was in such bad shape that he only weighed 98 pounds. As a last resort Ethel "Ma" Ewing brought him to live with "Doc" Sweet. Under the doctor's care, Jack was soon pedaling his bike around the valley doing odd jobs, and before long this young man had built his own home, married and commenced raising a family. His daughter Sharon (Hoffman) Floroi still lives in Lucerne Valley at the time of this writing.

Dr. Sweet sold her property to George and Alice Prince in 1945. The property was later inherited by their grandson, Chuck Bell, who became an active member of the community, still lives and farms there at the time of this writing.

According to the *San Bernardino County Sun* newspaper, the good doctor was 85- years-old when she passed away in January 1946 in a San Bernardino hospital. *The Sun* also stated that she was a native of New York and had resided in both San Bernardino and Lucerne Valley for the last 35 years of her life. The article also mentioned that in 1910 she owned a "rest home," at 3311 Temple Street (No town is listed, but that is the time when she was president of the Women's League in Los Angeles, so I am guessing that is where this "home" may have been.) A March 13, 1928, issue of the same newspaper, writes of her being a pioneer home owner in Lucerne Valley and one of the first to plant an orchard there.

Virginia and William Hemphill

Chronicler of Lucerne Valley's History – Virginia Hemphill

Written by Linda Gommel. Photos courtesy of J.S. Gobar Foundation

Lucerne Valley is a special little town with a surprisingly interesting and colorful history. Many of the stories that contribute to that history are sadly lost with those who took part in them. Others have been preserved, in newspaper articles, in other writings, and in two wonderful books, *Raising the Dust* and *Range One East*, both written by Virginia Hemphill Gobar.

In 1975, a mere three years after the publishing of *Range One East*, my folks and I moved to Lucerne Valley to operate Lucerne Valley Market as a service to this community. I kick myself now that I did not pay close attention to the many residents with long roots here; with stories to tell. I might even have been able to meet Virginia HemphillGobar, even though by then she lived in Utah. I lived in a shallow dimension of taking time only to solve the challenges of the day, and failed to take notice, listen, and hear, what people, the desert, and the critters of this place might say.

Thus, I did not allow myself the pleasure of "meeting" Virginia Hemphill Gobar for many years. I had lived in Lucerne Valley, probably 30 years, before reading these two books and regretted not having done so sooner.

Virginia (I hope she wouldn't mind my calling her that) is "Hemphill" because William Hemphill was her first husband who, in her words, "left us on October 21, 1952, after 24 years of almost constant illness." She was also "Gobar" because in 1959 she married Junie Gobar, one of the pioneers of Lucerne Valley, whom she admired and whose story she tells in *Raising the Dust*, having taken dictation from him as they traveled the country.

My favorite of the two books is Virginia's own story, *Range One East*, which begins when she, William and their son came to Lucerne Valley in 1931 to make a temporary home, while William recovered his health. They homesteaded 160 acres in the East End of Lucerne Valley, starting essentially from scratch. These city folks had to begin a life not only in the country, but in desert country that was alive with critters, with no close neighbors, and few of the basics of life without which we moderns would throw a fit: electricity, running water, indoor plumbing, etc.

Books by and about Virginia Hemphill

Virginia did not complain about the task of setting up a new life, nor did she whine or moan about her added burden of an invalid husband, whose ability to help was limited to the point that Virginia did most of the heavy lifting, literally. Initially, they lived in a wood shed turned into a dwelling and later Virginia decided that they should build a house as a permanent home, a point of difference between her and William. He always hoped to return to "normal life" down below. She had become attached to the desert and wanted to stay.

Desert sketch by Virginia Hemphill

In addition to her writing ability, Virginia could paint and sketch, so when she decided to build the house, she sketched her plans for the house and presented it to William as a done deal. Because wood was so scarce on the desert and therefore expensive, she followed the example of many other Lucerne Valley settlers during the Depression; she built the house with rock and used cement for mortar.

The Hemphills had to travel to Victorville to get the cement, which was weak and defective and they had to collect the rocks from around the valley. Then Virginia tackled the job and built the house essentially by herself. She had not told William of her plans for a fireplace in the west wall of the house, partly because it implied permanence and when the house was well along, she sprung it on him: "Oh, by the way, there is to be a fireplace in this wall." He resigned himself to her plans and made her a form for the fireplace that would draw the smoke properly. That was the extent to which he could help her build that house. With outside help, she managed to dig a cellar through rock-hard caliche clay, put up rafters, build a roof, and pour concrete floors. The house became known as Techatticup Cabin.

I cannot help but insert here my personal story of Techatticup Cabin. On many Saturdays, my dad and I enjoyed tootling around Lucerne Valley, just to see and feel the valley. One day we were out in the East End, east of Camp Rock Rd., driving slowly along a dirt road. We saw a building that was obviously abandoned and old, and drove

Hempill's Estate. B 1-17

up its long driveway to take a closer look. It was built mostly of stone and had a cellar dug out in the northwest corner. Another broken, stuccoed building stood to the north of the house. Sadly, broken glass and trash were strewn everywhere. I wondered if that could be Hemphill's' Techatticup Cabin, but dismissed the idea. I thought of the tiny picture of the cabin in Range One East that showed the outline of the buttes to the northeast. I excitedly looked it up on Google Earth Street View, and compared it to Virginia's picture. Wow! It was her cabin!

In 1945, as World War II ended, Virginia and William decided to publish a little paper about Lucerne Valley, to let outsiders know of this wonderful place. They landed on the name *The Desert Grapevine*, printing the first one on scrap yellow sheets, using a hand-printing press. It developed into the local paper until 1952, when they gave it up since others were starting publication of a more traditional newspaper called *The Lucerne Valley LEADER.*

Anyone who would like to meet Virginia, and I recommend that pleasure to any who loves Lucerne Valley or who simply likes good reading, may do so in her two books. One sees that she was a woman of wit and gentle humor, with spiritual depth and perception, and a love of this beautiful valley that many of us share. Her courage and strength reveal, by contrast, how spoiled we have become in this modern age of material comfort.

Virginia's stories of many other desert characters cannot help but make one smile and regret having missed this seemingly simpler life. The best remedy for such longing is to live mindfully in the present, aware of the unfolding of stories being written all around us. Rather than living blindly to all but our daily routines,

Desert Grapevine
March, 1950

we can learn from a person like Virginia to connect with the spirits around us, whether the human spirits and what they offer, the spirit of the desert in its barren solitude and quiet, or the Spirit of God, who speaks through all of it, teaching us to connect with Him. Thank you, Virginia, for pointing us in the right direction.

❖✿❖

Escape From Internment – Japanese Camp

Compiled by Bill Lembright. Photos courtesy of Bill Lembright

Years ago, I heard rumor of a Japanese camp southeast of Lucerne Valley that was used to avoid the internment camps during WWII. I asked several Johnson Valley residents and followed several leads, but to no avail. Finally an avid conservationist said I would find it, if I searched persistently, in the upper reaches of Bighorn Canyon. He told me in the Canyon, I would find a couple of mine tunnels, below the camp, that would have the remains of canning jars, with cabbage-based foods that could be either German or Asian.

Being a curious soul, I took my wife, Jan, a topo map, and plenty of water to explore. Sure enough, we came across two tunnels dug deep into the banks of Bighorn Wash. Outside the mouth of one were broken canning jars, with what looked like dried-up cabbage. Then came the guesswork. If the miners were camped nearby, where might their camp have been?

Up the wash there was a fork and, for some reason, I decided to go to the right. Above a little waterfall, the terrain became less steep; I thought there might have been a faint trail leaving the wash and heading uphill across a clearing. A little further along we came to the edge of a huge wash and found a trail climbing steeply up a ridge.

Animal pens. B 1-18

Japanese house. B 1-18

We finally came to a spring, with a half-inch rusty, galvanized pipe leaving it, and running alongside the trail as we climbed uphill. Where the hill leveled off into a flat, there were old structures in various stages of decay. We entered the main long house, with a roof so low that we had to keep ducking so as not to hit our heads. We became convinced that this was likely the Japanese camp.

There was also a chicken coop, livestock pens, and what looked like a bathhouse, and an outhouse. We were elated! What seemed to be an evasive rumor appeared to be true.

Professor Philip C. Brown, an expert in early and modern Japanese history, wrote that this group of Japanese built these structures under the pines to avoid detection from the air and to avoid being placed in internment camps. The residents would send a non-Japanese resident into town to buy needed supplies.

Stan Coutant, whose family homesteaded on Big Horn Road in 1957, remembers that in 1958, Sheriff Deputy Stillwell of Lucerne Valley was called to investigate one of the mine tunnels. They discovered a large stash of boxes full of canning jars. Some people said they saw Japanese handwriting on some newspapers found inside.

Lucerne Valley and the surrounding area has been, and continues to be, a haven for residents with a diverse mix of cultural heritage.

Bootlegging in Lucerne Valley During Prohibition Years

Compiled by Bill Lembright.
Information gathered from Cliff Walker's book One Eye Closed And
The Other Red, and from an interview with Allen Stanfield.

In 1919 the eighteenth amendment to the US Constitution was passed which banned the manufacture, transport, and sale of alcoholic beverages. Many felt it was none of the government's business, and distilled their own alcoholic beverages in defiance of the law.

Lucerne Valley was one of many locations where moonshine was distilled. Cliff Walker wrote: "In Lucerne Valley, a rancher had his stash buried in the driveway, covered over with a few tire tracks. When the bootlegger had a fight with his wife, she informed on him. Prohibition enforcers came, showed the warrant, and asked to borrow a pitchfork. They pitch-forked everything: the haystacks, hay bales, the grain, and the driveway. They finally gave up, returned the rancher's pitchfork and left. They had parked right over the part of the driveway that hid the booty".

Allen Stanfield tells of a store in the old stone building at the corner of Trade Post Road, just east of the building with the domed roof. One day a man came in looking for bootleggers. The store owner asked the visitor to sit down for a cup of coffee; meanwhile, he sent his oldest son to warn the bootleggers. Then he directed his visitor to other canyons where there were no "stills."

There were "stills" hidden in Furnace and Arctic Canyons. Bert Holcomb, a gold miner with claims all along the base of the San Bernardino Mountains, had a "still" in a mine tunnel and camouflaged the entrance with chicken coops. Stanfield said no one ever remembered seeing a chicken there.

The "still" in Furnace Canyon was eventually found and destroyed by law enforcement officials. Notice the bands from one of the barrels still lie outside.

Tunnel entrance. Photo courtesy of Scott Wallace.

Barrel bands at tunnel entrance.
Photo courtesy of Scott Wallace.

During Prohibition: Many "pints" held 11.4 to 12 ounces, hustling drinkers out of 4-5 or more ounces of liquor, (11.4 oz. Bootleg bottle on left, 16 oz. pre-prohibition bottles center, 11 oz. on right)

This axe-chopped washtub in mine was used in moonshine operation. Courtesy of Cliff Walker.

Another story told by old timers was that a gas station on Cushenbury Grade, between Lucerne Valley and Big Bear, had one tank that held moonshine, instead of gasoline. This fuel was dispensed, only, to trusted customers through a dedicated pump.

One thing we do know for sure, during the Prohibition, Lucerne Valley was arid, but not dry!

Lane Walker emerging from mine tunnel with still in Furnace Canyon. Courtesy of Cliff Walker.

Stone Monument to a Dream – Willis Well

*Compiled by Bill Lembright from the writings of Martha Coutant in Heart Bar Ranch,
Bill Mann in Guide to 50 Interesting and Mysterious Sites In the Mojave, Grace Loomis Odell in
A Piece of Baling Wire: Homesteading in the Desert, Dix Van Dyke in Daggett: Life in a Mojave
Frontier Town, and Walter Ford in Stone Monument to a Dream. Photos courtesy of Bill Lembright.*

George Willis had been a mining promoter in Nevada, until that job played out. By 1908 George and his wife, Mildred, were squatting on some worthless property along the banks of the Mojave River in Daggett, where they grew vegetables in a small garden. George made just enough for them to get by; gradually he accumulated a small herd of cattle and horses. In 1915 their campsite was washed out by a flood and they moved to Middle Ord Mountain.

Willis Well's walls are about 6' wide! B 1-19

At the base of Middle Ord Mountain, at an elevation of 4,000 ft., George spotted an Indian rock shelter covered with petroglyphs, surrounded by plenty of good grazing land for the cattle and horses. He surmised there was a spring nearby. George had lost the use of an arm in an accident, so Mildred dug down just 20 feet and found water. With water from the well, Mildred tended 300 head of cattle.

They hauled lumber to the site and built a crude cabin out from the face of the rock shelter. Visitors felt they were walking into a conventional cabin, only to find themselves inside a cave.

Although George's health was failing, he developed a nearby mine while, Mildred, only 5'3"and 125 pounds, performed most of the chores. George drove the horses, who hauled a drag, on which Mildred loaded around

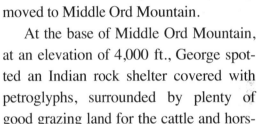

Willis Well still has water. B 1-19

1,372,000 pounds of rock to build a stone wall 660 feet long, four feet high, and almost six feet wide to keep livestock out of her gardens. George installed two planks over the well so Mildred could straddle the planks, lower a bucket on a rope between her legs, and raise water for the livestock, her garden, and to provide water for the cabin.

Mildred also built rock corrals and

*Willis Wells, Mildred and George Willis. B 1-19
Photo courtesy of Grace Loomis Odell.*

pens, plus a rock foundation for the cottage she dreamed of building on a slight rise near the well. Mildred kept pictures of Scottish castles from which she hoped to model her home and dreamed of planting massive desert flower gardens, protected from grazing animals by extensive rock walls.

Willis Wells, Mrs. Willis made all these rock walls herself. B 1-19

Willis Wells, Rock walls formed goat pens in early 1900's. B 1-19

In 1925 George became ill and had to be transported to San Diego for medical assistance, where he passed on. Soon after, Mildred sold their mining claims and cattle and never returned to complete her dream. These impressive, massive, rockworks stand today as a monument to this pioneer's dreams.

The Making of Barstow Road

Written for the Desert Grapevine Newspaper, January 31, 1949 by James Goulding.

Photo courtesy of J. S. Gobar Foundation.

"Dear Editor: I have been requested to state why I believe the present Bear Valley-Barstow road is the best of all the routes considered. But I have to look back to the beginning:

On April 14, 1914, the deputy county surveyor and a road crew had come as far as Stoddard Wells from Barstow, and were out on a preliminary survey from the Pass (now known as Sidewinder Road) as it is at present, to come across and connect with the Victorville-Bear Valley Road. Three preliminary surveys were made through Lucerne. The shortest way straight south across the dry lake was decided upon. On about the 24th of April, 1914, the county teams pulled into the north side of the dry lake and began work on the dyke across the lake. So you will know how road work was done in those days and how that and the dyke west of Strawberry Peak were built, I will tell you because I was there. Following the U. S. Section line, stakes 25 or 30 feet from the center of the proposed road were put down. With horse drawn equipment, this strip was plowed and mixed and then scraped to the center till the required height was reached. Then from the nearby hills, sand and gravel were hauled and packed down by the teams passing back and forth over the road-bed. The large rocks were pushed to each side to form a protective edge and prevent washings. Storm waters come from either east or west; culverts were put in but were not sufficiently protected from the cross currents. Even so, to my knowledge, there has been but one serious washout that made the road impassable, and that was when the storm water went thru and around a culvert and washed it out. The mud of this dry lake is known for its packing qualities. It has long been used by oil well drillers in hydraulic work. That road across the dry lake is as solid now as it was when built nearly 35 years ago; what the dyke needs is more culvert reinforcing. riprapping and black topping, all

This photo taken in January 1949, shows a scene not often seen in Lucerne Valley anymore. It was posted in the August 27, 1964 issue of the Leader Newspaper by Marjorie Reed who thought it might help the readers stay cool during the hottest season of the year. Photo courtesy of Lucerne Valley Leader Newspaper.

of which will be a lot less expensive than building a new road either east or west of the present road and around 5 or 6 miles shorter than these others would be, besides furnishing a direct road to stores and post office for 40 or 50 families living on the north side of this dry lake. These people will fight any change in the route, as a petition of 130 property owners and voters, to the supervisors, last fall, will testify. Now, personally, it won't help me any, only as a taxpayer. But I think the present road is the best for the present, all things considered. I have heard something about a shorter route. Sure, if the county would stand for about $80,000 for new grading. But try and get it. It is after election now, and I think you would hear plenty about "no funds for new grading."

The picture included is of Junie Gobar and friends building the dyke across Rabbit Dry Lake, for what was then, called the Victorville-Bear Valley Road and is now State Highway 18.

Current Barstow Road, heading North to Barstow from Lucerne Valley. Photos courtesy of Millie Rader.

Hercules Finger

Compiled by Bill Lembright. Photo courtesy of Lucerne Valley Leader Newspaper.

B 1-20

The first recorded climber of Hercules Finger or the Monument or the Pinnacle, whichever name you choose, was Kit Barnes, son of Dan and Marjorie Barnes. He was featured in this picture on the front page of the October 7, 1965 *Leader* newspaper. Kit stated in the article that he found other climbing pitons close to the top of the rock signaling that he was not the first to venture to the top. This landmark is located about 4.5 miles Camprock Road just south/west of the East Ord Mountain.

Too Much Civilization Coming to Lucerne Valley

Compiled by Bill Lembright. Photos courtesy of Bill Lembright.

Years ago, Dave Fisher, well-known cattle rancher of the Ord Mountains, told us a story his dad passed on to him. A former cattle rancher of the Ords rode his horse high in the mountains and looked out over Lucerne Valley to the south, as he often did. To his dismay, he spotted an electric light.

Goldfields flowers in wash along gas line road en route to the Ord Mtn Mines.

The story goes that he packed his belongings and moved his cattle to another range far to the east near Hole-In-The-Wall and Mitchell's Caverns. As far as he was concerned modern civilization had moved in and spoiled Lucerne Valley for those who loved the simple great outdoors.

Dave Fisher's Midwell ranch site, part of Shield F Ranch. B 1-21

North face at East Ord Mountain.

Cushenbury Grade, Famed "Back Road"

Story and Photos courtesy of Tom Core.

Cushenbury Grade James Johnston's Ranch House. B 1-6

Today the pleasant drive on State Highway 18 from Lucerne Valley to Big Bear may be done in only a few minutes. The distance is short, but the grade is steep with many sharp curves when compared to the other routes into the high country. However, the surface is good and several of the views are outstanding.

It was in 1865 that Superintendent John F. Nichols of the new and rich Moronga Silver Mine had this pioneer road built up through Cushenbury Canyon and across Cactus Flat to provide access to the mine in Lone Valley. All during this period of road construction, Nichols had his miners stock piling ore until the needed processing machinery could he hauled in.

With the wagon road completed by that fall, he soon had three smelters in operation.

It was early in the morning of February 2, 1865, that Nichols left the mine and hurried down the new road in his buckboard with a 50 pound bar of pure silver; the first of many loads he shipped from the roaring smelters. Two days later, when he delivered the shining bar to the Childs and Hiddens Mercantile Store in Los Angeles, there was much excitement and many shares of Moronga Mine stock were quickly sold.

When E. J. "Lucky" Baldwin began development of the Gold Mountain Mine in 1874 Chinese labor built a shelf road to the west that connected with the 1861 Holcomb Valley road to the desert and Cajon Pass. All the heavy machinery for this mine and its huge 40 stamp mill were hauled in over this wagon road. Later that year a road was built north from Gold Mountain City that switchbacked down to a junction with the Lone Valley/Cushenbury Canyon route in Cactus Flat.

Cushenbury Canyon and the grade were named after John Cushenbury, who was one of the earliest miners to arrive in Holcomb Valley after the May 1860 gold discovery. With bitter cold arriving that fall, most of the miners left for the duration of the winter.

One such group, making their way toward the desert, discovered a promising mineral deposit which they called the "Dickson Lead Silver Vein," and each staked a claim along

Cushenbury Grade photo of early road work.

Cactus Jim Johnson at Cactus Flats, 1912.

the exposed ore body.

Among this group was John Cushenbury, who was so impressed with this discovery that he laid out a town site and called it "Cushenbury City." Later, John established a ranch and built a home just below the present (Mitsubishi) cement plant. These old structures were later dismantled by Kaiser Permanent Cement in the 1970s after they purchased the property and springs.

Johnston Grade was named after pioneer miner James Johnston, who worked many mines in this country during his lifetime. He established a ranch at the top of Cushenbury Grade, and he is buried there on his ranch a few yards west of the modern highway.

The original road served for decades with only minimum maintenance until 1925 when 65 prisoners were put to work realigning and widening the famous old "Back road." One of the major improvements was the building of the switch backs and the shelf road uphill from Whiskey Springs. This greatly reduced the extremely steep grade from the bottom of the canyon to the crest at Cactus Flat.

Homesteading The Desert

Compiled by Millie Rader
Photos Courtesy, LV Museum, Robin McCartney and Claire Huck

Homesteading was the carrot that brought the early settlers to the valley, as it was the only way most could afford to purchase land of their own. Signed into law in May 1862 the Homestead Act opened up settlement in the western United States, allowing Americans, including freed slaves, to claim up to 160 free acres of federal land. To file a claim, an individual had to be at least 21 years of age, and be the head of household. This vagueness in the wording allowed women to file claims and own land. The act also required a person to be a citizen of the United States or declare intention to gain citizenship, which allowed many European immigrants to stake claims as well.

Davidson and Gobar

According to Junie Gobar in his book, *Raising the Dust*, Peter Davidson was the first homesteader in Lucerne Valley. He filed on land that included Rabbit Springs,

Peter Davidson's Cabin. B 1-13

where he created a Way Station for weary travelers headed for the gold fields. It is not known exactly when Davidson came to the valley but Gobar figured it to be sometime in the late 1870s.

In 1911 Junie and his brothers Harold and Dave drove here with their dad, Frank Joseph Gobar. Junie wrote that there was a lot of good land waiting as the desert was not in any hurry. They filed on parcels east of Rabbit Springs and on Camp Rock Road. They eventually let the Camp Rock Road claims go, but created the first large alfalfa ranch and dairy in Lucerne Valley on their homesteads located on Rabbit Springs, Lakeview and Gobar Roads.

What is a homestead?

The National Park Service website provides educational material that covers everything from animal habitats to American history. This interesting piece on homesteading is from that resource.

The cry went out in 1862, "Free Land for all who want it!" People came from the eastern United States and Europe, to the Great Plains to start new lives, staking their hopes and dreams on a claim for land. What they found was an ancient landscape of deep prairie grasses and unpredictable rain-fall. The

First Baldridge Cabin in Cove. B 1-16

free land they claimed came at a high cost, not just to themselves, but to the native people already living in the vast sea of grass. The native prairie itself was dramatically obliterated. Whole ways of life changed, some for better and some for worse.

The United States government wanted to see citizens settled in the interior territories to increase the wealth of the Nation. As Andrew Johnson, a Tennessee Senator, stated "... take one of these men, transplant him in the west upon 160 acres of fat, virgin soil, and in a few years ... you increase his ability to buy a great deal."

As the Civil War loomed closer, many other factors pushed the government into offering free land. The conflict over land increased between the South and North, with such laws as the Missouri Compromise and the Kansas-Nebraska Act of 1854. The South wanted to give the new territories and states the option of becoming slave areas; while the North wanted free states. The South, afraid of losing its voting power in Congress, did not want the new areas to be antislavery and opposed every new act that would give land away. As Galu-

Baldridge homestead in Sunset Cove. B 1-16

sha Grow, the father of the Homestead Act, stated ". . . why should not the legislation of the country be so changed as to prevent for the future, the evils of land monopoly, by setting apart the vast and unoccupied territories of the Union and consecrating them forever in free homes for free men?"

Orlando Jacobs Home Old Woman Springs Rd, drawing by Virginia Hemphill 1949, Desert Grapevine Newspaper. A 1-17

The coming of the Civil War assured passage of the Homestead Act. With the secession of the Southern states, there were few left in Congress to oppose the idea. On May 20, 1862, President Abraham Lincoln signed the Homestead Act into law, and became the champion of the free land idea.

Many railroads and western towns sent representatives to European countries to entice people to move to the United States. These representatives showed pictures of beautiful towns with tree-lined streets and rich soil for farming. The applicant of a claim had to file an affidavit with the local land office, stating they met the conditions required by the law. At this time, the claimant would pay a fee of $12 for filing the paperwork.

Once the filing was complete, there were additional requirements to receive the patent and title to the land. A person had to build a home, live on the land, make the land his/her permanent residence, and work the land for a period of five years.

After living on the land, building a home, and farming the land for five years, it was time to "prove

Typical Homesteader cabin circa 1950s.

up." This simply required the homesteader to find two individuals who would serve as witnesses. These witnesses had to state they had known the homesteader for five years, knew the claimant had built a home on the land, and that the claimant had tilled and worked so many acres of land for crops. With witnesses in tow, a claimant would proceed to the land office to "prove up," paying another small filing fee of $6 and having both witnesses sign the final documents. The claimant would then receive a final certificate or patent to the land.

There were several Homestead Acts after the Homestead Act of 1862, the Southern Homestead Act of 1866, the Timber Culture Act of 1873, the Kinkaid Amendment of 1904, the Enlarged Homestead Act of 1909 and the Stock-Raising Homestead Act passed in 1919.

In the early years of Lucerne Valley many newcomers here acquired land through the original Homestead Act. But meeting the act's requirement for cultivating 160 acres on a homestead was a challenge in the Mojave Desert. In the mid-1930s, a federal land inspector suggested a different set of rules were needed for the region. The Small Tract Act passed in 1938, provided homesteaders with five acres, requiring only that they construct a dwelling of at least 400 square feet within three years.

The Federal Land Policy and Management Act (FLPMA) phased out homesteading in the United States by repealing the pre-existing Homestead Acts in 1976, and declaring that these lands would re-

Bob Michael, Ada Michael and Parker Larum, clearing for foundation. B 1-18

main in public ownership. The National Forest Service, National Park Service, and now, the Bureau of Land Management, are commissioned in FLPMA to allow a variety of uses on those lands, while simultaneously trying to preserve the natural resources on them.

The Homestead Acts allowed the U.S. Government to give away 270 million acres of land in the west bringing many people to settle in this area.

McCartney and Huck

Many homesteaders came to Lucerne Valley following World War II, when the

need for affordable housing increased. They were able to homestead under the Small Tract Act. Many of those homesteader cabins can still be seen in their original state along the railroad track in the south-

ern foothills and throughout the Russell/ Lucerne Springs housing Tract and sur- rounding areas. Some of the cabins have been abandoned but many are still lived in today. Most of these homes have been enlarged but can still be recognized as a homesteader cabin by the one large room that comprised the original struc- ture. Many, but not all are constructed of cinder block.

In 2018 Robin McCartney still lives

Bob and Herman Michael building foundation. B 1-18

in an original homestead cabin built by her grandparents. Her grandparents were Herman Noble (Mike) Michael and Ada Elizabeth Skinner Michael. They were friends of Clark Gable, who in 1948 talked them into coming out to the desert to look at property. They drove up from the city to explore

Herman and Delmer Michael cooking dinner.

the area and spent the night in Lucerne Valley. They slept in sleeping bags on the floor of Ew- ing's Ballroom, the dome building on Highway 18 near Trade Post Road.

Gable ended up buying property in Palm Springs but the Michaels filed on three parcels, on Cherokee Trail in south/east Lucerne Valley. At that time each five-acre parcel was selling for $125 but they were able to buy three parcels together for $300. Robin's father and aunt ended up with the other two parcels. They began improvements in 1952.

Robin's family was living in La Crescenta at the time they homesteaded in Lucerne Valley and would drive out every other weekend to work on their properties. Her grandparents both worked for the Gladding McBean Pottery factory. Close friend and co-worker Claire Huck, along with her husband Parker Larum, also filed on a homestead parcel near the Michael's in 1952, and began building an improvement cabin. Claire who is 97, still lives in her cabin in 2018.

Several other friends and coworkers from the pottery factory also filed on homestead parcels and built homes there as well. The Michaels hired McDougall's Well Drilling to put

Sisters, Patty and Robin Michael.

in the first well. It was put down to 580 feet and the McDougall's allowed them to make payments. They soon formed a small private mutual water company called the Harmony Well Agreement and provided water to the friends who had built nearby. The other owners eventually put in their own wells. Robin and her two sisters, who inherited their grandparents place, are now the sole owners of the original well. Robin said that while they were constructing their improvement cabins, and before the well, they had to go up to Cushenbury Springs to collect water each day.

As a youngster, Robin came out to Lucerne Valley every weekend and continued the tradition after she got married. She, along with her siblings and dad helped her grandparents add a carport to the original structure. Later they had local contractor John Russell construct bedrooms and an indoor bathroom.

*Herman Michael proud
of new outhouse.*

Robin's parents bought the property across the street from her grandparents in 1952, and built a cabin in 1955. The Michaels all used cinder block in their construction while Claire and Parker used wood. Claire said they built the standard one big room by pouring the foundation, building a fireplace and then building around that. They too have added on throughout the years.

Robin McCartney and Claire Huck are only a small example of the many families in Lucerne Valley who are still benefiting from the early Homestead Acts.

Michael Cabin with Carport 1955. B 1-18

CHAPTER 2

Looking For Gold And More

Gold Mining In And Around Lucerne Valley

By Bill Lembright

A southern California gold rush began in 1860 when Bill Holcomb discovered a gold-bearing quartz ledge, in what is now called Holcomb Valley, while tracking a wounded grizzly bear. A few years later Big Bear experienced a record snowfall of 16 feet. Due to the freezing, many miners traveled down the north slopes of the San Bernardino Mountains seeking warmer climes. On their way down to the desert, some found deposits of gold and staked claims.

One of the richest finds was in Blackhawk Canyon exposed when the famous Blackhawk Landslide occurred eons ago. That story is told by Walter Del Mar later in this chapter.

Looking down on wagon-wheel wood arrastra and road you drive in on at the Fry Mountain mines. The mine at this arrastra was operating in 1911. Photo courtesy of Bill Lembright. B 2-1

Moving north across Lucerne Valley, some discovered gold in the Fry and Ord Mountains. Farther north they discovered gold and silver in the Alvords and Calicos. The Fry Mountains were named after Lucerne Valley resident "Dad" Fry who would head out alone in the night to his namesake mountains and return with bags of high grade ore. No one alive seems to know which prospects were his; but, there are many in the Fry's and prospectors continue to search there for gold, today.

Elsie Mine in the Fry Mountains, probably started by Dad Fry. Photo courtesy of Bill Lembright. B 2-2

The furnace at the Old Indian Springs Ranch, also known as Turner Ranch, is located above the Omya limestone plant and is the namesake of Furnace Canyon and Furnace Creek. It is believed to have been built by the Spanish for smelting ore out of the gold mines from the area of Wild Rose Canyon, such as Roy Garrison's Gold Point

Mine. The furnace measures about 5'x6' at the base and is 16' tall. It appears to have been used for years. The story is that the Spaniards enslaved the Indians to mine for gold and the Indians revolted, killed the Spaniards; and dumped the bodies in an abandoned mine tunnel, removed the timbers and collapsed it as a grave.

This picture taken in 1975 at Charcoal Furnace by Charles Rader includes several scouts from Boy Scout troop 150; Richard Rader, Ladd Parton, Ed Rader and David Rader.

B 2-3

George Lee's Lost Silver Mine

By Tom Core; printed originally in the Big Bear
Grizzly Newspaper on June 22 and 29, 2005; excerpted by Bill Lembright
with permission of Ruth and Ron Core and the Big Bear Grizzly.
Photos courtesy of Mojave River Valley Museum.

Robert Waterman

One evening around 1875, George Lee was in a saloon drinking and describing a good prospect for a silver mine he had found a couple of miles north of Barstow the previous week. It was there a chance meeting with politician Robert W. Waterman took place.

Before the evening was over Lee agreed to sell a half-interest in his claim, which they decided to call the Pencil Lead Mine. The next week the partners met again and Waterman asked to see the property before he paid for the half-interest. They met at the desert mine site a couple of days later and Waterman returned alone to San Bernardino with ore samples. When tested, the ore proved twice as valuable as Lee had claimed.

Lee remained at the mine as he wanted to dig out a larger quantity of the ore. A couple of weeks later he was back in San Bernardino with four burros loaded with ore. He was unable to locate Waterman, and bragged in the saloons that his new partner would have to pay twice as much for his half-interest.

In the meantime something strange transpired regarding the recording of the claim. Either Lee had gotten drunk and failed to file his claim, or Waterman had managed to have the paper removed from the records. The fact remained that Waterman was registered as the sole owner of the Pencil Lead Mine.

Never able to find his partner, Lee returned to the mine two weeks later with a dozen burros and sufficient supplies to last for more than a month. When he arrived at the mine he was confronted by three men armed with rifles who told him he was trespassing. Lee was furious, and said he had properly filed for the mine in San Bernardino. Not so, he was brusquely told, "This mine belongs to Robert Waterman."

Faced with no alternative, Lee was soon back in the courthouse, where he found Waterman was the owner of record. When he reported claim jumping to the sheriff, he was told the claim was legally

Waterman's, and Waterman had filed a complaint against Lee for robbing ore from the mine.

Seeking legal advice, Lee was told by his lawyer nothing could be done to get the mine back. He was also advised against taking the mine with armed force, as he could not gain by such an action.

In the following weeks Lee loudly and bitterly denounced Waterman in the local saloons. Word of the continuing tirade reached Waterman and he filed a lawsuit for slander against Lee. The effect of this was to intensify Lee's hatred, and he proclaimed when the matter reached the courtroom, he would prove Waterman crooked. Soon afterward, Waterman dropped the suit, but Lee continued his constant attack against Waterman.

The irate Lee resumed prospecting but was seldom gone for more than two weeks at a time. Whenever in town, he berated Waterman at every opportunity. The attacks infuriated Waterman and he told associates that Lee needed to be taught a lesson.

Head frame George Lee's Pencil Lead Mine.

About a year passed before Lee came in from a prospecting trip with a burro loaded with ore samples. Upon assay, they proved even richer than Pencil Lead ore. As before, Lee boasted of his discovery in the saloons, but said he would get this mine properly recorded in Los Angeles County where Waterman could not steal it. This attempt failed, as he was informed he had to record the claim in the county in which it was located. Lee decided not to register the claim at all; he would simply keep its location a secret.

During the following months, Lee regularly brought in his pack animals loaded with good ore. Working alone, he was able to support himself and his family from his secret silver mine. He claimed he would begin full-scale mining, but that Waterman was still having him trailed. He said Hans Hoffman, one of the armed men who had confronted him at the Pencil Lead, had twice followed him to Old Woman

Waterman Mill in Barstow where ore from George Lee's Pencil Lead Mine was processed.

Springs, a campsite on the way to his secret mine. This would later be recalled by the saloon crowd. One fall morning Lee headed up Cajon Pass on the way to his mine. The next day two riders were approaching Old Woman Springs when a horse and rider galloped from the trees and took the Barstow trail.

At the spring, the riders found a man sprawled on the ground with a large blood-stained rock in his hand. At first they thought he was dead as there was blood on his clothing, but after a brief examination they found his problem was being dead drunk. Shortly afterward, beneath a cottonwood tree they did find another body—this one dead from massive head injuries. They tied up the drunk, and one of the men rode off to San Bernardino to the sheriff. Later, the remaining traveler found three hobbled mules under some trees.

When Sheriff John Buckhart and three deputies finally arrived, they quickly determined the bloody rock had been the murder weapon. The tied-up drunk was now sober, and said his name was Hans Hoffman. When questioned about the dead man he explained it was a mistake that he was killed.

"Waterman only wanted him beaten until he told us where his mine was," Hoffman explained. "What's his name?" Buckhart asked. "George Lee" was the answer.

Under cloudy and dark skies, the body was loaded on one of the mules and Hoffman had to ride another mule as his horse had run away. Just as the group was about to leave the cottonwoods, three riders galloped up not knowing anyone else was at the spring. Buckhart shouted to halt, but they turned and swiftly rode away. Buckhart pulled his Colt, fired a single shot and one of the riders fell from his horse. Walking to the fallen man, the sheriff struck a match and saw a face he knew well. It was Regis Brown, a bodyguard for Waterman, and foreman of his Barstow Ranch.

In San Bernardino, Hoffman faced murder charges, with his expensive attorney fees paid by Waterman. He changed his story from what he had told Sheriff Buckhart, now claiming Lee had attacked him when they happened to meet at the spring. A first trial lasted six months and ended in a mistrial with 11-1 for conviction. The second shorter trial ended the same way. Hoffman was released on $15,000 bail, and after two days disappeared permanently.

Lee's wife sued Waterman for her husband's death and won an astoundingly large settlement of $300,000 for that time. Soon afterward, Waterman's brother sued Waterman for cheating him out of a 1/3 interest in the Pencil Lead Mine. The brother died before the trial date, but the heirs were awarded 1/3 the profits from the mine.

Waterman's cabin at the Pencil Lead Mine.

Waterman continued in politics and won an election in 1886 as Lieutenant governor of California. When Governor Washington Bartlett died a year later, Waterman became Governor of California.

More than a century and a quarter has now passed since old George Lee was murdered at Old Woman Springs. And in all of those decades, the rich silver mine he was working somewhere not too far away has not been found. Subsequently, silver was mined at Tip Top Mountain, and the Pioneer Moronga Mine. But, that ore did not match the richness of Lee's secret mine, which still remains lost on the desert side of the San Bernardino Mountains.

The Gold Mines of Blackhawk Canyon

By Walter Del Mar, excerpted by Bill Lembright. Photos courtesy of Walter Del Mar.

The Blackhawk Gold Company was formed in 1888 by Cook, Leach, Alexander Del Mar (Walter's grandfather, who was a world renowned mining engineer), and John McFee. Tunnels were bored in the west canyon walls and a ten-stamp mill operated for two years before the value of ore being mined fell off sharply. The Blackhawk mine lay idle for almost thirty years.

Cushenbury Ranch circa 1900 - Reine Rogers Wride, Belle Rogers Del Mar and friend to the left. B 1-6

Alexander's son, Algernon Del Mar, located the Blackhawk claims and directed the resumption of mining in 1921, along with his partner Roy Voorhies. Algernon incorporated the Blackhawk Canyon Mines into the Arlington Mining Corporation.

After Algernon married Adella Belle Rogers, Belle's brother, Bruce Rogers, bought Cushenbury Ranch for $10,000 in 1938 and built a house for a caretaker and the visiting Rogers and Del Mar families. They expanded the orchard and started raising turkeys commercially.

Algernon held the mineral claims to the vast limestone deposits south of the ranch. Kaiser Permanente Cement, who built the rail line from the Santa Fe rail line in Hesperia, later developed these deposits. The cement plant eventually purchased Cushenbury Ranch.

The weather at the Blackhawk Mines was harsh at times during the winter. Facilities were limited to wood stoves and creature comforts were few. Toilets were the two-hole variety behind the camp buildings. Bugs were a nuisance in winter and summer. There was a nasty bed bug we called Tigers, since their bite was painful, and the swelling lasted for some time.

The mines were very much a family attraction as the place that might make us rich some day. This did not happen, but the mine was a place to go and get the family together. Fourth of July holidays were a grand time with our fireworks and the firing of a small canon.

The winters were cold with occasional snow. We had a ready supply of pinyon pine wood that was rich with pitch to fire the potbellied stoves. To cool off in summer, we had the water storage tanks that served as a pool and bath, as there were no showers or bath tubs.

The mine always kept about four donkeys and a mule that carried the loads before the era of modern tractors and trucks. Walter's grandpa, George Rogers, used these animals to haul tanks, diesel engines, crushers, pipe, lumber, and tramway towers up the canyon trail to the base camp and mill, and then up the mountain to the ore deposits.

The Arlington Mill was powered by a 37-1/2 h.p. Fairbanks-Morse single cylin-

Ball mill arrives about one mile below the mill camp site. B 1-9

Blackhawk Mill - shows Cliff Mine tramway, blacksmith shop and donkey barn. B 1-9

der diesel engine, and electric power was obtained from a generator driven by a 25 h.p. diesel engine. To start the diesel engines, the cylinder was heated with a blowtorch and compressed air was used to turn the engine over several times. After a few bangs, the single cylinder engines would pound out a constant chug-chug. Clutches were closed, the big rubber belts turned the line shafts, and more pulleys and belts put the rock crushing and other machinery in motion.

In the dining room was a twenty-foot long table to serve up to twenty miners and the Del Mar family. Everyone had plenty to eat.

In 1931 the miners were paid three to five dollars a day, and one dollar fifty cents was deducted from that for board. The work day was 12 hours long. On Saturday the miners went to Victorville for a night out.

The underground workings totaled 12,000 feet in length and the ore was transported to mills by two aerial tramways; one being 5,100 feet in length and the other 4,300 feet in length. Each carried sixteen buckets that traveled over towers and cliffs. Gold was extracted from the ground ore by a sand-leaching-cyanide process.

In 1939, the Arlington Mine workings were taken over by the Santa Fe Gold Mines, Inc. which tried to speed up mineral extraction before the mine, and mill infrastructure was upgraded to handle higher volume. After two years of this ramped up schedule, most mining at the Santa Fe ended in 1941, as did most gold mines during WWII.

Santa Fe tunnels and workings. B 1-9

It was not until the 1980s when the price of gold approached $800 per ounce that serious mining returned to the Blackhawk Amerigold, Inc. and Del Peterson began a new venture that lasted several years. Trails became roads, a 300-foot well was drilled at the Arlington camp and mill site, and cya-

1939 - 600 ton sand-leaching-cyanide plant - located at mouth of Blackhawk Canyon. B 1-9

nide leaching ponds were constructed. Gold value dropped and work ceased.

In 1986 Del Peterson sold Amerigold, Inc. to Haber Inc. who built a test mill in 1987 at the Arlington Mill site; but due to the price of gold, not much came of it. Peterson reacquired the property in 2011. In 1985 Registered Professional Geologist Roger Ames documented the estimated reserves of the Blackhawk Mines to be 464,000 ounces of gold. At $1200 per ounce, that's valued at $556.8 million.

Early Miners – The Reed Family Story

By Clifford Reed, as told to Jan Lembright. Photos courtesy of Bill Lembright.

Doug Walton and Jan at Miner's cabin along Grapevine Creek. B 2-4

Clifford Reed's maternal grandfather, Maron Waller, suffered from health problems and moved here in 1920 or 1921 to benefit from the dry climate. He homesteaded off Camp Rock Road. Later, he and his wife moved to 20 acres between Baker and Trade Post Road and into the house near the VFW, where Cliff and his sister, Linda, now live. Maron grew alfalfa there.

Cliff's paternal grandfather, George C. Reed, was a miner who moved here in 1926. George lived on the hill at the top of Rabbit Springs Lane. He and his son, Harold (Cliff's father), went to work for the Arlington Santa Fe Mine from the late 1920s through the 1930s during the Great Depression. Then George discovered gold on the back side of Partin Limestone in Cactus Flats. He called his mine the Three Star Mine.

Cliff remembered that when he was a child there were cabins throughout Cactus Flats and up through Jacoby Canyon. While they were mining at the Three Star Mine, they ground the ore in an arrastra just below their cabin, and then hauled it out with mules. That arrastra (a circular grinding platform with a large stone in the middle was attached to a mule that pulled it around and to grind the ore into powder) is still there today.

All the boys who were old enough worked in the mine. There were eight boys and one girl. Troy was the youngest and too young to work. It was important for everyone to work, times were hard and the family needed the money.

The Black Hawk and the Arlington Santa Fe were the two mines where Cliff's father and grandfather worked; they hauled out silver and gold. It all ended when the gold standards stopped and World War II began. George had been a carpenter and went to work helping build George Air Force Base. Harold went to work at Pfizer Limestone Mine, which is now Specialty Minerals.

Arrastra just north of cabins and above creek. B 2-4

Cliff was born in 1940 in Bellflower, California. He worked for Kaiser Cement, and then worked for Bob McDougall for 20 years as a heavy equipment operator. Cliff and his sister, Linda, are both retired and still live in Lucerne Valley. Cliff now works for Center Water Company as a field worker and trouble shooter.

Kaiser / Mitsubishi Cement Corporation

Compiled by Millie Rader

The recorded history of the Cushenbury Plant began just after discovery of gold in Holcomb Valley, near the current Big Bear Lake, in 1860. The following year a prospector named John Cushenbury hiked down the north slope of what would later be called San Bernardino Mountains, in search of a warmer place to prospect through winter.

Modern Mitsubishi Plant. Photo courtesy of David Rader. B 1-6

Cushenbury was looking for gold and discovered a silver vein in limestone deposits of the future Mitsubishi Cement Corporation Cushenbury Quarry, located at the base of Cushenbury Canyon on Highway 18, seven miles southeast from the center of Lucerne Valley. A small silver rush occurred at that time with a large encampment of miners living at the springs below. They called their temporary home, Cushenbury City. Silver quickly played out, but people continued to occupy what we now call Cushenbury Springs because it provided a year-round water supply. Mitsubishi Cement Corporation now owns the land surrounding this artesian water supply and has designated Cushenbury Springs a Riparian Habitat and set it aside for local wildlife.

In 1888 The Blackhawk Gold Company was formed by Cook, Leach, Alexander Del Mar and John McFee. It was in operation only two years. In 1921 Del Mar's son, Algernon, resumed mining and according to a book written by his son, Walter, held the rights to all limestone claims south of Cushenbury Springs.

Algernon's brother-in-law, Bruce Rogers, bought Cushenbury Ranch in 1938 for $10,000 which included Cushenbury Springs. He built a newer house for a caretaker and the visiting Rogers and Del Mar Families. He also expanded an existing orchard and began raising turkeys there commercially.

Not long after Henry J. Kaiser built the Kaiser Cement Plant in Cushenbury Canyon in 1957, he also purchased the Cushenbury Springs property.

During World War II, Henry J. Kaiser was building Liberty Ships and needed a source of limestone, used at that time in the steel-making process. He found the nearest source along the northern flank of the San Bernardino Mountains near Lucerne Valley and purchased many mining claims there. He negotiated a deal with Santa Fe Railroad to build a spur from its mainline in Hesperia to Lucerne Valley to transport the ore. When the war ended, troops came home and a housing boom began. Kaiser realized lower grade limestone, not used in steel, was perfectly suitable for cement manufacture, and instructed his engineers to design and build the Cushenbury Cement Plant. On May 16, 1957, Kaiser staged a grand opening celebration, inviting dignitaries from all over California. Over 1200 guests are reported to have arrived by bus, plane, train, and automobile for the gala event.

Kaiser Permanente Cement Company Grand opening event. Photo courtesy of June Fuller. B 2-5

The third passenger train to travel across the 29.2 miles of railway track leading from the Santa Fe Mainline to Lucerne Valley arrived on May 19, 1957, for the dedication ceremonies of the new Kaiser Permanente Cement Company's Cushenbury Plant (now owned by Mitsubishi Cement Corporation). Visitors from all over Southern California left Los Angeles at 8:00 am making stops along the way for sightseeing and arrived at the Cushenbury Plant at

Third passenger train to Lucerne Valley May 19, 1957. Photo courtesy of June Fuller.

1:15 pm. Following the festivities, the group boarded the train and headed back to Los Angeles arriving there at 8:00 pm.

Pacific Railroad Society trip May 4, 1985. Photo courtesy of Lucerne Valley Museum Association.

According to an article written by Chris Guenzler for Trainweb.org, this Sunset Limited Amtrak was the fourth passenger train to ever visit Lucerne Valley. The trip was orchestrated by the Pacific Railroad Society. The train carried approximately 400 train enthusiasts, riding in a Santa Fe Hi-Level coach, from Fullerton to the Kaiser Permanente Plant in Lucerne Valley on May 4, 1985.

Kaiser 1957. Photo courtesy of
Mitsubishi Cement Corporation. B 2-5

This aerial photograph of the recently completed Kaiser Permanente Cement plant, located in Cushenbury Canyon on Highway 18, seven miles southeast from the center of Lucerne Valley, was posted in the *San Bernardino County Sun Telegram*. The caption stated "The $13,000,000 Permanente Cement Co. plant in Lucerne Valley was dedicated yesterday, May 16, 1957. The two 450-foot-long rotary kilns are in the center of the photo. At the right are 12 storage silos near the new Santa Fe Rail spur from Hesperia."

This May 2, 1957, *Leader* newspaper photograph was captioned "Distribution Superintendent of Lucerne Valley's (Kaiser) Permanente Cement Company, Bob Nieman (second from the left) shown presenting first sack of cement manufactured at the local plant to Chamber of Commerce officers. From left to right are President Al Morgan, Vice-President Jim Hansen and Secretary-Treasurer Marvin Bantz.

First sack of cement for chamber. Photo courtesy
of Lucerne Valley Leader Newspaper.

Mitsubishi Cement Corporation. Photo courtesy of
Lucerne Valley Leader Newspaper. B 2-5

This picture is of the Cushenbury Cement Plant as it appears today. In 1987 the plant was purchased by Hanson Plc, and was sold a year later to a group of Mitsubishi Companies whose leaders then formed the Mitsubishi Cement Corporation, USA. Mitsubishi immediately began upgrading the facility, significantly improving the cement quality, equipment reliability, and air quality.

The late local historian, Charles (Chuck) F. Rader, drove for the Shell Oil Company in 1957, when this photo was taken. He is shown here with an unnamed Kaiser driller, refueling the Joy Drill that was working just south of the Primary Crusher. The drill was used for test and blasting holes.

Joy Drill. Photo courtesy of Chuck Rader. B 2-5

In the early years, Kaiser Cement kept its own fleet of trucks for shipping its product. The Cushenbury Plant was patterned after and considered to be the sister Plant of Kaiser Permanente Cement plant in Cupertino, California. At the completion of the Cushenbury Plant, many of the Cupertino truck drivers were transferred from the bay area to Lucerne Valley to transport cement to local markets. Most of those drivers chose to make Lucerne Valley their new home, raising their families and retiring here.

Kaiser truck fleet. Photo courtesy of June Fuller. B 2-5

Mill and equipment operators 1959. Photo courtesy of Chuck Rader.

Only the names of two Kaiser employees in this picture were available at the time of this writing. The man standing to the far right is Bob Tevis and the man with the broom, next to him, is Chuck Rader who worked 28 years for the company. He was the safety supervisor when he retired. Chuck's son, David Rader, is the safety supervisor at the plant at the time of this writing, and Bob Tevis's grandson, Roy Tevis, works in the quarry.

Omya / La Habra / Lucerne Valley Lime-Rock Products

Compiled by Millie Rader. Photos courtesy of the Veale Family Trust.

According to the March 11, 1960, edition of the *San Bernardino Sun Telegram*, the County Planning Commission approved a zoning change for 1440 acres of land, located near the top of Crystal Creek Road, just south of the Santa Fe Rail spur, from M-1 light manufacturing to M-2 heavy manufacturing. George W. Veale Sr. of Lake Arrowhead, President of Sentinel Mining Corporation, told the planner the company was proposing a quarter million dollar ore processing plant at that location.

Main Plant. B 2-6

The ore processing would be done in conjunction with Hall, Hall & Petty Corporation's processing of dolomite to allow mining of the more precious limestone deposits below. This plant would be called Lucerne Valley Lime-Rock Products.

Sentinel Shareholders

Wilbur C. Veale, Elick M. Bowler and Clifford Hamblin, three of the eight Sentinel Mining Corporation shareholders, examine the first calcium carbonate or limestone rock processed through the newly constructed primary crusher at the Lucerne Valley Lime-Rock Plant in the spring of 1960. The other original shareholders were George W. Veale Sr., Edi Juan, Les Grove, Harry Pike and August W. Bowler.

Primary Crusher. B 2-6

This photo was taken in May 1960 of the Lucerne Valley Lime-Rock primary crusher during its trial run. The crane stands by to make any necessary adjustments. By October 1960, the new plant was producing approximately 400 tons of limestone weekly, which was used by Kennedy Metals Co. in paint whitening.

In this photo, also dated May 1960 Sentinel shareholder Wilbur Veale, and an unnamed employee, set the final sheet of steel into the primary crusher hopper, while a haul truck full of rock waits to make the first dump. Veale was the catalyst behind the formation of the Sentinel Mining Corporation. While at the Pirates Den, a nightclub of which he was part owner, he met many miners with claims in the San Bernardino Mountains. Their stories inspired him to head for the desert to prospect for uranium. During one of his prospecting trips on the hillside above Lucerne Valley, he noticed there was more limestone than uranium, and about 1955

Wilbur Veale Setting Steel

he began to establish claims in the Furnace Creek and Crystal Creek canyons. Sometime in 1966, he realized that he had struck white gold. With the housing boom at that time, limestone was in high demand. He talked his brother, George, and others into forming a mining company. The group then pooled their resources to build a processing plant to handle ore they were mining. That processing plant was the foundation of what is now Omya's limestone processing plant on Crystal Creek Road just above the BSNF Railroad tracks in Lucerne Valley.

In 1959 Wilbur's nephew, George Veale Jr., shown here dismounting a TD 48 dozer, graduated from USC. The Sentinel partners talked him into joining the group and being the hands-on operator until the company sold the plant to LaHabra Products Inc. in the early 1970s. George Jr. stayed with the plant through the LaHabra and Pluess Staufer/ Omya, (CA) changes in ownership. He was the Omya Safety Coordinator and Public Relations Rep-

George Veale Jr.

resentative when he passed away in 1989, having been with the operation over 30 years.

First truck load.

This truck load of sacked limestone was the first shipment produced by the new Lucerne Valley Lime-Rock plant in 1960. The company, at that time, had only one customer. Now this same limestone processing plant is owned by Omya, an international company, with customers worldwide. Omya leases its claims from several different claim holders, but the majority of its limestone still comes from the Sentinel Mining Corporation owned and operated by the heirs of the original eight partners.

The August 18, 1960, *Lucerne Valley Leader* newspaper featured this picture on the front page, with an article about William "Mac" McAllister who lived in the cave in the background, which he had dug out from the side of the hill. McAllister was known as one of the best bulldozer operators in the area. He pioneered most of the early roads to the Furnace Canyon limestone claims as well as to the Sentinel claims south of what is now the Omya Limestone Plant. McAllister lived in the cave year round. Much of his cooking was done on his hand-built, rock barbe-

Furnace Canyon Cabin. B 2-7

cue/oven that can be viewed near the cabin. Three outdoor visitor cots are visible in this picture. A spring flowed from the side of the hill just behind the person with a camera. The spring still seeps from the ground in this area, but the cave and cabin have long since been covered by overburden material from the Specialty Minerals Inc./ Limestone quarries. In this article, McAllister told the reporter that the old, run-down miner's cabin was there long before he showed up. While renovating the cabin, he found that it had been insulated with newspapers dating back to the early 1900s.

Furnace Canyon Cave interior.

This picture shows the interior of the Furnace Canyon cave that McAllister had created and called home for many years. According to Bill Veale, son of Wilbur Veale, the cave was quite ingenious. He had visited the cave many times and mentioned the 55 gallon drum woodstove, the cot to the left and the revolver hanging on the wall, all visible in this picture. The cave was used by McAllister and the Sentinel partners until a mining claim dispute in the late 1950s caused the company to focus its efforts on the Crystal Creek Canyon claims which, according to the descendents of the original Sentinel shareholders, turned out to be where the richer deposits of limestone were to be found. Photos courtesy of Barbara Veale.

Texas Granite Quarry

Compiled by Millie Rader.

An article in the June 30, 1940, *San Bernardino Daily Sun* stated that Texas Quarries Inc., located in Victorville, California had recently doubled their plant size. The company had a backlog of $250,000 in unfilled orders and had just signed a contract with the U.S. War Department to fill orders requiring Golden Vein Granite; the world's sole source was located in Lucerne Valley.

Texas Quarry gold vein blocks. Photo courtesy of David Rader. B 2-8

The Lucerne Valley Texas Granite quarry was located near Cougar Buttes. The granite blocks were blasted out and cut on site, then trucked to the Victorville facility to be polished. This photo was taken sometime in the 1940s on Rabbit Springs road near Midway School.

Granite Truck. Photo courtesy of Sam Clark.

Crane. Photo courtesy of David Rader. B 2-8

The Sun newspaper article also stated that a 50 ton derrick was to be installed at the Lucerne Valley site raising the production capacity. The Golden Vein Granite from Lucerne Valley was also used in construction of the Santa Fe Hospital in Los Angeles, the Mormon Temple in Idaho Falls, and St. Vincent's Hospital in Seattle. In three previous years, the company had supplied over 40 post offices throughout the nation with granite facades, steps, cornices, and decorations. Though no history was found for the date the quarry ceased to operate, the crane is said to have withstood the elements until the mid-1980s, when it mysteriously disappeared.

Victorville Limrock / Pfizer / Specialty Minerals Inc.

Compiled by Millie Rader. Photos courtesy of Lucerne Valley Museum Association.

According to the *San Bernardino Sun Newspaper*, the Victorville Lime Rock Company (now Specialty Minerals Inc.) opened its million dollar Lucerne Valley Plant in April, 1961. The plant is located at the top of Meridian Road, six miles south of Highway 18, on the Santa

Victorville Limerock. B 2-9

Fe Rail line. 50 employees were hired at that time to operate the lime rock processing mill, quarries and maintenance shops. The company projected to have up to 200 employees within five years. Engineering and core drilling had begun almost four years earlier and it had taken a year to construct the plant. Victorville Lime Rock was owned by C.K. Williams and Co. of St Louis. The Victorville plant was one of the largest lime rock suppliers in California at that time.

Victorville Lime Rock Co. announced the transfer of ownership in October 25, 1962, edition of the *Lucerne Valley Leader* newspaper after the sale of C.K. Williams and Co. to Charles Pfizer Co., Inc. Executives of the two companies met in New York on October 15 to complete the transaction, which involved 7,232 shares of Pfizer common stock. Pfizer officials said no

Ownership change.

changes in management, personnel or the operation of the Victorville and Lucerne Valley Plants were being considered. This picture shows a shovel loading a haul truck in the newly acquired Pfizer quarry.

New Design. B 2-9

John P. Bartels, director of operations at Pfizer Lucerne Valley Limestone Plant (center) points to new units in the chemical lime complex. He cites design features to J.W. Ayers, general manager left and B.J. Quinn vice president. In 1964, the new $7 million operation had over 100 employees.

Small Mines

Compiled by Millie Rader. Photos courtesy of Lucerne Valley Leader Newspaper.

Lucerne Valley Rock Products

Lucerne Valley Rock Products received a zone change from the San Bernardino County Planning Commission in 1957, allowing the owner Ernest Herrmann to begin light to heavy manufacturing on 40 acres. According to the *San Bernardino County Sun Telegram*, it was located three fourths of a mile east of Crystal Creek Road and two miles south of Old Woman Springs Road. The rock and sand plant, now known as Hi-Grade Materials, is located on Meridian Road, south of Highway 18. The plant is currently owned and operated by Robar Enterprises in Hesperia.

Hi-Grade Materials. A 2-10

Silver Creek Mine. B 2-11

Silver Creek Mine

This picture of the old Silver Creek Mine was featured on the front page of the June, 17, 1965, *Leader* newspaper as a tourist attraction. At that time there were mine shafts and old miner cabins. These have long since disappeared. The mine site, located north of the Santa Fe Rail line near White Knob is now part of the Omya (Ca) limestone mine claims.

C M & H Mining Company

In 1957 the C M & H Mining Company planned to go into operation, shipping ore by rail from the Kaiser Permanente Cement Plant loading ramp, with an estimated 200 tons per day as the initial shipments. Shown here is the site located at the Bessemer Iron Mine, 31 miles east of Lucerne Valley. Fred H. Crosby from Toelle, Utah was the mine superintendent.

Bessemer Iron Mine. B 2-12

Silver Reef Mine located on Bessemer Mine Road. According to westernmininghistory.com its primary ore is zinc. Photo courtesy of Lucerne Valley Leader. B 1-7

Mill at Silver Cliffs Mine at the east end of the Rodman Mountains. Photo courtesy of Bill Lembright. B 2-13

Miners cabin east of Troy Road in the Newberry Mountains. Photo courtesy of Bill Lembright. B 2-14

Cyanide vats at Copper Strand Mine at ne end of the Fry Mountains. Photo courtesy of Bill Lembright. B 2-15

Mill terraces at Gold Belt Mine near Goat Mountain Pass. Photo courtesy of Bill Lembright. B 2-16

Lester Dale ore hopper adjacent to Partin Lime Quarry. Photo by of Bill Lembright. B 2-17

*Main house at Lester Dale
mining camp. Photo courtesy
of Bill Lembright. B 2-17*

Blackhawk Landslide

Blackhawk Landslide. B 1-8

In 1959, Ronald Lee Shreve published a thesis, titled *Geology and Mechanics of the Blackhawk Landslide, Lucerne Valley, California*. He presents the geological and mechanical evidence to conclude that this two mile wide by one hundred foot thick landslide lobe, that extends five miles from the mouth of Blackhawk Canyon to the floor of the valley, was propelled by a natural air-lubrication mechanism. This explains not only the high speed and undeforming nature of the sliding sheet, but also the compositional structure. The Blackhawk Landslide can easily be viewed from Highway 247, 10 miles east from the center of Lucerne Valley, near Santa Fe Fire Road.

CHAPTER 3

Cowpunchers and Clodhoppers

Old Woman Springs Historic Ranch

Written by Virginia Hemphill and published in the Desert Grapevine newspaper, February and March 1947. Photo courtesy of Lucerne Valley Museum Association.

Old Woman Springs Ranch reservoir. B 3-1

To the uninitiated, a desert spring is expected to bubble gently from a depression in the flat sands. Out in this part of the Mojave, springs are found in the foothills. Those of Old Woman Springs come from the heart of a clay hill. The location was first mapped and given a name nearly a century ago.

In 1907 Albert Swarthout homesteaded the land at Old Woman Springs and had the government establish his boundaries. Then he fully developed the springs that supplied water in abundance for the 400 acre stock ranch.

A tunnel was bored in the largest of the springs, through a 40 foot thickness of clay, back 200 feet into the hill. This is known as a clay gouge. At 75 feet from the entrance, in the tunnel, a shaft 22 feet deep was sunk and an 8-inch pipe let down. This increases the flow to 60 inches continuously for a 10-day irrigation. Ordinarily, there is 16 inches of water flowing from the spring. At the time this arrangement was completed, an engineer by the name of Hoye of Santa Ana wrote an article about it for an engineering journal.

The water goes into a large reservoir and to irrigate the fields, Swarthout built a simple and effective system. From the reservoir, the fall is 26 feet to a concrete basin of two compartments. In the first section, a cutoff controls the speed of the flow of the intake. The second compartment has three gates that feed the laterals to the different fields. At intervals of 30 feet, gate valves on these laterals control the flow into the checks. All this was accomplished at considerable expense, as any rancher knows from experience. But, there is the enviable fact that this wonderful lot of sparkling water costs absolutely nothing to lift. The music of running water is heard everywhere about the ranch. It is a nice experience to stand beside the reservoir, cooled by the gentle afternoon breezes and shaded by overhanging boughs of rich green. Glimpsed through the trees is the white, barren des-

Albert Swarthout.

ert and hemming that, is a string of pale, lilac hills at the base of which are bands of heat waves that dance one's eyes out of focus. But here, the water sings a greeting to the light of day, and we murmur a gay response, because we know its borning is not costing a red penny.

Albert R. Swarthout was born in San Bernardino, February 11, 1872. He is from Mormon stock, his grandfather having helped to build the Temple at Salt Lake before the family migrated to San Bernardino in

1937 Cattlemen gathering. L-R: Cliff Shay, Dale Gentry, Harry Allison, Al Swarthout, John Cram, John & Will Talmadge, Will Shay, Sheriff Emmett Shay. From Kendall Stone's "Foxfire, 100 years of Cow Ranching in the San Barnardino Mountains/Mojave Desert."

the early part of the century. In 1895 as a young man, dreaming of a cattle empire, he wandered into this valley and filed on land now known as Box S Ranch. Swarthout dug a well and built a cabin, then decided the location wasn't suitable for a cattle ranch, and relinquished the claim, which James (Dad) Goulding later homesteaded.

Swarthout then filed on the land at Old Woman Springs and started a herd of white-faced herefords. The stock was pastured at Old Woman Springs during the winter, and at Big Meadows, at the head of Santa Ana Canyon during the summer months. When the herd reached around 1200 head, the pasturage at the ranch proved inadequate. In order to produce a portion of the winter feed, Swarthout built the irrigation system. While the water is plentiful and free at Old Woman Springs, the fields are wide, pipelines are long and cowhands insist upon pay and good horses, so Swarthout took in a partner. This arrangement worked for a time.

Bob Kaiser, last round-up circa 1940s.

The Swarthout brand, Heart Bar, has no special significance. Swarthout explained that he wanted a brand that would not blotch when applied and chose this for no other reason. We changed the subject, knowing the man would sooner be heard laughing out loud than admit to sentiment of any kind.

Old Woman Springs Ranch alone consists of 400 acres, plus he and his present partner own 2600 acres at Big Meadows. Not all the land of the desert ranch was homesteaded; a part of it was bought with script from the State. This consisted of about 20 sections over the desert. They drilled wells on these sections, put up windmills and built watering troughs. A perfect setup that worked successfully until homesteaders, seeing that water was to be had, took up land in adjoining sections and got water at the watering troughs. This was all right with Swarthout until, either through fear of the cattle (cows with young calves are not too friendly) or just plain lawlessness, the stock was eventually driven away. Often constructive acts attract a certain amount of opposition; perhaps this was Swarthout's particular barrier - one of many. In desert well skirmishes, homesteaders came out second best, because Swarthout had the windmills dismantled and stored at the ranch.

Not all the homesteaders in that part of the desert were of the type who chased pretty white-and-red cattle from their very own drinking water. One, by the name of Martin, had an idea. He was an electrical engineer and came to the desert to experiment with sunlight, believing the rays could be used for heating and a few other purposes. Though his experiments failed, Martin passed away recently, still believing that someone would succeed in harnessing the sun's rays for the benefit of mankind.

Back in the days when the herds were really large and the roads mere trails, the Swarthout outfit trained wild burros as pack animals. When changing the stock from the desert to the Big Meadows Range, loaded with supplies, the patient little burros walked slowly among the cattle without causing a stampede, and returned to camp of their own accord. Horses were too fast for this purpose.

At that time, wild burros and horses roamed the area from Old Woman Springs to Cushenbury. The wild horses were known as "broomtails" because their manes and tails were one mass of burrs and cactus thorns. The band at Cushenbury became the target for Sunday big game hunters and cat and dog food dealers, until the law stepped in four or five years ago.

A few young horses fled to the safer area of Horsethief Flat. Every now and then some of these stray down to the desert. One or two promising specimens have been captured and trained as cow ponies.

Old Woman Springs was given its name by a surveying party that came in 1856 and found a number of old Indian squaws at the springs. That situation suggested the name that has been on the

Stone meat house and ranch house. Photo courtesy of Martha Coutant. B 3-1

maps for nearly a century. As to why only old women were at the Springs, there are two different reasons handed down through the years, and no one can be certain that either is correct. We prefer the reason Mr. Swarthout gives. It was customary for Indians of this section of the Mojave to leave their old women and very young children at these springs while they went up into the hills to hunt and gather nuts. While it is true that the survey party is said to have mentioned only old women, there could have been children there also. They may have been hidden when the surveying party appeared. The other known story does not give the Mojave Indian too much in the way of social responsibility. It states that when the women got very old they were taken to a location far removed from the large encampment, where they were left to themselves until death came. Let us credit the Indians with this much; they chose the camping place of the old squaws with care. If Old Woman Springs was really the last home of the discarded tribe members, we think their lot was not so bad.

We saw tomato plants here in December still bearing. And who knows, but that these old women looked forward to their exile where they would be free from the lazy, overbearing men-folk.

Bunk house. Photo courtesy of Martha Coutant. B 3-1

To digress a bit, our knowledge of Mojave Indian lore is almost nil. We discount much that has been written, sketchily, in most instances, about the Paiutes. The old scrapbooks kept by Mrs. Jones from the newspapers, as far back as 37 years (1910), makes but one mention of an Indian. That was in connection with the 2 year-old boy that strayed to Muffin Mountain.

From old settlers we get Indian data that can be considered worthwhile. These people lived with the Indians, and do not recall the experience with the same enthusiasm of the late James Fenimore Cooper, the beloved author. Swarthout knew these Paiutes and they trusted him. He believes, for instance, that had he been here at the time Willie-Boy went haywire, he could have brought the Indian in without the aid of the posse. This was not a boast. Swarthout simply stated a fact without, in any way, wishing to appear braver than the members of the posse.

In 2018 the Old Woman Springs Ranch is still in existence with three ponds and many of the original buildings still in place. It is privately owned and is not open to public viewing.

Wild Horses

By Frances Hanken, Edited by Jan Lembright August 2017
(This article was first published in the Lucerne Valley newspaper July 18, 1957)

For many years, herds of wild horses roamed the hillsides and canyons south of Lucerne Valley. Thundering hoofs, whistling stallions and the typical trailing manes and tails of wild mustangs were still common sights in the mountains here as late as 1938.

Back in 1900, nearly 200 horses were branded with the Triangle J-H and belonged to a Mexican cattleman called "Felipe." When he sold out to Ed Grime in 1909, the open range was discontinued and dozens of colts grew up without ever seeing a white man.

Homer Urton, one of the cowboys of the Ihmsen Ranch in Apple Valley, was quoted as saying, "There is only a handful of the big herd of wild horses left in the hills. About two dozen can be seen grazing in the neighborhood of Coxey Ranch; another dozen roam the Cushenbury grade hillside. None of the old ones, marked with the Felipe iron, are left. But those left on the range today are plenty wild!" Homer added, "they are so interbred that none of them weigh more than 750 pounds, but boy are they still wild."

The wild horses presented quite a problem to the cattlemen, although it was agreed among them that the band of horses presented a picturesque sight whenever they came into view. The horses were so wild they frightened the range cattle, and at the water holes their sharp hooves muddied the tiny streams, often clogging up the outlets.

Frequently, Lucerne Valley residents caught wild colts and raised them, later breaking them to the saddle or for use on the ranches. Aaron Whaller, in the late twenties, caught a wild colt in the hills back of his homestead in the Camp Rock Road area east of town, and sold it after breaking it to the saddle.

A number of wild horses came to the brush in back of Rosa and John Koehly's barn. Twelve year old John Koehly Jr. got close enough to pet one of the colts, but promptly was bitten on the arm by the mare, the mother of the colt.

Later, young John chased a herd of wild horses he found while riding across the valley, driving them until he was able to separate a colt from its mother. When he had thrown and tied the colt he rode home, got his father and with the family's Model T Ford sedan, in which the unwilling colt was put, the colt was brought to the Koehly barn. The colt, named "Danger," grew to be a beautiful riding horse that was later sold to another Lucerne Valley rancher.

Until fairly recent, wild grape vines grew in profusion in Crystal Creek. Ranch families, of Lucerne Valley, often went up into the canyon to pick the ripe grapes, which they made into jelly or wine. Frequently wild horses were seen in this canyon. Once, a group of people were terribly frightened by some of the horses that came to drink from a small spring near where a picnic lunch had been spread out.

Guy Williams of Baker Road, who came to Lucerne Valley in 1935, said recently that when he arrived there were two heavy mules running with the herd of wild horses.

Bruce Tyler, who lived at Cushenbury Springs at the time, caught several of the wild horses and one of them, after being tamed, became an excellent riding horse.

The wild horses have disappeared from the hillsides south of our valley and none have been reported for at least ten years.

Water Rights - Miller Ranch

Compiled by Jan Lembright from anecdotes of Greg Carpenter, Gene Hedly, Kathryn Anema and Virginia Hemphill's article Ranches of the Valley, Desert Grapevine August 1946.

The Miller B bar Ranch is five miles southwest of the center (of town) and is one of the older ranches of the valley. Its elevation is 300 feet higher than the floor of the valley, which moderates the temperature so that pepper and eucalyptus trees thrive, unusual for the Mojave desert.

The ranch was first owned by Mary Frances Bird, who homesteaded the land in 1925 and secured the water rights to Ruby Spring a few years later. This water was piped 2 1/2 miles down to the ranch for its livestock, orchard and five houses.

In 1964 the cottages were widely separated, each being secluded by a growth of shade and fruit trees. The Miller brothers occupy the ranch house and El Repose, and others are rented furnished.

The Millers bought the ranch around 1938. H.G. Miller, who came from Canada to the valley, has lived on the ranch continuously and raised giant baby bronze turkeys. He has his usual 1,000 birds this year.

Sam Clark added that Henry Guy Miller and his wife, Myrtle are buried here. Mr. Miller went out to tend his turkeys one day and when he didn't come back, they went out looking for him. They found him lying in his turkey pen; his death was apparent result of a heart attack.

In the late 1800s and early 1900s, there was cattle ranching in the foothills of Lucerne Valley and Johnson Valley. Miller Ranch was located at the top of High Road, south of Highway 18.

I was told by Greg Carpenter that he had lived in a old guest house on the Miller Ranch property. He found out about the house, which was located on an old ungraded road and very isolated, from a realtor. Greg was pleased with it since it was to be a weekend house. The water came from a spring in the foothills about a mile from the house. He told me a lady had cleaned out the spring with simple kitchen tools and used cement to divert the water to her house.

According to local history, in 1931 a conflict arose over water rights and the pipeline right-of-way between the Miller's, Mary Francis Bird, and a homesteader, who claimed the spring had not been properly taken care of and that he owned the pipeline right-of-way. They were still fighting these issues in 1937, when a judge finally awarded Mary Francis Bird full rights to the water. It is not known when she sold the water rights.

Greg said the house is a block house with no insulation. He had purchased some solar panels and was able to provide power to the property, as there was no power to that area. He made a number of improvements to the house to make it livable. Greg had the idea of using solar power long before it was popular.

Water issues have continued to be a problem with the property owners in that area.

Cattle Rancher - Frank A. "Mike" Crawford

Compiled by Millie Rader.
Photos and information courtesy of Sam Clark.

Esther Haddan's brother, Frank A. "Mike" Crawford, was a cattle rancher in the north part of the valley. He was born in Oklahoma City in 1910 and came to California when he was about 10 years old. His father was a druggist in Fontana. Mike became a resident of Lucerne Valley in about 1932. In 1940 he and Jean Miller, daughter of Henry G. Miller, were married and lived on his ranch on Gobar Road. From 1944 to 1946, Mike served as a pharmacist mate in the U.S. Navy. Upon his return to civilian life, he raised cattle in Tyler Valley, on the north side of Ord Mountains, accessed by Camp Rock Road. He and Jean lived on a place near Willis Wells until 1949 when they built a home on Christenson Road in Lucerne Valley.

Mike Crawford, and windmill in Tyler Valley.

According to Sam Clark, the photo (on the next page) is of the inside of Mike and Jean Crawford's door. Mike had borrowed and inscribed the brands of the local cattlemen in the area. He did this when he built their house next to the Clark family home on Christianson Road in 1950. Sam does not know all of the brands

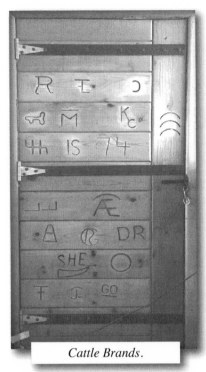

Cattle Brands.

but has identified those he is familiar with. The top row center brand is "FC" with a backward "F," this was Mike and Jean's brand. FC are the initials of Frank Crawford which was Mike's real name. The "74" brand was Buck and Esther Haddan's brand. Sam had heard that Buck had tried several brands which were rejected by the commission as already in use or too close to brands already in use. He tried 74 and it went through. Sam doesn't think that it had any real meaning, it was just an "off the cuff" try. The "SHE" with the horn under it was Shehorn's brand. Like Buck and Esther, the Shehorns were still running cattle on the east range on Old Woman Springs Road, in Sam's younger days. Sam is pretty sure that the "GO" with a bar below was the Gobar brand.

Mike loved raising cattle and would have continued on in Tyler Valley but was forced to call it quits when their water dried up after an earthquake. The unsuccessful attempts to get water by re-drilling wells there is written up in *Raising the Dust*, by Junie and Virginia Gobar. Local Geologist, Don Fife has suggested that maybe a dry lake fissure was opened by the quake causing the water to drain into the basin.

According to Sam Clark, this photo of Jean and Mike Crawford was probably taken around 1959 after Mike had taken over grounds-keeping at Midway and Pioneer Parks. For about a year before Mike died in 1960, they lived in the center section of the Midway School building, which had been converted for their residence probably as a supplement to a "not overly generous," compensation plan. Jean's mother Myrtle Miller, of Miller Ranch lived there with them.

Mike served as Desert District Vice President of the Christian Endeavor Society of San Bernardino County and for years was very active in the church work. He spent many hours working on the well, pump house and building of the new church completed on Crystal Creek Road. Mike passed away on December 28, 1960 at the age of 50. According to Sam Clark, Mike was in Ensenada with Eddie Richardson, a Christian friend from Fotana. They brought clothing to the people there, but their primary purpose was to disseminate Gospel Tracks. They traveled and camped in Eddie's VW Bus and slept on the floor of the vehicle. They used a charcoal briquette heater to keep warm at night. As a result of that, Mike succumbed to Carbon Monoxide poisoning while sleeping. Eddie Richardson survived. Jean then moved back to their home on Christianson Road and went to work as a librarian for the Lucerne Valley Elementary School. She also supplemented her income with work at the local San Bernardino County Branch Library. Jean passed away June 30, 1982. She and Mike are both buried in the Lucerne Valley Memorial Park.

Jean and Mike at Midway Park.

First Ranch of the Ords
Haddan Ranch

Compiled by Bill Lembright. Information from Martha Coutant's account in Heart Bar Ranch. Photos courtesy of Martha Coutant.

Corral at Haddan Ranch. B 3-2

Buck Haddan was born Robert Wesley Haddan in Stonewall, Colorado. He learned to ride horses as soon as he could walk and was nicknamed Buck by an uncle. Buck's father was a rancher and moved to New Mexico to manage a couple of ranches. Later Buck moved to Arizona where he ran cattle for Phelps-Dodge. After that, he moved to California and ran cattle for Albert Swarthout at Big Meadow, near Seven Oaks, and around Old Woman Springs Ranch in Johnson Valley.

Soon after actor Rudolph Valentino died in 1926, Buck moved down the hill to the Kellogg Arabian Horse Ranch in Pomona. He rode Valentino's famous horse, with a silver ornamented saddle and flowing robes, in a numbers of shows and, even in the Rose Parade.

After a few years as an Arabian sheik, he returned to the high desert to put a herd of cattle together. That's where he met Esther Crawford who was visiting her brother's ranch in Lucerne Valley. They married in 1939, and Buck's wandering days were over. At first they ran cattle in North Valley,

Old cabin at Haddan well. B 3-2

but people were moving in, raising alfalfa, and the Haddan's cattle kept breaking through the barbed wire to graze on the oceans of alfalfa. So, they moved into an old miner's cabin on federal grazing lands north of Middle Ord Mountain.

Later they moved that cabin onto their own property, enlarged it, and dug the well that is still called Haddan Well on topography maps.

They operated the ranch through good times and bad, but always were able to make a living, while many cattle ranches folded. They were content to live simply, far from neighbors; evenings were often spent reading. Later Esther acquired the luxury of a gasoline-powered washing machine, but she was also Buck's ranch hand. When Buck rounded up his cattle, Esther drove the truck with equipment and feed. The cattle ranged across the valley to Willis Well.

The Haddans spent thirty years on the ranch, driving to Barstow or Lucerne Valley for supplies. However, in 1946, Albert W. Harris, a wealthy Chicago businessman, established an Arabian horse ranch in Chino, and persuaded Buck to move there to run the ranch. Buck would travel back to Haddan Ranch as often as possible to check on his own animals. After two years of this challenging arrangement, the Haddans moved back to the Haddan Ranch. Buck's health began to fail in 1974, so they disposed of the cattle. Buck's horse, Franklin D., was also showing signs of slowing down. When Franklin D. could barely move, Buck asked a friend to shoot the poor animal. Three days later, Buck died at the ranch house.

After that, Esther moved back near the center of Lucerne Valley. While she and a friend were loading the last of her belongings onto a truck, the old ranch house burst into flames and burned to the ground. It is unknown what started the fire. In 1986, she still lived with a view of the south face of Ord Mountain and maintained her mementos, photos, and books. She missed the old place and would drive back to the Haddan Ranch for visits. A corral and shed, which Buck built, were still in use. While visiting, she said she felt as if she had never left.

Louis Basura, Daily Press

Family of Ranch Hands – Basuras

As told to Bill and Jan Lembright.
Photos courtesy of the Daily Press Newspaper.

Louis was born in 1932, in Los Angeles and moved to Lucerne Valley with his family in 1938. He went to Lucerne School, which was located in the heart of town, where Crossroads Chapel stands today. Miss Mary B. Crawford was his first teacher and lived in the house behind the school. The students were later transferred to Midway school. Robert Clark, nicknamed "Slim", was his bus driver, who Lou remembers with great fondness. Mary Lou Jacobs was in his class and he would dip her pigtail in the inkwell. The Jacobs had a store next to the Box S Ranch; the Box S had an apple orchard and artesian well, with a big reservoir. Louis also remembers buying ice cream at Lew Cowan's restaurant, which was at the "Y."

He remembers how beautiful the Junie Gobar Ranch was, which was located on the corner of Rabbit Springs and Barstow Roads. Junie's father was a doctor and lived farther down the road.

When Louis was 12 years old, he rode the range with Buck Haddan, Leonard Terry, and the Koehlys. Louis worked for Buck, at 75 cents per hour, to brand cattle. He recalled the mountains were lush with grass and the cattle had a lot to eat. At that time, Dale Gentry owned Old Woman Springs Ranch and a hotel in San Bernardino called, The California Hotel. When Louis was 12-13 years old, he worked for Gentry and helped build the main house at the Old Woman Springs Ranch.

Bob Clark driving the first School Bus

The Basuras lived on 120 acres at the base of White Horse Mountain. Louis, his brother, father and grandfather dug a well that was 130 feet deep and installed a windmill. His father bought a huge wine vat with metal bands to hold water. He and his brother waited outside all night for the first water to be pumped. Their job, after school, was to fill the kerosene lamps and chop wood for the stove and hearth. Louis's father worked at the Santa Fe Mine in the 1930s.

Louis and his brother helped their father and grandfather, George Lackitt, develop a spring and erect a windmill in the Cove near the Baldridge Estate. Other people helped, who were then able to get water when they needed it. He recalled, in those days, most people were friendly and neighborly.

When Louis and his brother were working cattle with Buck, their family had 10 head of cattle in the area east of Dallas Road. At that time, they lived in a house that his grandfather, father and others built. One day Louis let the cattle out to graze and their neighbor rounded up the cattle and put them in his own coral. Louis saw what happened, told his grandfather,

Four members of Victorville Marshal Leo Uhl's office from left: Deputy Marshal Louis S. Basura, Uhl, clerk Joan Ailshie and Deputy Marshal Gale W. Slauson.

who directed Louis to retrieve the cattle. When Louis opened the neighbor's corral to get the cattle, the neighbor came out with a shotgun. Louis told him they were his cattle and that he was taking them back. The neighbor responded that he had found and fed them and that Louis owed him for his trouble. Louis and his grandfather notified the deputy in Victorville, and the deputy and Louis went to the neighbor's house. After much posturing on the neighbor's part, the cattle were returned to Louis with the help of the deputy. Louis was so impressed by the deputy, who was 6 feet tall and mean looking, that he wanted to become a deputy.

Louis was 19 years old when he graduated from Victor Valley High School in 1951. He then joined the air force and fought in the Korean War. After returning home from Korea, Louis became a deputy marshal with the San Bernardino County Judicial System and Sheriff's Department.

At the age of 82, Louis received the Ambassador of Peace Medal from the Republic of Korea, with a letter that expressed that country's everlasting gratitude for restoring and preserving their freedom and democracy.

Slash X Ranch - Lee Barry

Compiled by Bill Lembright
Information from the Desert Dispatch, the Billy Holcomb Chapter of
E. Clampus Vitus, and Martha Coutant's book: Heart Bar Ranch

From the 1930's through the 1950's, Lee "Sourdough" Barry had one of the largest cattle ranches in San Bernardino County, with about 70,000 acres. In 1942, Lee and his wife, Mary, started the Slash X Ranch. He became known as the "Cattle Baron" of the Mojave Desert. His brand /X became the name of the ranch. At its peak, the Slash X ran about 3,000 head of cattle.

He had timber shipped from Oregon and with the help of his ranch hands, he built the Slash X Café and Bar in 1953 across from his house on Barstow Road.

In the 1970s, a group of us that were operating Lucerne Valley Market, along with Cora Belt Tidwell drove to the Slash X. On the way we stopped to see the foundation of her old ranch house in North Lucerne Valley, where she and her husband AP

Lee Barry with fiddle.
Photo courtesy of Slash X.

"Ted" Tidwell, ran cattle. A concrete step outside the back door had the words "Step high, wide, and handsome" etched in it. Cora did not remember that saying being there; but, that step is now on display at Crossroads Center in an alcove between Lucerne Valley Market and Hardware and the Wash'n Shop coin laundry.

Slash X Ranch truck. Courtesy of Bill Lembright. B 3-3

As we drove back to SH247, Cora pointed to the rusty steel water tower standing just south of the stone reservoir on the east side of the highway, and said that Ted had built both of them. (Around 2010, someone cut down the water tower for scrap metal and we lost a long-standing landmark). From the site of Tidwell's water tower and reservoir,

Slash X Saloon and Cafe Lee Barry built for his ranch hands. Photo Courtesy of Bill Lembright. B 3-3

we drove north on SH247 over Goat Mountain Pass and descended seven miles to the Slash X Café in Stoddard Valley. As we entered, Cora looked around, spotted a thin, old bowlegged cowboy and asked, "Lee Barry, is that you?" They were old friends, as the Tidwell cattle range had bordered the Slash X near the ridge of Goat Mountain pass. The two of them went on for quite a while reminiscing of days long past.

In 1986, Martha Coutant, in her book *Heart Bar Ranch*, said Lee and his wife, Mary, still host trail rides from Slash X. He also welcomes bikers, truckers, campers, and tourists. Lee enjoys showing visitors mementos from his cowboy days, including photos, a well-used forge, a sourdough pot…he'll still fiddle and sing songs about girls and cattle, girls and cowboys, and girls and Slash X. All good things must come to an end and in 1988 Lee passed on. His memory lives on at the Slash X.

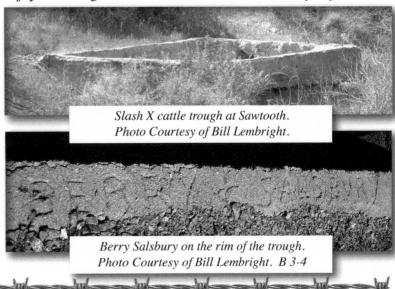

Slash X cattle trough at Sawtooth. Photo Courtesy of Bill Lembright.

Berry Salsbury on the rim of the trough. Photo Courtesy of Bill Lembright. B 3-4

While exploring a side canyon north of Sawtooth Canyon, Jan and I found a concrete trough, once fed by a spring, with the inscription: /X CATTLE CO – FEB 52 BARRY & SALSBURY.

AT Ranch - Tidwells

*By Bill Lembright from an interview with Floyd Tidwell
by Millie Rader and Chuck Bell.*

In 1936, Alla Powers "Ted" Tidwell, who was Postmaster at the Metcalf Bay Post Office in Big Bear, bought a cabin in The Cove in Lucerne Valley for a winter home. In 1945, Ted bought a place in North Lucerne Valley, started buying up all the cattle grazing leases there, and established the AT brand, the letters from Alla Tidwell. His consolidated range added up to about 80,000 acres and ran from Sawtooth Mountain to a ridge south of Stoddard Wells to Fairview Valley in East Apple Valley to Whitehorse Mountain to Peterman Hill.

For four years, he was in a partnership with Bob Wian, the founder of the Bob's Big Boy Restaurant franchise, to supply beef for Big Boy hamburgers. Bob Wian decided it was not worth the investment of his time and money, and backed out of the cattle business. In 1949, Ted started leasing steers from Bo Zimmerman's Ranch in Hinkley, CA. Those were wet years and the grass was lush on the AT range. From spring to early summer, Ted would let the cattle graze. He developed wells and even installed a water tank on a tower on the east side of Barstow Road next to a stone reservoir, just a quarter mile east of the Tidwell house. Bill Knickerbocker of Big Bear built that water tank with him.

*Floyd Tidwell with Julia and Chuck Bell.
Photo courtesy of Millie Rader.*

*Tidwell's Water Tank. Photo
courtesy of Bill Lembright. B 3-5*

When the grasses dried up, Ted would drive the cattle south to Junie Gobar's alfalfa ranch and stables, at what is currently called Rancho Lucerne, north of the high school. Junie's brother, Dave, owned and operated the dairy, still standing, but collapsing, just west of the intersection of Gobar Rd. and Barstow Rd. The cattle would ship from there and Ted would be paid, by the pound by Bob, for any weight gained from grazing.

Ted's cattle herd peaked at around 500 and his

*Gobar Dairy. Photo courtesy
of Bill Lembright. B 3-6*

*Gobar house north of high school.
Photo courtesy of Bill Lembright. B 3-7*

Tidwell's cattle. Photo courtesy of Floyd Tidwell.

range butted up against Lee Barry's Slash X. Ted installed fencing all the way from Fairview Valley, in the west, to the Ord Mountains, in the east, to keep his cattle separated from Lee Barry's, Buck Haddan's, and Dave Fisher's.

Ted kept McGinnis Spring, on the Johnson Grade en route to Fairview Valley flowing, as well as Badger Spring in Sawtooth Canyon. One of his wells was located at a World War II bombing target in North Valley.

Tidwell's cattle escape. Photo courtesy of Floyd Tidwell.

By 1950, Ted was ready to retire from cattle ranching and his son, Floyd, turned away from cattle ranching and began a career in law enforcement, later to retire as the elected Sheriff of San Bernardino County.

A small group, that included the Gommels and Lembrights, had operated the Hitchin Post Market in Reche Canyon between Grand Terrace and Loma Linda, CA. Floyd and Janet Tidwell, and Floyd's mother, Cora, lived nearby and shopped at the store. That's how we were acquainted; it IS a small world. At the ground-breaking of Lucerne Valley Market and

Cattle branding. Courtesy of Floyd Tidwell.

Cattle branding. Courtesy of Floyd Tidwell.

Hardware, Floyd donated the front step of Ted Tidwell's North Valley home, located between the store and the Wash'n Shop Coin Laundry.

Cushenbury Ranch at Cushenbury Springs

By Lynn Dee Hilton, summarized by Jan Lembright

Cushenbury Ranch 1917, public Domain image. B 1-6

My grandparents, Ralph and Isla Miller, leased the Cushenbury Ranch in the early 1950s. Grandfather continued to care for Mr. Cushenbury's herd of cattle on the ranch; and also put in long rows of chicken coops to raise chickens for Foster Farms. Mr. Cushenbury purchased another ranch at the bottom of the Cajon Pass. I only remember going there once as a small child, when grandfather delivered some steers for Mr. Cushenbury. I remember him to be a kind man, generous to many that cared for his animals.

When the upper portion of the ranch was sold by Mr. Cushenbury to the cement plant, a huge cattle drive was held. I think it was the last large cattle drive ever held in California. My brother, Dale who lived with my grandparents, was 13 or 14 years old at the time. The cattle drive occurred around 1960 or 1961; my brother was allowed to go with the other ranchers who had hired on to help drive the cattle. This was in the fall and his teachers gave him permission, with the stipulation, he had to give an oral report on the cattle drive in all his classes. My grandfather and my uncle Gene also hired on as hands for the drive, which went from Cushenbury down the Cajon Pass to Mr. Cushenbury's ranch; it took a week.

Cushenbury Creek after severe storm, 1958. Photo courtesy of Lucerne Valley Leader.

Sometime in the 1950s, during the time my grandparents were leasing the ranch, there was a huge forest fire. It came very near the main ranch house area. I remember the blackened trees all over the upper ranch area and also near the stream. The smell was heavy for weeks afterwards. My uncle, father and older brother, along with my grandmother, fought flames using the ranch hoses. The U.S. Forest service fought in the areas above the ranch. If not for all their efforts, the ranch house would have burned to the ground that day. I remember the long row of chicken coops were also in danger and they hosed down the ones on the outer edges constantly. Shortly after the cement plant was built, the underground water for the main ranch dried up, so my grandparents gave up the lease and moved. Mr. Cushenbury then sold the rest of the ranch to the cement plant. Around this time, most of the ranchers who had turned to raising chickens went bankrupt.

Lucerne Valley was a ranching community during this time, as well as Apple Valley and Hesperia. There were still a few ranches in Victorville and Big Bear.

Cushenbury Chicken Ranch 1956. Photo courtesy of Mitsubishi Cement Corporation.

The ranchers worked long, hard hours and played hard at events that involved work and pleasure horses. Many entered in rodeos at the Victorville fairgrounds and in parades held before the events began. My grandfather, Uncle Gene, and my Aunt Lynda entered many of the rodeo events. Some of the women entered the baking and canning events as well.

Ralph Miller working cattle, 1950s.
Photo courtesy of Lynn Dee Hilton.

In 1970 and 1971, when the bottom fell out of ranching, many moved to other areas and my family chose to go to Idaho.

I remember the Burro Days held in late August, 1962. They stopped when the animal activists stepped in, saying it was cruel to the burros.

We had such fun as children. When I was four years old, I remember they hung my Uncle Gene at Deadman's Point. It was so real looking I cried bloody murder, especially since my Grandfather, Ralph, playing the sheriff, slapped the horse out from under him. My mother was totally embarrassed. She had to take me to the sheriff's office to prove to me my uncle was not dead! A collar had been hidden in his shirt to protect him. It took me 30 minutes to calm down while my uncle held me.

Cushenbury house circa 1970.
Photo courtesy of Lynn Dee Hilton. B 1-6

In the 1950s a Pony Express Riders relay race was part of the Old Miners days celebration in Big Bear. My Grandfather, Ralph Miller, and his brother, Charles Miller, and my oldest brother, Obray, participated in passing the mail bag during the race. The participants were from the Big Bear, Apple Valley and Lucerne Valley Mounted Sheriff's Posses.

Lucerne Valley in those days was a thriving community, now it's just a small town with characters. During the early days, Lucerne Valley struggled to survive and everyone felt the strain. Many struggled with ranching and growing alfalfa; many fields now lay barren and dry. In Apple Valley, Jess Ranch, once the largest turkey ranch, is now gone. On Rabbit Springs Road, there were turkey ranches and turkey barns, which were so lit up at night, it looked like a landing strip.

Men came to this valley with their wives and children from many parts of the United States; they lived here through the depression years. Some were the people who had the guest ranches and when gas rationing made it impossible to travel too far, Hollywood stars vacationed in Big Bear and also came to the guest ranches.

Cushenbury east side circa 1970.
Photo courtesy of Lynn Dee Hilton. B 1-6

In those days, local residents did whatever it took to get the job done, they were grand people, neighbors helping neighbors, friends helping friends. I cherished knowing them as a child. They were the backbone of this nation. Back then the word lazy was only used in connection to city dwellers.

Five Generations of Ranchers in Lucerne Valley
The Priester/Hoffman Family

By Veda Mae Hoffman. Photos courtesy of Cindy (Hoffman) Anderson.

Five generations of the Priester/Hoffman family have been residents of Lucerne Valley. My grandfather, Louis Priester, owned the Holmes Ranch before World War I. His sons, Albert and Harry, called the desert home for several years. Albert owned the Crystal Creek Ranch and Harry owned an alfalfa ranch on Lincoln Avenue. My sister, Lenore, and her husband, Gordon Disney, and their 7 children lived on that ranch until 1957, when they moved to Northwest Montana with Harry.

Cabin and Poultry Barn at Crystal Creek Ranch. B 3-8

My husband, Jack, had been plagued with asthma since his childhood in Seattle and in Poulsbo, WA and later in Los Angeles. At age 22, he weighed only 98 pounds. As a last resort, Ethel "Ma" Ewing, brought him to Lucerne Valley in 1932. He stayed with "Doc" Henrietta Sweet, who owned the property where Chuck Bell and family now live. She was a retired physician, and under her expertise, Jack was soon pedaling his bike around the valley, doing odd jobs. Remember, these were "Depression Days!"

As soon as Jack was able, he fixed up an abandoned cabin to live in. It was across from the Fratt homestead east of Midway School on Rabbit Springs Road. Later, Ernie Moe built a nice home for his family across from the school.

Verne and Irene Fratt were instrumental in our meeting each other. They were working for my father, Harry Priester, on his ranch on Lincoln Avenue. I had just graduated from Hollywood High School and

Crystal Creek Ranch. B 3-8

they introduced us in the summer of 1937. Jack was working at the Von Breton ranch for Hazlett Anderson. The Andersons had several children and a new baby, so when Anna Deacon, who had been working for them, had to go back to school, I got the job. Needless to say, a romance developed between Jack and me, and we were married in Los Angeles in May, 1938. In March, 1939, our son, Jack was born in the Rose Maternity Hospital in Los Angeles. But we missed the desert, so we moved back as caretakers of my father's ranch. When we learned another little Hoffman was due in 1941, Jack took a second job at the Texas Quarries in the buttes east of Lucerne Valley. It closed on February 5th, the day Sharon was born, but that paid the hospital and doctor bills.

We moved away from the valley several times to where the pay was more lucrative, but Jack's asthma would return, so we always returned to the clean, dry air of Lucerne Valley. Jack worked at several jobs around the valley, including laying gas lines and working with his father-in-law, Harry, putting power lines to Big Bear. That job financed us buying five acres from Harry and Sedona Oberlin in the early 1940s. We worked very hard clearing, by hand, a long driveway to our property and our homesite. Jack drilled our first well with a posthole augur. In 1958 Junie Gobar drilled a deeper well for us. We

Hoffman house, 1949. A 3-9

started out small but planned our home to grow as we could afford it. I planted apple trees I had started in milk cartons when we lived in Monrovia and watered them, one bucket of water at a time. We moved in

during the summer of 1947, and on March 3rd, 1948, our second son, Glen was born. As the years went by, our home did grow

Priester Ranch, Lincoln Road 1929. B 3-10

to four bedrooms, two bathrooms, a large kitchen and dining room, a spacious living room with fireplace and a roomy basement and washroom, all built by Jack; not to mention the reservoir which doubled as a swimming pool and a water source for our large garden.

The house is now owned by the Probert family, who were kind enough to let us have a peek around during our visit in May, 2002.

In 1953 Lorraine Koehly and her husband made a homemade television and when Jack saw it, he had to have a TV, too. So we had the first store-bought TV in Lucerne Valley. We went to many dances at

Priester homestead 1929. B 3-10

Midway School and the old Women's Club, where the Kingdom Hall now is. Junie Gobar played the drums in a 3-piece band. We also enjoyed the dances at the Ewings' Desert Dome.

Jack Jr. and Sharon attended the Midway School and remember favorite teachers Alice Barnett, Susanne Mueller and Ethel Windchanz. Glen attended the Lucerne Valley Elementary school. Jack was hired at Kaiser Permanente Cement and Gypsum when it began operations around 1957 and he continued there until his retirement in 1975.

Our family has grown to

Cattle pens at Priester Ranch.

Priester family.

ler.) Our daughter, Sharon Floroi still lives in the valley; she started working at the Pfizer/Specialty Minerals in 1963, and was there for over 30 years. Our son, Glen and his wife, Laura, have 3 children, Glen, Alina and Andreana.

My father, Harry, and sister, Lenore, wanted us to move to five wooded acres in Libby, Montana, which we did in 1977, but this time we had our house built for us. Harry died in 1988, at the age of 96 and Lenore died in 1996. Jack Sr. died on December 23, 2000 at the age of 90 and our son, Jack, died on December 23, 2002.

Priester horse.

include son Jack and his children, Roger, Cindy, Craig, Crystal, Charles and Clint. Jack Jr. was married to Sherry Chesshire, daughter of Ernie and Edith Chesshire, former valley residents. He also worked for Sherry's brother-in-law, Jim Ward, at the Shell Station where the Sinclair Station is now. His daughter, Cindy, attended the Lucerne Valley Elementary school through 3rd grade before moving to Montana. (His daughter, Crystal, and her husband, Brad Miller, and our two great grandchildren, Makayla and Tyler.)

Alfalfa field. Veda, Mae, and Lenore Priester, 1929.

Old Oasis Ranch.

I made the trip back to the valley in May, 2002 with my son, Jack, and granddaughter, Cindy. We brought my husband's ashes back to the desert and also got to visit many old friends: Jake and Bonnie Stanfield, Bill and Pearl Martin and their family, Bob Delperdang, whom Jack had known for years and Darlene Schultz Field, who went to school with Cindy, among many others.

Priester Ranch water, 1929

Shield F Ranch
Dave Fisher

Written by Bill Lembright.
Photos courtesy of Kendall Stone.

In the late 1960s, Dave Fisher moved to Hinkley to help his dad, Guy, with his alfalfa ranch. Then Dave bought the Black Ranch on Black Canyon Road and named it the Shield F, maintaining that brand for the rest of his life.

Dave acquired the Ord Mountain Range from Charles Mitchell in the late 1970s, and later picked up the Rattlesnake Canyon Range. His herd peaked at about 400 head.

In the 1980s, Jan and I took a trip in search of the legendary cattle rancher of the Ord Mountain Range, Dave Fisher. He was a fifth generation cattle rancher in the challenging Mojave Desert. He was chairman of the High Desert Cattlemen's Association and respected by all cattlemen. He grazed cattle on over 5,000 acres of his own land and 154,000 acres of BLM land; on which he held the grazing rights.

Dave Fisher, President of High Desert Cattleman's Association

We found him at his headquarters ranch house and corrals at Haddan Well, far north of Lucerne Valley, off Camp Rock Road. After introductions, he showed us around and answered numerous questions. He was a profound man with depth, wit, humility, and a deep respect for God. We were transfixed by his stories and listened to him for a couple of hours.

He told of one day, as he rode on horseback up to the Ord Mountain Mine to check on the condition of Sweetwater Spring, a mean looking dude came toward him pointing an assault rifle. He was on guard duty for an illegal drug lab in a mine tunnel and ordered Dave to leave. Dave stared him down and told him he would be riding up to check the status of the spring. He turned his back to the armed thug and rode on.

Another time he was crawling under the wicked catclaw bushes surrounding Sheep Spring, when he came face to face with a mountain lion. Sweating profusely, he reached back through the thorny branches, for what seemed like an eternity, to reach his trusty rifle and lived to tell this story.

I would have liked to listen to him all day, but felt guilty tying him up so long and suggested we leave so he could get back to work.

Branding party at the Slash X.

Dave shared a lot of history and tips on nearby sites to explore. We often met him in his pickup as we were out exploring the Ord Mountain Range. One day, when I got a flat tire way out on his range, he spotted us by the glare from our windshield. He drove for miles to see if we were alright. Looking down at our tire, he dryly said, "You shouldn't drive around on those wimpy city tires out here." I took his advice and had very few flats after that.

Dragging calves to branding fire.

Dave did a lot of digging into springs that weren't flowing, until the water flowed freely and then would give them names. On one occasion, he and a partner worked on a spring all day; when they finally succeeded they celebrated over a bottle of tequila. Then they argued about what to name the spring and finally agreed on, you guessed it, Tequila Spring.

Shield F Ranch cattle off CampRock Road. B 3-11

He was a nature lover and provided water for all kinds of wildlife, which in response, thrived on his range. As Jan and I would drive slowly along Camp Rock Road, in the vicinity of Dave's grazing herd, we often saw desert tortoises eating amongst his cattle. The cattle didn't graze desert vegetation all the way to the ground, so the lower plants were perfect grazing for the low profile tortoise, and perhaps, also for sheltering them from the ravens; which devour defenseless baby tortoises. We are tortoise lovers and never once saw one harmed on Dave's huge range, except at the base of rocky cliffs, where the ravens dropped the babies to crack open their shells.

Nonetheless, in 1990 the Sierra Club, Center for Biological Diversity, and Audubon Society became fixated on the idea of "cattle free" rangeland and spent a half million dollars trying to drive Dave out of business, by legal harassment. Tragically, it may have resulted in driving him to an early grave.

Goat spring. Photo courtesy of Bill Lembright. B 3-12

Dave Fisher remains a legend and a hero in Mojave Desert history. He lived for God's right, truth, and justice and practiced it daily.

Trough at Kane Springs. Photo courtesy of Bill Lembright. B 3-13

A Dream Deferred – Rancho Lucerne

Compiled by Millie Rader

According to Julian (Junie) Gobar's book *Raising the Dust*, the property at the corner of Rabbit Springs and Barstow Roads, now known as "Rancho Lucerne," was first purchased as bare land from the Santa Fe Railroad in 1931 by Hayden and Anna Winford. Annie named it the "Oasis," and had Junie put in the first well. The Winfords built a guest house to live in, while the main house, a double garage

Old Oasis ranch house. Photo courtesy of Chuck Rader. A 3-7

and a barn large enough for two cows, and a brooder house large enough to hold 500 laying hens was being built. The main house was the first house of its kind in the valley. With 24 inch thick cement block walls, steel window frames, lintels of railroad cross ties, plastered walls, floors and kitchen counters all laid with colorful tile, and red tile on the roof, it became the showplace of Lucerne Valley. It was Anna's dream to retire there, but ole Hayden was not in agreement, so they sold the place to Elaine Larimore in early 1934. Fortunately for Junie Gobar, Elaine soon realized that she did not have the experience to run the ranch, and before the year was out, she sold it to Junie. He lived there until 1941.

After Junie, the ranch went through several owners over the years. The most notable, for running it as an alfalfa ranch, were John and Elaine Wren, who had it in the early 1980s, if memory serves. It was called Rabbit Springs Ranch at that time. The Wrens also raised buffalo there and owned a feed store at the corner of Old Woman Springs and Barstow Roads, called Wren's Hay and Grain.

Then along came the Pacific Golf Community Development LLC, who sold municipal bond investors on the merits of funding, what they called, Rancho Lucerne (The old Oasis and a few other ranches to the east). According to its advertising in the early 2000s, Rancho Lucerne was to be a quality development and was to feature a 27- Hole Pro quality Golf Course, 4200 lots of varying sizes, horse trails and a community friendly club house. There was also a proposed new market and shopping center, hotel, and gas station. All of these things were projected to bring commercial competition, more jobs,

Palm trees. Photo courtesy of Photographer Diana Anderson.

and more local tax revenue for residents and consumers in Lucerne Valley.

The area was soon leveled, roads graded, palm trees and evergreens were planted, drainage and other basic infrastructure put into place and many local residents were excited at the prospect of this new community and, especially, the golf course.

In 2002 everything stopped, and as of this writing (2017) the project has not been completed.

Finally the *LA Times* reported on September 25, 2004, that a federal judge had ordered a California real estate developer and its manager to pay $5.9 million in penalties for misleading municipal bond investors about the prospective value of the project, the Securities and Exchange Commission announced. U.S. District Judge Cormac J. Carney had ordered Pacific Golf Community Development and its manager, Manoucher Sarbaz, to pay $4.9 million and $980,000, respectively.

Through the years, the community would hear rumors that the project might once again move forward, but nothing ever happened. Most of the trees have died, leaving only a handful of palms struggling to put out green shoots each spring. The dead ones have long ago lost their heads to the wind and now stretch their long dry stalks to the sky creating a forlorn and forgotten appearance. It is sad to see the once green and thriving alfalfa fields, sitting dry and desolate. But the dead trees have become useful to local photographers and even out-of-town advertising agencies have used them as backdrops for commercial shoots.

There was some recent action on the property, with grading and heavy equipment at work, and the May 10, 2017, issue of the Lucerne Valley Leader stated, "Last week workers paved a stretch of Club View Avenue in Lucerne Valley. The area, near the Lucerne Valley Middle High School, is where the proposed Ranch Lucerne project was expected to go in. It is not known whether the paving is related to that project. It is currently unclear if the paving is an indication that the Rancho Lucerne project is back on track. The Leader will report as details come in."

No more information has been presented and it has been speculated that the owner of the property is continuing to make improvements to keep the permits open. Will the planned community of Rancho Lucerne ever become a reality? Only time will tell.

Billy Mitchell, Julie, and Serenity Mitchell

Last Cowboy in Lucerne Valley - Billy Mitchell

By Bill Lembright. Photos courtesy of Billy and Julie Mitchell.

Billy's grandfather, Charles Arthur Mitchell, was Billy's role model. His was one of the founding families in Barstow. He owned four of the six largest ranches in the Mojave Desert: Coyote Lake, Valley Wells, the Kingstons, and Ord Mountain Ranch in Lucerne Valley. He also worked on the PK and Black Ranches north of Hinkley.

At the age of 10, Billy started going to his grandfather's PK Ranch (overlapping Ft. Irwin) during summers and during school vacations. He grew up working his granddad's ranch with many other ranchers he met along the way. One of them, Dave Fisher of the Shield F Ranch, was Billy's best friend.

Buck and Esther Haddan had acquired the Ord Mountain grazing allotment and drove around their range in a VW Beetle. After Buck passed, Esther sold the Haddan Ranch properties at Mid Well and Haddan Well, plus her range rights to Charles Mitchell. Charles had all the range he could handle and let Dave Fisher acquire Haddan's Ord Mountain Range so it would be kept in friendly hands.

Billy operated heavy farm equipment for his granddad for years, so in 1969 when massive, destructive floods hit Southern California, at age 22 he started work with the Operating Engineers Local 12 union. It became his day job for the next 40 years. Two of the projects he worked on were the construction of the Solar One facility and the Gasification Plant, both in Daggett. However, his passion in life was cattle ranching.

When Billy visited his granddad, Charles, who was on his deathbed, Charles grabbed Billy's hand and asked, "Do you see that angel in the corner waiting for me?" God takes care of His own.

At age 38, around 1985, Billy bought his first ranch, the PK (named after Pilot Knob

Billy Mitchell cattle roundup.

north of Hinkley). In the early 1990's, environmental activists decided the desert tortoise was an endangered species and that range cattle ranching was accelerating their demise. One of their targets

Branding calf.

was Billy on the PK Range, of which 90% of its acreage was deemed prime tortoise habitat. This turned into a range war, something not paralleled in threats and potential violence since the days of the Wild West. One night Billy was alerted to noises coming from his cattle pens. When the intruders refused to answer him, Billy fired over their heads and they took off. In response to the escalating crisis, in 1995, the Tortoise Council and Wildlands Conservancy stepped in to diffuse the growing tensions and bought Billy's PK Ranch and range rights. In 1996, he bought the 29,000

acre Rattlesnake Canyon Ranch between Lucerne Valley and Johnson Valley from Dave Fisher. He bought the private land, house, and barn from miner, John Bolf. Billy's herd peaked at 400 head.

He has served on San Bernardino County's Range Improvement Advisory Committee since 1992 and has been its chairman since the passing of Dave Fisher. He continues to work with other ranchers and government officials to maintain a working relationship between ranchers, the County, and the Bureau of Land Management.

At 70, he is still going strong seeking water and feed for his current herd of 100 cattle. He works to ensure the safety of his herd against predators, both human and animal. He has also learned to adapt to ever increasing rules and regulations aimed at eliminating open range cattle ranching. There is a strain of environmentalists who look at range

Rattlesnake Spring in Rattlesnake Canyon. B 3-14

cattle ranchers as an enemy of the environment; but, nothing could be further from the truth. Billy provides water and security for other wildlife, such as the desert tortoise and the bighorn sheep.

He still leads cattle drives during which he rounds up his cattle, brands them and castrates the bulls. He can even make cattle sounds to get their attention. It is tough work but he loves the challenge and the freedom. Billy and Julie's children and grandchildren are making plans to carry on the family ranching tradition with the help of their good friends, the Bohmans at the Rattlesnake Canyon Ranch. They feel this life is what God has in mind for His people. And I wouldn't argue with that.

CHAPTER 4

Going to School

Compiled by Millie Rader.

Introduction

James "Dad" Goulding, known as the "Father" of Lucerne Valley, was also the founding father of the valley's school system. On November 1, 1904 he was issued a homestead for 160 acres that included the "Box S" Ranch where his cabin and first well were located.

That same year Goulding sent his children for schooling to the little mining community of Doble, located 35 miles up the mountain at the north end of Baldwin Lake, near Big Bear, California. In 1906 Goulding went to the San Bernardino School Board asking to form a school district at Box S, the area soon to be renamed Lucerne Valley. He was told a minimum of six children were required to form a school district, and that the county had no money for a building. Goulding's five children Mamie, George, Nellie, James and Theodore, were the only children in the valley of school age so he borrowed their cousin Hanna Brown, who lived near Oro Grande. Hannah came to live with the Gouldings and made up the sixth student necessary to form a new district. The new school district was the beginning of what is now the Lucerne Valley Unified School District that consists of three campuses and a total of 700 students. In this little town, that's progress.

First School House

To get the first students in, out of the weather, James Goulding bought an old, green, wood, cook shack, with a rusty tin roof, on wheels, to house the school. He pulled the shack off the wheels, then leveled and braced it in his yard. He painted one interior wall black for a chalkboard and built crude benches and tables from rough lumber to furnish it. Just imagine how many splinters were picked up along with the three Rs.

First School House. Photo courtesy of LVMA (Lucerne Valley Museum Association.) A 1-4

First Teacher

When the school house was in place, the county provided the first teacher, Miss McIntosh, who boarded with the Goulding family as part of her pay. On September 9, 1907, Lucerne Valley's first school opened with school supplies furnished by the Gouldings and the teacher. Miss McIntosh, shown here with her students, stayed for only one year. The next year Miss Helen Sevier was hired.

First Teacher. Photo courtesy of LVMA.

Teacher transport. Photo courtesy of LVMA.

Teacher Transport

Early teacher, Olga Johnson Rosenau and her mode of transportation. Teachers didn't last long. In the early years most teachers stayed for only one year for a reason. In selecting a school teacher, teachers sent applications by mail with a photograph included. Selection was often based more on the picture than other considerations, so the children had some nice looking teachers. The drawback, however, was that many times before the year was out the teacher would be married, leaving the position open once again.

Second School House

In 1910 the valley was growing. More students had moved to the area, and the little cook shack was about to burst. To remedy the matter, Goulding bought a house from a widow to provide room for the school to grow. "Shorty" Mulholland had agreed to move it to Goulding's four acres across the road from Box S. Before the move was accomplished Shorty married the widow, and decided to move the house to his own

Second School House. Photo courtesy of LVMA. A 4-1

property. To replace it he then built a larger building, and the first actual "Lucerne School house" opened. To clarify, the first school was called Lucerne School because the "valley" portion of this town's name was not added until later.

Third School House. Photos courtesy of LVMA. A 4-1

Third and Fourth School Houses

In 1914 the school was once again overcrowded, requiring the first school bond of $2,000 to be approved. A 43x48 foot cement block building was erected and a well drilled. In January 1916 after the students went home a windstorm took the roof off, and carried it across the road. It knocked the west wall in, breaking the wood stove and setting the building on fire, only the piano and books were saved. An-

Third School House looking south. A 4-1

Third School House court yard with students.

other bond for $3,500 was approved, and a new block building was completed in 1917. This one had a bell house. In 1918 World War I caused the Lucerne School to close and the students then all attended Rodman School in North Valley. Lucerne School was reopened in 1920. This school was located west of Highland Road where the current Crossroads Chapel Foursquare church sits today. The church youth center there was the original "teacherage" built to house the teacher in 1938.

Third School House. Photos courtesy of LVMA. A 4-1

First School Bell

In 1910 after the new school building was completed, Goulding asked the school board to buy a bell for the school. They refused, so he bought it himself from Sears and Roebuck. The first belfry was built on the ground so that students could ring the bell. It was said to have been heard for miles around. In 1916, the bell was placed on the roof of the school. Ownership of the bell passed to the Baptist Church when they bought the school and property. The bell was still on the building when it burned in 1953. When the

First School bell located at Lucerne Valley Elementary School.
Photo courtesy of Lucerne Valley Museum Association. A 4-2

church was rebuilt it did not build a belfry and the bell was stored for years. In 1973, through the diligent efforts of Pam Turner, who was PTA president at the time, the bell was returned to the school district. It is now displayed on the front lawn of the Lucerne Valley Elementary School on Barstow Road. In June of 1975, a commemorative plaque was added to the bell.

Rodman School History

By Frances Hanken. This story was taken from The History of The Schools and PTA in Lucerne Valley,
compiled in 1977 by Pam Turner, Harriet Yetto and Martha Rader. Permission to use by Martha Rader.

The Rodman School district was formed September 1915, and closed in November 1919. School bonds were voted on and unanimously carried on November 1916, in the amount of $700. The money was used to finish the building. The school itself was located on the north side of Lucerne Valley Dry Lake, in North Valley.

Three families lived there: Scott, Campbell and Dunigan. When World War I broke out both Midway and Lucerne schools shut down because the young men went to war and their families returned to the city where the parents of the women lived. Rodman School was the only one running during those years. Miss Lydell Michener taught 1917 to 1918 and recalls "I rode to school on a donkey which I chose from those rounded up by Junie Gobar. I called her Damascus. I could either ride or walk because the road was only two deep ruts and my feet almost touched the ground in the center of the road. I boarded with the Phleghardt family, about 2 ¼ miles from the school. A few times I had to walk the whole way to school and it was so cold I would stop and set some brush on fire to get warmed by it."

Inside the school house the children sat on long benches with writing desks in front of them. I taught six grades.

In warm weather Ruth Phleghardt and I scoured the horse trough with a wire brush and soap, put on bathing suits and took a bath in it.

There were a lot of wild grapes in Cushenbury Canyon, so we would pick grapes for canning. We'd hitch up a farm wagon and camp overnight in the canyon. Mrs. Scott invited a group over and brought out ice cream made by freezing the ice cream mixture with ice taken from the water in the horse trough.

Rodman School in North Valley. Photo courtesy of Lucerne Valley Museum Association. B 4-3

The valley gave me a 'hot dog party' when I had to leave because my father was ill, and I went to live with him. I liked my address in Lucerne Valley; it was 'Near Daggett Road, between Biscuit Mountain (Muffin Mtn.) and Calico Butte."

Mildred Poorman was a teacher at Rodman School and she too boarded with the Phleghardt family. She was 19 years old and this was her first "taste" of teaching.

Instead of bringing apples to the teacher, the Scott boys would bring rattlesnake buttons and she had a box full of them before the 8 months she taught were over.

The teachers pay was $69 a month but with a supplement of foodstuffs her mother sent her every week in the mail, she managed all right.

The night of the Christmas program Miss Poorman had to walk all the way home because there was a misunderstanding as to who would give the teacher a ride home and its propriety. It was a 3 mile journey from 10 p.m. till midnight, in the snow, and she cried as she walked in the dark, and the tears formed chunks of ice that she had to keep brushing away.

People later marveled over the fact that she had not fallen down one of the abandoned holes that had been started as wells.

Miss Poorman recalled the "visitor" at the Rodman School; a red fox. This fox would come to the door of the schoolhouse, on a regular basis, and she would say "okay, children, you may go." They would run around and around the schoolhouse after the fox and after about 10 minutes they would all come back into the school and the fox returned to the desert, until the next time.

Mildred had eight grades and said she had the worst of teaching conditions, but would not give anything for her experience. She learned stamina, courage and how the rugged life affected children. She also learned how to make use of material at hand. For lessons on nature, everyone would just go out into the desert, and sit down on a carpet of wild flowers and learn about the things they could see and feel.

The original Rodman School building was subsequently auctioned off in 1920 after its closure. Mrs. Koehly bought it for her daughter, Helene, and moved it to the property across the road from their place on Rabbit Springs Road, where it became one room of the small house.

Teacher Alice Barnett

Alice Barnett was Lucerne Valley's first school principal. Her parents moved to Lucerne Valley in 1942 for health reasons and she followed in 1945, when she became the principal/teacher at Midway School. She was the principal and a teacher at Midway until 1954, when the school was moved from what is now Midway Park at the corner of Rabbit Springs and Midway Roads, to its present location on Barstow Road. There she was a principal and teacher until 1956, when the school grew large enough to require seven teachers and had the budget to afford a principal who did not also have the responsibility of a classroom. At that time, Miss Barnett chose to stay in the classroom, and the school hired its first male principal, Mr. Raymond Jackson.

Miss Barnett was using the same classroom building at the current elementary school site that she had used at the Midway site. That building had been moved in 1954, and now houses the principal and office staff.

Alice Barnett. Photos courtesy of Veale Family Trust

Allen Stanfield, who moved to Lucerne Valley in 1946, when he was seven years old, said his first teacher was Alice Barnett.

"I think we moved here halfway through the school year and I remember her as one of the best teachers I ever had. I also remember that as principal, she had to make some hard decisions. She did what she needed to do and nobody ever disputed her judgments because they were always right," Allen said.

Miss Barnett continued to teach first grade or a first/second combination class at the new site until she retired in 1959.

The last permanent structure constructed at the Lucerne Valley Elementary School site, was the First Grade wing. After the building's completion in 1967, it was dedicated to Alice Barnett, just months after she had passed away. A bronze plaque is still attached to the south/east corner of the building with her name on it. Many students have passed through the three classrooms located in that wing including four of her great-nieces and nephews, and six great-great-nieces and nephews.

She left a lasting legacy for the community and for her family, many of whom still reside in Lucerne Valley.

Named on the back of George Knowlton's class picture is left to

Alice Barnett's Class Picture, courtesy George Knowlton.

right starting at the back: Christine Terry, Geneva Barnes, Tommy Hill, Jimmy Slecomb, Caroline Wheeler, Sarah Clark, Caroline Webster, Miss Barnett, Cecil Bailes, Susan Pacatti, Kenneth Clark, Raymond Holforth, Robert Bailes, Jimmy Clark, Deanna Gross, Ray Carter, Byron Reed.

Newspaper captioned this photo "Ladies First" is apparently the motto of the gentlemen in this photo. Local school board member, Agnes Clark, digs the scene with a silver plated shovel at the ground breaking last Thursday (September 7, 1967) for the Alice Barnett Primary Building. Much free labor was donated as leaders of most of the organization in the valley turned over a shovel of sod. Also shown in the picture is left to right: Ken Davis, Superintendent of Construction for the Stan Nelson Construction Company of Loma Linda, Contractor Stan Nelson, Agnes Clark, Administrator Darold Henry and Senior Custodian and Caretaker of Shovel Al Roberts.

School Board breaking ground for the Alice Barnett Primary Building. Photo courtesy of Lucerne Valley Leader Newspaper.

Midway School

In 1912, after a lengthy dispute between Goulding and those living on the east side of town over the placement of the school, those on the east side decided to form a new school district. This new district would eventually be known as Midway. For over a year classes were held in private homes, including the Garrot, Fratt and Rice homes, while the Midway School House was under construction. The school was built on property donated by the Fratt and Rice families, with Mr. Hans Therklesen and Malcolm Rice in charge of construction. The building was ready for use in 1914. In 1915 Midway became a branch of the San Bernardino County Free Library, allowing the community to borrow books after school hours. The same 1916 storm that caused the fire at the Lucerne School also did some damage at Midway. Midway was closed for a year during World War I, and all Lucerne Valley students attended Rodman School at that time.

Midway School, 1935. Photo courtesy of Lucerne Valley Museum Association. B 4-4

1930 School Bus. Photo courtesy of George Knowlton.

1930 School Bus

This 1930 photo from the album of Rosa Koehly, shows one of Victorville's early school buses, picking up high school students in the Koehly yard on the Post Office Road. Lorraine Koehly Knowlton, is named as one of the passengers looking out the back windows. If you look close you can read Victor Valley Union High School on the side of the bus. Lucerne Valley students above the eighth grade, first attended higher grades in Victorville, and then in Apple Valley, until they had enough students to support a local middle / high school.

Eighth Grade Graduating Class

By 1929 the valley had grown enough to supply ten eighth graders to Midway School. Pictured in this graduating class are: left to right, Lorraine Maher, Ruth Horton, Nina Baumgardner, Madeline Jones (valedicto-

Eigth grade graduating class. Photo courtesy of George Knowlton.

rian), Donald Middlehurst, Lloyd Bailes, Paul Busick, Dick Owen, George Baumgardner and Walter Carter. Their teacher was Miss Cheeseboro. After eighth grade, Lucerne Valley students, along with Apple Valley, Bell Mountain, Hesperia, Oro Grande, Adelanto and Wrightwood students were bused to Victor Valley High School (VVHS), which had opened in 1915, on the corner of 7th and Forrest Streets. At first, VVHS included 9th-12th grades. In 1946 Lucerne Valley 7th and 8th grade students began attending VVHS. In 1953, a new Victor Val-

Allen Stanfield and Jack Hoffman.

Photos courtesy of Jack Hoffman.

Mexico project actors.

ley High School was built on the corner of Mojave and 6th Streets. In a letter to James Goulding inviting him to the May 12, 1954, dedication program, he was commended as a charter school board member who had participated in the development of the educational program and the planning of facilities to meet the constantly growing enrollments.

Midway Grows

In 1938 Midway school was renovated and enlarged, giving it the architectural lines that we are familiar with today. 1n 1939 Midway and Lucerne School Districts combined, to become Lucerne Valley Union Elementary School District. In the early 1940s an extra building was erected behind the main school house for added classroom space. This building was moved to the current elementary school site in 1954. First and second grades

Midway School, 1938. Photo courtesy of Lucerne Valley Museum Assoc. B 4-4

stayed at Midway, after the new elementary school was built. These classes were moved over to the new site in 1957, after the addition of four new classrooms. In 1957 the Midway School property was moved into the CSA 29 County Park system and became Midway Park. It was briefly resurrected as a school

Midway (School) Park, 2015. These 3 photos are courtesy of LVMA. B 4-4

once again, in the years 1985-1988, due to overcrowding at the elementary school, when it was used as a satellite campus for lower grades.

Midway School teacher Mrs. Mueller and friends.

Midway School teacher Mrs. Mueller on swing.

Lucerne Valley Elementary School

Ground breaking ceremonies were held in November, 1956 for the construction of four new classrooms to be added to the current Lucerne Valley Elementary School site. In January, 1957 the buildings were completed, and the first and second graders still attending Midway School were moved to the new site, bringing total enrollment up to 140 students. These class-rooms are still in use today, housing second and third grade classrooms. In 1958 the Lucerne Valley School Board began negotiations with San Bernardino County Schools, to bring the students of

New Classrooms. Photos courtesy of Leader Newspaper. A 4-2

Timco Acres, and Johnson Valley into the Lucerne Valley School District. Many students from those areas were already attending Lucerne Valley Elementary, but the area was considered part of the Newberry School District. The transaction was completed in 1959, adding another 252 square miles to the district.

More Construction

In June 1958 the slabs for the multipurpose room, and the new kindergarten room, were poured and construction was completed in 1959. The multipurpose room was later named "Goulding Hall," in memory of James Goulding in a dedication ceremony

Administration Building. A 4-2

on May 15, 1993. Also, in 1959, the building that had been moved from the Midway School site, to be used as the kindergarten room, was converted into the administration building and is still used

Goulding Hall. Photos courtesy of Millie Rader. A 4-2

for that purpose today. In 1963 the district built a bus garage/shop just west of the elementary school yard. In 1967 and 1968 they added basketball and handball courts, where the Early Childhood Learning Center is today. That same year, the last permanent classroom building, the Alice Barnett wing, was completed to house first graders. In 1988 the first portable classrooms were added, allowing the kindergarten and first grade students to move back from Midway.

A 1965 newspaper caption reads, "The interest in good food is shown on the face of Tommy Stokes," who is anticipating the generous serving that Mrs. Kumley and Mrs. McHenry are about to give him. The children from left to right are Penny Smith, Kathy Hert, Tommy Stokes and Denise Tamplen.

School Cafeteria.

In 1969 this big bug had just been added to the playground for shoulder and arm development of primary children. Vincent Paseri is the first grader on the equipment.

These 3 photos are courtesy of Lucerne Valley Leader Newspaper.

Playground Spider.

A 1969 Lucerne Valley Elementary School Flutaphone Ensemble. Top: Terri Malcolm, Kathleen Warnock, Colleen LaChance, Robin Weldon, Robin Walton, Debbie Martin, Nancy Roesch, Vance Perdue, David Fry, Tim Larson, Calvin Sisk, Chris Rickli, David Rader, Daniel Kost and Mark Carpenter.

Flutaphone Ensemble.

Middle School / Mountain View / District Office / High School

The original Lucerne Valley Middle School, opened on Aliento Road in 1987, for grades 7-8, with 145 students, adding sixth grade in 1990. In 1985, Lucerne Valley Union Elementary District became a Unified School District. In 1988, the Pfizer Limestone Plant, donated 80 acres on Rabbit Springs Road to build a high school, which opened for grades 8, 9

District Office, Alt Ed Center. Photo courtesy of Lucerne Valley Unified School District. B 4-5

and 10, on September 10, 1992, leaving those students attending 11th and 12th grades to finish up at Apple Valley High School. The Lucerne Valley High School celebrated its first graduation ceremony in 1995. The middle school was moved from the Aliento Road campus, to the high school campus in 1998, creating a middle/high school, serving grades 7-12. Mountain View (continuation) High School, was operated in portables at LVHS until 1998, when it moved to the Aliento Road campus now the District Office and Alternative Education Center.

Lucerne Valley High School. Photo courtesy of David Rader. B 4-5

Midway School Reunion
Compiled by Millie Rader

In 1988, Allen Stanfield who moved to Lucerne Valley in 1946 thought it would be fun to pull all of his Midway School chums together for a class or rather school reunion. He began planning a three-day event to take place around Lucerne Valley's annual Independence Day Celebration in 1989. Now according to Allen, you don't much hear of grade school reunions. But this was not just any grade school. This was Midway School. This school was made up of children whose parents were pi-

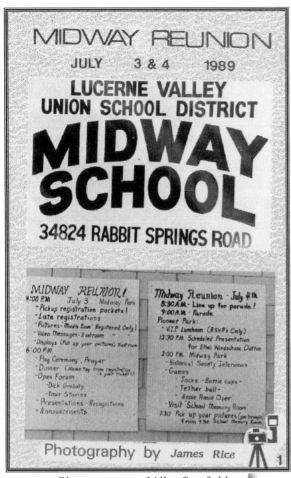

Photo courtesy of Allen Stanfield.

oneers in what back then was the primitive little town of Lucerne Valley. These kids went to school barefoot, got paddled by the teacher if they misbehaved and learned how to read and write without the aid of a computer or cell phone. They learned history before it was rewritten by the politically correct, and were taught how to be respectful, contributing members of society.

For many years Allen was the town's only barber. Anytime his old school chums were in town, they would stop by for a haircut and most would ask about the kids they had gone to school with. Finally Allen began to organize this monumental task with the help of Margie (Delperdang) Nickols, Sally (Donaldson) Emerson, Charlene (Stott) Horton, and of course his wife Roberta, who Allen said got saddled with the largest portion of the work. The biggest challenge Allen said was finding the long, lost Midway students.

Allen made many, many calls. "At first everybody told me that they already had plans for that July 4th weekend, and I thought *Oh no, nobody will come*," said Allen. "But as we got closer to the date, I began to get messages stating that people were changing their plans so that they could come to Lucerne Valley instead."

There was much thought to detail. T-shirts had been ordered with an original cartoon of a teacher with a paddle and the school in the background, and a Big Rig with a flatbed had to be borrowed for the parade float. Jack Ewing, who had been the biggest and most rambunctious kid in the class, was dressed up as an angel complete with halo as he rode on the float. Many years prior, a favorite teacher, Mrs. Mueller, had picked Jack to be the star of the Christmas play, "The Littlest Angel," even though he had been no angel. Allen said that she could see his heart.

Mrs. Susanne W. Mueller was born March 20, 1889 in Dresden, Germany. She passed away February 14, 1989, just a month before her 100 birthday, and just five months before the reunion. Her daughter Ilse attended the reunion in her place. At the reunion she thanked the students for their loyalty over the years. "You helped make Mutti's life a happy one – you cared for her," she said.

Agnes Clark, whose children attended Mid-

Bonnie Stanfield and Lorraine Knowlton visit at reunion. Photo courtesy of George Knowlton.

way, was presented with a survivor T- shirt for her longtime membership on the Lucerne Valley Union School Board.

When they found out that teacher, Ethel Windschanz Clafton, who taught at Midway 1949-1953, was coming, the Chamber of Commerce decided she would be the parade Grand Marshall. Midway student Chuck Francis provided the convertible to carry her and Allen rode shotgun.

Helene Koehly Wood was the earliest Midway student to attend the reunion. She attended 8th grade there in 1918, and was the first student to graduate from Midway.

There were 93 Alumni who participated along with their families. A total of 250 people attended the dinner on the 3rd. Some of the old family names represented were: Bailes, Barnes, Barnett, Clark, Donaldson, Ely, Ewing, Foell, Fife, Francis, Garrett, Gross, Hahs, Hayes, Hettick, Hudson, Huffman, Johnston, Koehly, Knowlton, Klaus, Kolbly, Michaels, Owens, Pangburn, Pederson, Pittman, Reed, Sieswerda, Sherman, Smillie, Stanfield, Steingal, Stott, Therkelsen, Thompson, Tyler, and Wilson.

This group was part of what historians call "The Silent" generation. They did not whine or complain, they just put their heads down and got the job done. Sadly, there are not many of them left.

That Independence weekend 29 years ago, they all came back to the old Midway School house to celebrate their past, reminisce and renew old acquaintances, and all were grateful for the opportunity.

Lucerne Valley Christian School

Photo courtesy of Allen Stanfield.

CHAPTER 5

A Town of Characters

Heralding Our Home Grown Residents
. . . Lucerne Valley has nurtured some long-time family ties!
By Pat Judkins, 1993

As the sun shone brightly overhead, as it does nearly 365 days a year in Lucerne Valley, a small group of men tied a rag around a wagon spoke and busily counted each turn along the 22 mile dusty road between Box S and Victor. The year was 1911, and William Russell was among the pioneers measuring the distance between the communities, now known as Lucerne Valley and Victorville. Their measurement was recorded with the County of San Bernardino in order to get the dirt road accepted. William Russell came here from Los Angeles for health reasons. He was partially paralyzed on his right side, and he was cured in one year. His son, John Russell, is today as involved in this community as was his father, who homesteaded 320 acres here and opened the first restaurant in Victor.

Also in the year 1911 Theodore P. Owen filed on 640 acres two miles north of Midway Road (first known as Owen Road). He moved here due to an acute bronchial condition, and after three nights on the desert he didn't cough anymore. Theodore Owen later operated a turkey ranch which boasted possibly the largest turkey hatchery in the nation with a flock of 3,000 turkeys. His son, Dick, still resides locally and has been very involved in civic activities over the years. Dick was the first Boy Scout here and the first volunteer fireman. His wife, Ethel, opened the first beauty shop in Lucerne Valley.

George and Laura Reed homesteaded 160 acres here in 1926. They moved from Fresno for the health benefits that a drier climate offered George, who suffered with malaria. Their nine children all lived here at one time. George and Laura are buried at Lucerne Valley Memorial Park. Two of their sons currently reside in Lucerne Valley; Troy and Harold. Harold's daughters, Becky and Linda, and his son, Cliff, and his family, also reside locally. Bill Reed lives in Victorville. The Reed family, especially Bill, are mentioned in Gobar's *Raising the Dust*. Troy, who was born here, and his wife, Betty, have also contributed much to this valley.

Troy, Betty, her sister and husband, Mildred and Fred Tyler, are all extremely active in community affairs. All have volunteered endless hours annually to the San Bernardino County Fair held in Victorville. Betty and Mildred have worked with fair exhibits for 13 consecutive years. The ladies parents, Clarence and Dorothy Donaldson, first resided here in 1939. During the war they moved to L.A. for awhile. Fred and Mildred visited her aunt and uncle, Lonnie and Mabel James, who had homesteaded 160 acres. The Tylers moved in and out of this valley a few times before settling in permanently. They bought property here in 1947 and had a well drilled for $250.

Jim Sherman Sieswerda kept both parents last names; a custom in Holland. His parents brought their family to the U.S. where they first settled in Michigan. While serving in the army in 1916 Jim saw advertisements about Lucerne Valley, California, and moved here with his brother in 1917. They bought 40 acres across from the Von Breton Ranch on Rabbit Springs near Camp Rock Road, building their first home there. Jim met Athene Sharpley, a nurse who was caring for Dr. Henrietta Sweet. They were married in 1920 and had five children born in this community. Their father delivered many of them in their cellar because the doctor couldn't make it past Rabbit Dry Lake due to flooding.

In 1930 Jim homesteaded 180 acres, and son Joe and his wife, Glenda, still live on some of that acreage. When Joe was a teenager, it was his job to hand-pump water into a black 50-gallon-drum which was in the sunlight so the water would heat up for dishwashing and bathing. The valley's first solar water heater? He also pumped water into a white 50-gallon drum for domestic water. They had a kitchen cupboard that protruded outside on the north side of the house. It was made of tin and burlap so water could trickle over the burlap and cool food stored inside. A forerunner to the ice box?

"The valley was a lot different in those day," Joe remembers. "Everybody helped one another. In the 1930s people here were pretty poor. People would give my dad .22 shells, and he would go hunting and furnish almost everyone in the valley with venison."

Joe remembers when he was about seven years old, everyone would go to Koehly's post office on the east side of Post Office Road, just south of Rabbit Springs. They would get their mail and stay to enjoy a social and dance. "Some folks would bring watermelons, others would bring hand-cranked ice cream, and some would bring fiddles, guitars, and accordions."

The Risler family has owned property here since the 1920s when Tom and his brother, Lee, and their mother, Agnes, lived here. Lee and Tom have passed away, but sisters-in-law, Iona and Nee are neighbors. Nee is busy on behalf of the Moose Lodge, and Iona just won the 1993 Woman of the Year award. Nee's son, Lee, and his family reside locally and own the popular business which makes Kiwi Sandals.

Maureen Pederson was born in the back room of her father's newspaper office in Slaton, Texas. She worked on her high school paper and for the Nogales Herald in Arizona. Many residents here first met Maurine at the L.V. *Leader* where she worked for 17 years before retiring in 1991. Maurine first visited Lucerne Valley in 1934, and has made it her home for about 47 years.

Bob Clark and his late wife, Agnes, arrived in the valley over 56 years ago. They raised six children; and their son, Sam, still lives here. Bob's doctor sent him to the high desert for his health in 1937, suggesting the desert climate might possibly help him. Considering Bob has celebrated his 84th birthday in September, it appears to have done wonders for him. Agnes was on the L.V. School Board for 23 years. Bob drove the school bus for Midway and Lucerne Schools. Many grandfathers living here still, rode Bob's school bus when they were children. Bob was a volunteer fireman, too.

Other families like the Barnetts, Delperdangs, and Stanfields contributed greatly to this valley, and their children and grandchildren are following suit.

Whether it was 1911 or 1993, these families enjoyed the same majestic sunsets and brilliant stars, nearly 365 days of radiant sunshine, and cool, breezy summer nights here at the Crossroads of the High Desert. They have all enjoyed the howling of coyotes and the nocturnal serenade of crickets. Many residents disliked the area when viewing it the first time, some claim you either love it or hate it, but most learned, given time - the desert draws you in and claims you!

Barber, Pastor, Teacher – Allen and Roberta Stanfield

By Allen Stanfield as told to Jan Lembright, March 11, 2016. Photos courtesy of Valerie (Stanfield) Rice.

Allen and Roberta Stanfield, who are both still living in Lucerne Valley at the time of this writing, have a family history in this town that spans over 70 years. Their children, Les and Valerie, are the fourth generation of this family to live in this valley. Les has moved on, but Valerie not only lives here, but has long been the only chiropractor in town.

It all began when Allen's uncle, Ralph and his wife, Lola Stanfield saw a Lucerne Valley brochure shortly after World War II; encouraged by what they saw, they showed it to Ralph's brother Jacob and his wife Bonnie, and Allen's parents, who were interested as well. Together they contacted a Lucerne Valley realtor named Batelle and promptly bought 20 acres on Laramie Road, which

Allen and Roberta Stanfield with Allen's grandmother Maud Ralls

they divided between themselves. They divided the land right down the middle by putting electrical power, a well and a divided reservoir on the property line. Over the years there were never any arguments as to where the property lines were.

Allen was born in 1938 in Covina, and moved to Lucerne Valley along with his parents and sister, Alice in 1946 when he was 8 years old. His family planted mulberry trees to raise silk worms, but soon after the war synthetic plastics were made available putting an end to the silk trade. Allen's dad then got a job mining limestone on the east side of Highway 18 across from what is now Mitsubishi Cement Corporation. He worked there about five years, and then Kaiser Cement came along and hired him as an electrician, where he worked until he retired.

Allen attended Midway school, and then was bussed to Victorville for junior and senior high school. He married his high school sweetheart, Roberta Richards at Lucerne Valley's First Baptist Church in 1958. At the time of this interview they had been married 58 years.

Roberta's Lucerne Valley story started in 1948 when her Grandmother, Eva Richards, homesteaded five acres on Haynes Road in North Valley. The family came as a result of real estate information obtained from Dennis Medici's grandfather who was a realtor at that time. They enjoyed many week-

Allen Stanfield with his favorite book.

ends here, camping out, while developing the site. Roberta's parents, Milo and Goldia Richards built a house and moved with Roberta and her sister Eva May to the property in 1955. Roberta was 15-years-old at the time. Back then, one could leave Santa Ana, where Roberta's family lived, and drive to North Valley, encounter only one stop sign, and never see another car on the way. Times have changed just a bit.

Allen first opened a barbering business in Lucerne Valley 1958. At first he was in a little building on the SW cor-

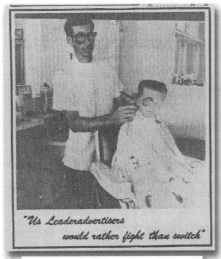

*Stanfield Barber Ad in
Lucerne Valley Leader*

ner of Crystal Creek and Highway 247. Then in 1959, Roberta's parents built what is still the barbershop building on the sw corner of Old Woman Springs and Oracle. Thus Allen began cutting hair in a brand new barbershop. After cutting hair for 16 years, he felt God calling him to the ministry, and he sold the shop to Bud Miller. The building now belongs to Carla Turner and still houses a barbershop run by John Cosato, and a gift boutique called "My Vintage Heart" run by Cindy Surber.

Allen served as youth pastor in Apple Valley and then in Hesperia while he was attending Bible college. They lived in Victorville and Hesperia during that time.

Roberta taught at Lucerne Valley Elementary School for 10 years. But her dream was to have a Christian School. To fulfill that dream Allen's grandmother Maud Ralls, donated the money to build Lucerne Valley Christian School on the nine acres adjacent to Allen's parents property on Laramie.

Allen and Roberta then moved back to Lucerne Valley to run the Christian School. Roberta was the teacher and Allen the administrator. They operated the school from 1980-2000.

Allen was the associate pastor of The First Baptist Church in 1991 when he was first realized that the church should be keeping the Saturday Sabbath. He was the senior pastor in 1999 when the church voted to become Sabbath Keepers. In 2000, the congregation realized their

*Stanfield miniature donkey,
Shorty and the kids*

building and property on Highway 18 was too large for their needs and sold it to Crossroads Chapel Foursquare Church for $1.00; moved their church into the Lucerne Valley Christian School building on Laramie, renaming themselves Old Paths Assembly. The school at that time was only a homeschool base and they renamed it Old Paths Academy.

According to their daughter Valerie, Old Paths Assembly is a Torah pursuant group of Messianic Israelites, who believe the pre-incarnate Messiah Yahshua is the physical manifestation of YHVH, and they keep the feasts of Israel. Allen was the leader or shepherd of this church for many years. David Gibson is now the current shepherd of this group.

*L to R: Roberta's parents Milo and Goldia
Richards, Roberta, Bonnie and Jake Stanfield,
and Allen at China House 1980s*

Whether teaching reading, writing and arithmetic or teaching God's word, Allen and Roberta have put in their teaching time here. They have now both retired and with the help of their daughter, Valerie Rice, they enjoy raising many different kinds of farm animals on their small ranch across from the church.

Jack the Hatter

By Allen Stanfield as told to Millie Rader.
A boyhood memory of Allen Stanfield, lifetime resident of Lucerne Valley.

My mom worked for Ethel Ewing at Ethel's Cafe in the early 1950s, and I would get dropped off the bus there with Clifford Reed, Jack Hoffman and Jackie (Jack) Ewing. In the spring we would run down the road and meet up across from where the Valero Gas Station is now, just west of the "Y"

The tree is but a memory now, but Allen's friend from church Debbie Foster was kind enough to reproduce it in this drawing, the boys legs dangling belong to a couple of the gang, they could be Allen's or Jack's or Cliff's or Jackie's.

intersection and east of the flood control channel. A giant Mulberry tree grew there and the fruit came on early in the season, so we would climb up there and hide in the leaves. Late spring was best because the Cottonwood snowstorms were over, the apples not quite ripe yet, but the mulberries were, and we could sit there in the shade of the leaves eating berries until we thought we would pop. Then we would throw the berries at passing cars. We may have seen a car go by every 10 minutes or so, and had plenty of time to gather ammo.

This Mulberry tree was our hideout. If I was bored, with nothing to do, while my Mom worked, I knew that all through the lazy summer months I could find at least one of the guys sitting in that tree. We had laid claim to this wonderful tree. It was our tree, or so we thought, until a new guy blew into town in a brand new 1940 Dodge pickup pulling a brand new trailer that he parked in the shade of our Mulberry tree; right where we climbed the trunk to reach the branches above. According to the sign on the side of the trailer, this was 'Jack the Hatter' who did hat cleaning, blocking and sales.

This new trailer was not a welcome addition to our prized location, but soon cinderblocks began to stack up and the building that now houses Adelita's Mexican Restaurant began to take shape. This was great entertainment and the gang then became construction inspectors whenever the new owner was away.

Jack the Hatter turned out to be Jack Smith, who along with his wife, Ellen, opened their hat blocking business in May 1947, as verified by an ad found in Virginia Hemphill's newspaper *The Desert Grapevine*. Jack was in the community for quite awhile, but I don't remember what ever happened to him. He never shooed us boys out of "our" tree, but never developed a relationship with us either. He must have known that we small boys would soon grow up to be big boys and then the tree would be abandoned for other interests such as cars and girls. He was right, but now, almost 70 years later the memories made in that tree still bring a smile to an old man's face.

The Desert Grapevine, 1947.

A Living Encyclopedia – Sam Clark Remembers

As told to Bill and Jan Lembright

More than eighty years have now passed since Robert, Agnes and little Bobbie Clark, first made their way east on an unpaved Bear Valley Road, heading toward Lucerne Valley. Sam's dad would recount that in their earliest days they could "look out across the valley at night, and count only two lights."

In 1937, Sam's father Robert, mother Agnes, and oldest brother Bob Clark came to Lucerne Valley, from La Crescenta, Californa. Robert was recovering from TB and was advised to move to the desert for his health. He always reported that his Doctors had "sent him to the desert to die." And he did die in the desert, but not until 1996, at age 86.

Through a mutual friend, the Clarks met Wilbur Phelps and his first wife Mary, who lived in Lucerne Valley. Wilbur was the foreman at the Sewell Ranch, and he invited them to stay there while they looked things over.

After spending their first night in Lucerne Valley at the Sewell Ranch, the Clarks made arrangements to rent and occupy the east half of the Fratt House. The house is still standing and is located on the north side of Rabbit Springs Road, east of Midway Park (formerly Midway School) .

Verne Fratt and his wife, Irene, owned the house, and occupied the west half. This living arrangement, for both families, spanned the years from 1937 to 1941. Verne Fratt was a genuine cowboy and rode a horse everywhere he went. Verne also did ranch work for others.

Fratt place. Photo courtesy of Sam Clark. B 5-1

During the Clark family sojourn at the Fratt House, it was common to see trucks rumbling past, laden with large granite blocks, traveling west on Rabbit Springs Road. The granite was cut from the Texas Granite Quarry east of Lucerne Valley. One photograph that Robert took at that time, of such a Granite hauling truck, still exists. (See ch. 3 The Miners)

In 1939 Sam's second brother, Ed ,was born at Monsanto Hospital in the Los Angeles area, where he remained for a period of time before he was able to come home to the Fratt House.

The Clarks next lived in one of the ranch houses on the Von Breton Ranch, from 1941 until sometime in 1943. A daughter was born there in 1941 and a third son in 1942. Both were born at home with the assistance of a neighbor, Lucy Ann Yearout. In advance of the first of those two births, Robert would recount that he drove to town to call the doctor, who would have to drive out from Victorville. The call was placed from the only public telephone in town, which was located at the Jackrabbit Cafe.

The doctor, who served a dual role as an area sheriff, arrived after the baby was born and began to fume when he learned that fact. He was still steaming as he entered the house. He forcefully unfastened his holster and pistol, and slammed them down on top of a table in the entry hall.

He soon cooled off, and went on to provide medical help to mother and newborn, before he left the premises.

Clark Family.
Photo courtesy of Sam Clark.

The Von Breton Ranch had been very well developed and still had a huge reservoir that was fed by a very high capacity agricultural well. At 320 acres in size, the Von Breton Ranch had perhaps been the largest of the ranches in Lucerne Valley. With the exception of a 40 acre parcel, located southwest of the intersection of Rabbit Springs and Camp Rock Roads, the Von Breton Ranch stretched between Old Woman Springs and Rabbit Springs Roads, bounded on the west by Joshua Avenue, and on the east by Camp Rock Road. Added to that was an adjacent 40 acre parcel, located on the east side of Camp Rock Road.

Sometime in 1943 the Clark family moved to the homestead house of the Frew Ranch, which was located on Valley View Road, six tenths of a mile north of Highway 18. They first rented, and then in 1945, purchased the little house and the surrounding 3 acres.

In 1945, another daughter was born into the Clark family, and in 1952 Sam was born. Both of these last two children were born in the nearest hospital at that time, which was the old Barstow Hospital.

Valley View Road had been named for the highly developed Valley View Ranch, adjacent on the south, to the Frew Ranch. The 40 acre Valley View Ranch had been homesteaded and developed by David Christensen and was, after David died, owned by his older sister Anna (Christensen) Winford. (Harry Christensen, known as "Duke," was the brother of David and Anna). In the later 1940s, when someone pointed out that there was another Valley View Road in Lucerne Valley, the county changed the name to Christensen Road. Through the years, the county street signs have displayed a few spelling variations, leaving us at last with the misspelling Christenson Road.

Sam remembers the Haddans:

Sometime in the 1930s, Frank A. "Mike" Crawford (1910-1960) and his sister, Esther Crawford, (1907-2002) moved to Lucerne Valley from Fontana, California. Their father operated the Crawford Drug Store there, which he had founded. The Crawford family had come to California from Oklahoma in the 1920s.

Both Mike and Esther took up residence on the Gobar Ranch. Mike did handy work, like carpentry and painting; Esther raised turkeys in pens near her house.

Robert W. "Buck" Haddan (1893-1974) was born in Colorado into a ranching family. He had learned to care for horses and cattle there and in New Mexico. He came to California sometime in the

1920s, and worked with Arabian horses at the W.K. Kellogg Ranch in Pomona, California.

He came to Lucerne Valley sometime in the 1930s. Buck was a genuine cowboy and found work with the cattlemen in this area. He also had some cattle of his own on his ranch in North Valley.

Buck and Esther met here in Lucerne Valley; in time they decided to get married. Esther summarized the story about their wedding day as follows: she went out early in the morning and cleaned her turkey pens, she went in and cleaned herself up, Buck came to get her, they drove over to Las Vegas, Nevada, and they got married.

As the number of Haddan cows increased, so did the number of neighboring ranchers growing alfalfa in North Valley. The temptation of fresh green fields nearby was too much for the Haddan cows, so Buck was spending more and more of his time catching cows, mending the fences they were breaking down and making reparations for the general commotion the cows were causing.

Esther reported that Buck always liked small cars, since "all he needed in a car was enough room to carry a saddle and a bale of hay." At that time Buck and Esther owned a mid-1930's Austin Bantam, slightly modified to haul those necessities. In that little car they set out one day to explore some less inhabited territory, about halfway between Lucerne Valley and Daggett, in which their cattle might have the freedom to graze.

They came upon an old timer north of East Ord Mountain, who had built a small cabin on a 40-acre parcel surrounded by government land. The old fellow said that he had "lived there so long that he was beginning to talk like the quail." He immediately took a fancy to their car. They soon reached an agreement wherein the old timer would relinquish his "Ranch" in exchange for the Bantam and $20 (or possibly it was $40).

When all was settled, the old timer drove off in the prized Bantam, with the cash payment in hand, and Buck and Esther and their cattle were soon established on the old timers claim, with not a neighbor in sight.

There they stayed, and their cattle happily grazed on the surrounding government range, until Buck died in 1974.

Esther then moved back to Lucerne Valley, to a new single-wide mobile home, on property adjacent to her sister-in-law, Leora "Jean" (Miller) Crawford (1915-1982), and also adjacent to the Clark family home on Christenson Road .

Esther moved to live with family in Fontana in 1987 or 1988; and she died there in 2002.

Sam's mother, Agnes Clark, assisted Esther in removing her household goods and accumulated contents from the old Haddan Ranch. On the last day of their endeavors, they were burning a large number of old papers in the woodstove. The heat generated was too much for the old chimney to bear, and the cabin caught fire and burned to the ground.

Dave Fisher acquired the Haddan ranch and took over their cattle grazing range.

Sam remembers that whenever Esther came to town, she was always quaintly attired in a pioneer sunbonnet, a calico dress, and cowboy boots.

Sam remembers the "Old Miners Days Burro Races":

In the 1950s (and perhaps into the 1960s), these exciting three-day contests were held annually, during the first few days of August.

The burro races commenced in Apple Valley in a field at the base of Bass Hill, west of the Apple Valley Inn. On the morning of the first day of the race, the sizable number of untamed burros, which had been collected from the wild for the event, were held in a corral and then parceled out to the wranglers, by the luck of the draw. The burros each had numbers painted on them, and they each wore a small pack, blazoned on left and right sides with advertising signs for each animal's sponsor. Their wrangler, who also traveled on foot, would lead (or attempt to lead) the burro with a short rope.

The race proceeded east from the starting point, on Highway 18, to the lunch stop at Dead Man's Point. After lunch, they continued east on Highway 18, until arriving at the field on the southwest corner of the Lucerne

Burro races. Photo courtesy of Lucerne Valley Leader Newspaper.

Valley "Y," where the McDougall's Well Drilling building now stands. There they had dinner and camped for the night.

On the second day, the race continued on Highway 18, the men and burros began the climb to the lunch stop at Cushenbury. After lunch the real climbing began, until they reached a field to the northeast of Baldwin Lake, where they again had dinner and camped for the night.

On the third day, the wrangler and burro teams that had survived the rigors thus far, reached for the conclusion of the race, trekking on to the finish line in what is now Big Bear Lake Village.

Sam remembers Service Stations:

Sam remembers that in the 1950s, Dale and Margie Wilson operated the Union 76 Service Station on the north side of Highway 18, northwest of the "Y." Dale was an energetic fellow and would tackle mechanical repairs of any kind.

In a separate building to the north of the Service Station, Dale and Margie had an Ice Producing facility. Patrons could approach at any hour, insert a quarter into the coin slot, and a large block of ice would come crashing down the chute.

In the late 1960s, Dale Wilson operated a water hauling service. Water was supplied from a well near their home, southwest of the intersection of Highway 18 and Kendall Road.

Dale and Margie had come to Lucerne Valley prior to 1940.

Dale had enlisted in the military in 1943 and had served in the Army Air Force for the duration of World War II. He was thereafter a vigorous supporter of Military Veterans. The present V.F.W. Post 5551 is located at (or near to) the former Wilson home.

On the southeast corner of Highway 18 and Ox Bow Road was another Service Station. Sam "remembers his dad's recollections," that this had been a Shell Service Station, started and operated for some period of time, by F. M. Van Norman .

Archer's Shell Service operated at the location in the later 1950s. In the later 1960s, Al and Lyndall Archer continued to operate Archer's Auto Parts in the same building. Sam remembers that when it was no longer an active Service Station, a gas pump island (without the pumps) was still present in front of the building.

And until recent years, the Lucerne Valley NAPA Auto Parts store was located in that building. On the northeast corner of Highway 18 and Trade Post Road, the building is still standing that was a service station. The multi-bay auto service building to the north, that was an adjunct of the service station operation, is also still standing.

A very modern Chevron Service Station was built on the southwest corner of Highway 18 and Baker Road in the 1950s. Sam remembers that Russell Strunk operated this station from the time it was new, and for perhaps a year or two after that, until he suddenly died. Frank Czerwonka operated the Chevron Station for many years after that.

Also on the south side of Highway 18, about midway between Baker Road and Cody Road, there was the Richfield Service Station. This was owned and operated by Jesse and Alice Blair. Alice was cheerful and usually greeted the customers, checked their water and oil, and pumped gas for them. Jesse did some service work and sold and installed tires, in a bay on the east side of the building. The Blair's Richfield station was in existence from Sam's earliest memories; certainly from the earlier 1950s. Sometime after Jesse died in 1969, Alice returned to Texas, remarried, and died there.

A great attraction for small boys—and just about everyone else, was a pen that extended out from the west and north walls of the Blair's Service Station. The pen was a few feet wide and the surrounding block wall was perhaps two feet high. This was populated by a goodly number of desert tortoises—of all sizes—from a few old giants to smaller specimens a few inches in length.

Sam remembers Grocery Stores:

The building immediately west of Blair's Richfield Service Station housed Leo's Market when Sam was a small boy. In the early 1950s, Elma Regensberg (1908-1995) seemed to be always pleasantly tending the store by herself.

In the mid-1950s, the installation of the Kaiser Permanente Cement Plant set many other changes in motion. One quite noticeable change, on the local landscape, was the construction of the Lucerne Valley Shopping Center. In about 1956, Leo's Market expanded into its new and spacious quarters on the west side of that compound.

Around 1960, the West End Market opened. This was located on the south side of Highway 18, a short ways east of Baker Road. Owners Lew (Luther B.) and Bess Cowan, lived in the house just to the west of the store building. Lew and Bess were hard workers and ran the business quite professionally. Sam remembers that Lew and Bess were always attired in light brown grocer's aprons, and that Lew always wore a dress shirt and a tie under his apron. Jake (last name lost to memory) very capably ran the full service meat counter at the rear (south end) of the store.

It would seem that the Cowan's had been residents of Lucerne Valley since about 1946, and had been active in business for most of that time. Lew and Bess Cowan were divorced in 1969. Bess continued to operate the West End Market for some years after that.

The building that housed the Homestead Bakery and Grocery is still standing. It is located on the north side of Highway 18, due north of the intersection of Highland Avenue.

The Homestead Bakery and Grocery, also known as Jakes Market or Jacobs Market, was operated at that location for a number of years—probably commencing about the mid-1930s, and continuing well into the 1940s. The proprietors were Orlando "Jake" and Mildred Jacobs.

The Jacobs had come to Lucerne Valley in about 1928, and until 1936 lived on their homesteaded land—southeast of the intersection of Northside and Meridian Roads. It was there that, "Jake baked

60 or 70 loaves of bread, sweet rolls, cakes and pies on Saturdays and sold them through Max Lewis' grocery store."

Around 1936 the Jacobs purchased a large parcel of land located southeast of the intersection of Barstow Road and Old Woman Springs Road. Their North Valley house was moved to this new location, and there it is still standing. It is the first residence east of Barstow Road; on the south side of Old Woman Springs Road.

Lucerne Valley's Pioneer Park is situated on 10 acres, donated by the Jacobs for that purpose.

Preceding the Jacobs venture, the Lucerne Valley Supply Company was a hardware and grocery store operated by Max Lewis, for a period of seven years. It was located in the building on the southwest corner of Highway 18 and Ox Bow Road, and the tall tank house is still standing there behind it. Max Lewis came to Lucerne Valley in 1926.

Homesteaders - Donaldson Family

By Sally Donaldson Emerson, condensed version.
Photos courtesy of Sally (Donaldson) Emerson and Janet (Donaldson) Miller.

We start with the first generation of Lucerne Valley Donaldsons, Clarence and Dorothy:

Clarence Donaldson was born in Alabama in 1900 and came to California about 1920, where he met Dorothy Rufert, a native Californian, whose family came here from Kansas about 1890. They were married in 1923 in Selma, Fresno County, lived in Selma for a short time and then moved to the Los Angeles and Glendale area, where their first child was born in 1924. The family began to grow and they added four more children while living in that general area. They moved to Lucerne Valley about 1936, where their last two daughters (Sally and Janet) were born at home. During WWII, they again moved to Los Angeles until the war was over and in 1947 returned to their home in Lucerne Valley.

Dorothy's sister, Mabel Rufert, married Lonnie James and they homesteaded a parcel of land in Lucerne Valley, giving a portion to the growing Donaldson family, where they began to build a home on what is now known as Donaldson Road. In those early days, there was no electricity, no water and no pavement to that area, and very few neighbors; today it is still a dirt road with very

Donaldsons, 1947, Back, Betty, Irene, (Mom and Dad) Dorothy & Clarence, Mildred, Front Emma, Sally, Janet and Don.

few neighbors. They started by building a 20 x 20-foot wooden room, where the young family lived. The wood that was used was taken from a railroad box car that had been used in a movie set at Dead Man's Point. In about 1938 they added another room built from rock gathered from the nearby hills, and then started to add a third room also built of rock gathered again from the area, but this time it was from a volcanic area northeast of their property. The home is still in use and owned by relatives of the family,

Building the third room with help from family and neighbors, 1939. B 5-2

although the road from the highway is still dirt to the homes in that area. Modern times did not catch up to them until the late 1950s, when electricity was finally installed. Up to that time, they relied on kerosene lamps and lanterns for light and a wood burning stove for heat.

They dug a well about 1949 and until that time, water had to be hauled seven miles from the artesian well at the Box S Ranch, owned by the Goulding family. The Gouldings supplied many families

Dad working on the third room, 1939. B 5-2

with water as needed. Food was kept cold in an ice box on the front porch; the ice melt ran under the house and the dogs loved that cool area. They also had a cooler that was a box covered in burlap that was kept wet to keep some food cool. The washing machine was run by an old Star motor. The necessary (outhouse) was built quite a distance from the home. Ironing was done by heating the irons on the stove. Bathwater also had to be heated on the stove. It was not until the 1960s, that a real bathroom was finally added to the house, as well as another room that became the kitchen.

"Town," in those early days consisted of a gas station, and restaurant The Jackrabbit Cafe, one small grocery store, a post office, a school in town, a community center, a couple of churches, library, the Malt Shop, the Desert Dome Dance Hall, and not much else that I can remember.

Clarence was partly disabled while working in Glendale during the war years, but was able to do odd jobs around town. Dorothy Donaldson worked to support the family as a cook at the Jackrabbit Cafe, until it burned down, then worked in various other coffee shops until her retirement. After she retired, she became active in the Garden Club in Lucerne Valley. She and Clarence are both buried in the Lucerne Valley Cemetery.

As for the Donaldson family - Mildred was the oldest child and graduated from Victor Valley High School in 1942. In 1943 she was married to

Family returning to Lucerne Valley, 1947. B 5-2

Donaldson homestead. B 5-2

Frederick Tyler in Seattle, Washington. He was in the navy at that time, and when he finished his navy career, he joined the air force and the family moved around the world, as he continued to serve until his retirement. Then they moved back to Lucerne Valley, built a home and lived there until their deaths. They were both well known in town. Fred was a volunteer with the veterans organizations and Mildred worked for several years in Victorville, at the S.B. County Welfare Department. She was also involved in the local Garden Club. They had two children, Douglas and John, and seven grandchildren and seven great-grandchildren.

J. Elizabeth "Betty" Donaldson graduated from Victor Valley High School and married Granville "Granny" Reed in 1944 in Lucerne Valley. They lived on a ranch in the area, then moved north to Yreka, where Granville died in an accident in 1948. Betty, with two small children, moved to Glendale and in 1949 married Granville's brother, Troy Reed. Together they had two more children. They lived in La Crescenta, California until Troy retired from the city of Glendale and then moved back to Lucerne Valley, where they built their home and are well known in the valley. Their one son, Michael, and his family also live in the same area. Troy was also raised in Lucerne Valley and other members of the Reed family are still here.

Irene, the third child went to the local schools, and for a time went to Victor Valley School, then went to live with family friends in Los Angeles, where she graduated. She married in 1949. She and her husband, Ray Poquette raised their family in the San Fernando Valley.

Son, Don Donaldson graduated from Victor Valley High School in 1951, and joined the marines for one tour of duty, then joined the air force where he served until retirement. He currently lives in Canon City, Colorado.

Emma attended schools locally until 1951 when she moved to Washington State; graduated from high school there in 1953, married Clyde Douglas in 1955 and had two girls. After Clyde's death she remarried. Her late husband, Bernie Carey, was well known in the valley. Many of her children and grandchildren still live in the area.

Sally was born in the family home in Lucerne Valley, and attended Midway School from 3rd through the 6th grade and then went to Victor Valley Junior High School for 7th grade. She then left to live with a married sister and her family for 3 1/2 years, returned to Lucerne Valley and graduated from Victor Valley High School in 1957. She moved to La Crescenta, where she met her husband, Richard Emerson. They raised their two children in La Canada.

Janet was also born in the family home and attended Midway School. She graduated from Victor Valley High School in 1960.

Dorothy and Sally Donaldson, 1943.

She married Allen Miller in 1962, who was in the U.S. Air Force stationed at George AFB at that time. He worked for Kaiser Cement and McDougall's Well Drilling until he became a paid call Firefighter at the Lucerne Valley Fire Department in 1964. In 1967 he became a full time Firefighter and was promoted to Captain in 1970. By 1971 he had been promoted to Assistant Fire Chief and in 1986, he became Lucerne Valley Fire Chief and District Manager. Lucerne Valley Fire was under the umbrella of the San Bernardino County Fire Agency, but transitioned into the San Bernardino County Fire Department in 1994. Allen was promoted to Battalion Chief at that time. He retired in 2003 after 39 years of fire service. He passed away in 2009. Janet worked for 25 years until her retirement from Lucerne Valley Market. They have three children who have raised their families in the area.

Independence Learned Early – The Risler Family

Recorded by Jan Lembright October 13, 2015. Photos courtesy of the Risler Family.

This is a fun story that includes four generations of Rislers, the last two of which are still quite active in the valley. Please don't feel bad if you have a hard time following this family line as it includes five generations who could not let the first name "Lee" die out.

We will start with the first who was Lee William Risler Sr. He married Agnes Jackley and this is an account of early settlers in Lucerne Valley as told to me by Lee Risler, III. His father came to California from Ohio in

Lee III's Grandma feeding the animals 1927.

1904, traveling by car and ended up in San Pedro. It was there he worked as a longshoreman.

He and his family came to Lucerne Valley to homestead in 1925. They homesteaded 160 acres on Rabbit Springs Road near the little volcanic buttes, east of Lincoln road. They had to live on the land for three to five years while making improvements. They built a house, put up a barn, and fencing. He had two sons, Tom the oldest at 13, and Lee Jr. who was 11 years old. Later they bought a neighbor's land and ended up with 640 acres. In the 1950s they subdivided their land and sold all but the 100

First Risler house. B 5-3

acres, on which the family still lives. Their main reason for coming to Lucerne Valley was to have a place to stay while hunting in Big Bear.

Because they still had to work, Lee Sr. and Agnes went back down the hill and left the two boys here. The boys would

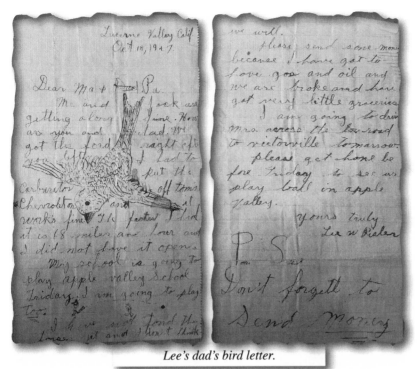

Lee's dad's bird letter.

write their mother for money and basic needs, drawing pictures on the letter. Once young Lee Jr. asked for a saddle for the horse as he kept getting bucked off.

The brothers, being boys, fought a lot. When things got bad, Lee Jr. went to live with neighbors until things cooled down, or his mother came and put things straight.

Once when the boys were going to school, they saw some wild horses, they spent the day chasing them.

Film crews used Lucerne Valley to film westerns and came out to make a movie while the boys were there; and the movie makers asked the locals to dress as Indians and ride their horses around. Tom and Lee made a little money playing natives.

Years later they would only come on weekends to hunt. They hunted deer in the foothills and duck in Big Bear. They also cut firewood in Big Bear and hauled it down by wagon. They would attach a couple of long logs to the back of the wagon as a brake. When they got to the bottom, they would cut them up and throw them in the back with the other logs.

In 1975 Tom, and his wife Iona,

Lee Risler's grandpa panning for Gold, Cactus Flats.

built a house on the family acreage in Lucerne Valley, just north of Rabbit Springs Road. In 1986 Tom passed on, but Iona stayed active in the Grange and her church until her passing in 2005.

In 1978 Lee Jr. retired and moved with his wife Neona to the homestead in Lucerne Valley. Lee Jr. and Neona belonged to the Moose Club, helped build the current lodge, and was also active in the Roadrunners. Lee Jr. passed on in 1988 and Neona in 2001.

In 1963 Neona's son Lee III had graduated from high school and started his own business making custom leather sandals, purses, and wallets under the brand LeeGin Leather. By 1972 with a lot of luck and hard

Lee Risler Sr. and friends hunting party.

Lee III's Grandpa and friends.

work, he had three retail stores and a wholesale division in the Redondo Beach and Hermosa Beach areas. After 10 years as a businessman, he began traveling around the world surfing and enjoying his freedom. He even lived in New Zealand for two years. During this time Lee was married for a short time and had his oldest son the fourth Lee, who now has a son of his own named, you guessed it, Lee V.

In 1974 he returned to build his dream house in Lucerne Valley. Local Contractor Bobby Delperdang set the forms and poured the slab, and over the next two years, Lee III and his friends built the house.

After running low on funds, Lee started another sandal shop using the brand Kiwi Sandals. In 1976 he met his second wife Bryn Kingston, and they were married in 1979. Bryn is an RN and has worked as the local school nurse. She also designed and started the first St. Mary's Hospital mobile medical van that still serves Lucerne Valley residents. Bryn still works for St. Mary's Hospital. She also served two terms on the Lucerne Valley Unified School District Board.

Artist at work, Lee III, 1979.

Rhett, Jessica and Aydin Risler.

Lee III and Bryn have three grown children. The oldest Rhett and his wife, Jessica, along with their son, Aydin, took over the sandal business in 2005. Rhett had been raised in the shop and Jessica soon became an eager student in the art of sandal making. Lee worked with them for three years before fully retiring. Rhett and Jessica continue to operate the business, traveling to sales shows and selling over the internet. Like Bryn, Jessica has recently become a school board member for the Lucerne Valley Unified School District. Bryn and Lee's daughter, Elaine, lives in Apple Valley where she works as a beautician, and son, Vincent, followed his mom into the nursing field.

As you can see, the Rislers are fast approaching 100 years of active community involvement in Lucerne Valley.

Bryn with new St Mary's health van 1996.

Scouts, Beautician, Historian – Dick and Ethel Owen

By Pat Judkins

Dick Owen, courtesy LV Leader.

Ethel Johnson married Dick Owen at the Community Church in November of 1950; Rev. Charles Coon officiated. In 1946 Ethel began setting hair in her kitchen and later built a beauty shop on the front of the property. (Sadly, it is now an abandoned building near the Desert Mini-Mart Gas Station on Highway 18, about 100 yards west of Baker Road). Ethel was the first hair stylist and barber here.

Ethel told me they went to San Bernardino, paid $1 for a building permit and started building. She said there were no inspections; you just filed a Notice of Completion when you finished.

She met Dick on a blind date. They attended a Lions Club party in Helendale. On their second date, they went dancing at the newly opened Apple Valley Inn. Dick's father used to say they did their courting in the hay fields, as after each date, Dick took Ethel to various fields where he was to bale hay the next morning. "He said he wanted to see if the dew was putting the proper moisture content in the alfalfa he was supposed to bale," Ethel said.

Quite a hearty gal she was. Before she married Dick, Ethel was alone one night when her two horses got out; one horse returned with a 7" long and 3" deep gash in its chest. No vet was available for 24-hours, and Ethel wasn't sure about leaving the wound open that long.

What would a pioneer woman do? she wondered. Then she realized she was a pioneer woman for that point in time, so she got out her curved upholstery needle and a spool of button and carpet thread, then soaked them in alcohol. She washed the wound with cotton and a lysol solution. Next, she got busy stitching up the horse. "I pulled a lot of meat together," Ethel said. "Fortunately, the horse cooperated!" The vet commended her and her Hamiltonian ex-cavalry horse recovered.

She also had encounters with a rattlesnake and other varmints. One time she noticed the waste basket under the sink was not in the same place each morning as she had left it the night before. She

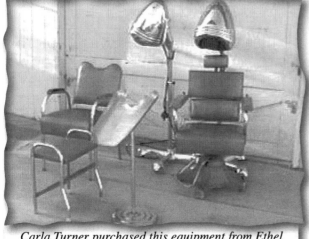

Carla Turner purchased this equipment from Ethel Owen. Ethel used them in her beauty shop on Hwy. 18.

figured she had a rat, so she went to Dan Stewart's General Store (where Behind the Chutes was at that time, the building is now owned by Mark Riddle). She purchased a rat trap and put it in place. She said there was a board missing behind the sink. She heard a commotion and ran over just in time to see the back end of a skunk going down the hole with its hind leg caught in the trap. With a few kicks, it left the trap behind. "That wasn't all it left behind, but we managed to get through the night," she said. I could write about Dick and Ethel Owen all night. They were true characters; delightful!

Librarian, Historian – Frances Hanken

Remembered by Pat Judkins

Frances Hanken was born July 9, 1907. She died April 27, 1990 at the Queen of the Valley Hospital in West Covina after a long illness. Frances will be remembered in this community as a truly dedicated, deeply involved, civic-minded contributor to her beloved Lucerne Valley.

Her many friends here describe her as " creative, colorful, fascinating, adored, and a great asset to this community."

Field Trip with Lucerne Valley Museum.
Front Row: L-R Joe Elnicky, Flo Elnicky, Frances Hanken, Mrs. Tegelberg, Irene Welband, Janice Horst. Second Row: Gil Tegelberg Sr., Gil Tegelberg Jr., Ethel Watson, Ida May Chamberlin, Joe Horst. Photo courtesy of Lucerne Valley Museum Association.

Part of her legacy to her children and to this community may be found in her many contributions here. She left a lot of herself in the varied projects she undertook lovingly on the behalf of Lucerne Valley. Frances, who arrived here around 1929, was honored as Citizen of the Year. She worked for the library in various capacities for several years, and is credited with working alongside Joe and Janice Horst to provide a Lucerne Valley chapter of the San Bernardino County Museum Association.

Lena Barnett remembered attending a church picnic at the home of Frances and Joe Hanken when they lived up at Cushenbury in the late l940s. "The trees were beautiful, and we had a great time," Lena recalled.

Robert Clark's reminiscences include driving Frances' children on his school bus when they attended Midway School. His wife Agnes and Frances served together at numerous PTA functions. The Clarks who moved to this community in 1937, said some of the first residents they met were Francis Hankens' parents. "Her father was a minister who helped found the United Church, which met in the little building on Highway 18, where Art Bishop later sold antiques," Agnes said. (This building is now part of the Jack O'Landia complex just west of Crossroads Chapel.)

Francis is most remembered for her deep love for Lucerne Valley. She was constantly gathering myriad facts about the history of our community. She hoped to write a book and had many files and manuscripts filled with local memorabilia. She fascinated many with her tales about her beloved valley. She used this knowledge to impart much of her interesting local facts to the citizenry by writing articles for The *Lucerne Valley Leader* newspaper,

"Frances and I were kindred spirits as far as wanting to write a book is concerned," said her friend, Millie Edwards. Millie, who was captivated by the lore Frances would spin, perhaps summed it up best, quoting from Gray's Elegy, written in a country church yard: "Full many a flower is born to blush unseen and waste its sweetness on the desert air." Frances never got a chance to complete her book, but she steadily shared her findings with interested parties through her narrations and articles. Her friends would say that her heart remained in Lucerne Valley, even after she had to leave for much needed health care. (Though Frances never published a book of her own, her writings and research are now woven through the pages of this book. She was definitely a contributing "Town Character."-Editor)

Gil Tegelberg Sr. in his cactus greenhouse. B 5-4

Cactus King –
Gil Tegelberg

By Bill Lembright

When Jan and I moved to Lucerne Valley in 1981, we met a friendly, knowledgeable gentleman at the museum named Gil Tegelberg. He was one of a handful of long term residents who took us around to some of the area's wonderful and interesting historic landmarks. We began to understand that the Lucerne Valley region is brimming with historical landmarks and geographical wonders. Gil was a pioneer in the eyes of us newcomers.

Gil was born in 1897 in Iowa, where as a boy he started raising cactus. In World War I, he served in the American Balloon Corps until he was gassed. He spent three months recovering in a hospital at Cannes, France. That French hospital had a cactus garden which rekindled his interest in the plants. After his discharge, he began growing and selling cacti commercially.

In 1930 he homesteaded 320 acres along, what is now, Camp Rock Road. Gil's father graded the wagon road to bypass their acreage. During a flood, the nicely graded road had a 6 foot deep rut cut into it, but the Tegelbergs were able to use their plow to refill it. After that, the county agreed to take over the maintenance of the road. Tegelberg's old grader is now on display in the outdoor section of the Lucerne Valley Museum.

Gil built three large hothouses where he grew and sold cacti. This business kept his family off the government dole during the Great Depression and kept food on the table for over fifty years. Gil became known as the Cactus King because he went into the business earlier than most others. He grew and/or developed more than 1500 species. He sold common species at discount prices, but rare species sold for $500 to $2,000 per plant.

Today, his old hot houses and antique grader serve as monuments to this famous character from our past.

Tegelberg's road grader that now sits in the Lucerne Valley Museum's outdoor display. Photo courtesy of Millie Rader. A 5-5

Recollections of a Lucerne Valley Native Son – Frank Francis

Interviewed by Bill and Jan Lembright

Rod and Chuck Francis, where Burger Depot sits today

Frank's dad, Lloyd Francis, worked for a railroad in Los Angeles. He suffered from emphysema and moved to Lucerne Valley in 1946, with the hope of recovering. In 1951 Lloyd and his pregnant wife were visiting relatives in LA when Frank was born.

The Francis family rented the house that still stands just south and adjacent to the Burger Depot on Custer. Then the Francis family moved to a house located where Butcher's Block Hardware and Lumber now stands. Across Highway 18. on the north side facing the Francis home, stood the Ewing's Muffin Mountain Motel, now the Ace Motel.

Around 1957 Bobby Delperdang would ride a motor scooter from his home on Haven's Rest to the Francis's home.

At eight years old Frank broke a small window on the Francis's home. Just west of their home, Vern James, who would later open Vern's Mobile Glass, had opened a glass shop. So, Frank, who made about 25 cents a week picking up bottles, asked for a piece of glass. Feeling sorry for the boy, Vern supplied the glass and followed Frank home to teach him how to install glass. Vern's only stipulation was that Frank would quit throwing rocks. Lew and Bess Cowan opened an appliance store in a building next to Vern James' glass shop.

Frank Francis, Francis house next to old West End Market, now Butchers Block. A 5-6

One day Lloyd was burning a thick stand of bamboo on their property as it was a hiding place for snakes. Unbeknownst to Lloyd, there were some old tires hidden in the bamboo which created a plume of heavy black smoke. At the sight of the smoke, Dale Wilson, the Chief of the L.V. Volunteer Fire Department, jumped in his water pumper truck to put out the fire. Floyd couldn't afford the fire call fee and offered Del a six pack in payment.

Del Wilson was the fire chief, possibly because he was the only resident who owned a water pumper truck which he kept at his and Marge's Shell Station where G & G Auto now stands. One day the Baptist Church caught on fire which then touched off a vegetation fire. Del's pumper truck and the other volunteers put out that big blaze.

Frank recalls being told that Chimney Rock got its name from the smoke of all the Indian campfires around it. He also remembers Grandma Arnie, Bob Hayes' great-great grandma living at a cabin called the Eagle's Nest near a spring at the base of White Mountain.

Frank remembers a Sheriff's deputy (possibly named Mr. Thompson) who patrolled Lucerne Valley before the arrival of Red

Chimney Rock. B 1-11

Stillwell and would track suspects from horseback. He would be gone for up to two weeks and would let Leo Regensberg know where he was going.

He also recalled that Al Marty ran the Trading Post on the sw corner of Tradepost and SH18. A Texaco Station stood at the northeast corner of the intersection of SH18 and Tradepost.

Al and Vivian Archer, Sara Delperdang's parents, operated a Shell Station with auto parts. One day Frank's mother sent him to pick up an evaporative cooler v-belt on credit. Two years later Al gave the Francis' a statement that they had a debt outstanding. When questioned, Al came up with a statement that included the cost of the v-belt, plus interest.

Frank & Shelly Francis' Christmas Tree Forest Tree farm in 1990

In the building on Box S land, north of the intersection of Highland Road and SH18 was a Real Estate office run by realtor Don Williams. Next it was a union hall, and then a video rental store.

Mr. Blair built a Richfield Service Station where the Desert Minimart and Gas Station is now located. Years later, Pete Hert, Scott Hert's dad, bought the Richfield station from Mrs. Blair who moved to Texas. Scott worked at the station.

Frank recalls that the dome building west of the intersection of Tradepost and SH18 was a dance hall moved from LA. It became a roller skating rink, then Moose Hall, and then a church with tent revivals.

Rodeos used to be held on the vacant land (where the cemetery is now located) south and adjacent to the Baptist Church west of the modern Post Office, now housing Crossroads Chapel. In the 1950s

Frank Francis, 12/26/67.

and 1960s, the rodeo was held on the first Saturday of the month. Lloyd Francis transported local kids to the rodeos on a homemade flatbed he had constructed on the back of a 1951 Chevy.

When not in school, Frank found plenty of work with the local Paly Farms Co-op of Lucerne Valley chicken ranches.

Lloyd Francis worked for turkey rancher Stoddard Jess in Apple Valley, where the Jess Ranch housing development is now located. Lloyd also worked for Ross Dana, whose company paved many High Desert roads. In the 1960s Ross sold out to the Cooley brothers.

Frank attended Victor High, then finished high school at Apple Valley High in 1969. Travel time on the school bus was up to 2.5 hours twice a day. Soon after, he became an auto mechanic. He also often worked with Carl Kraft and Glen Moretz on several odd jobs. Frank was a school bus driver 23 years for the Victor Valley Unified School District.

Frank remembers that Frenchman Rene Belbenoit, who had escaped from the penal colony on Devil's Island, off the coast of French Guiana, had operated a men's clothing store in the building just west of the Lucerne Valley Shopping Center. Rene was found dead of a heart attack inside the store. Later, Dick Grobaty bought the business and operated the store.

A Gold Mining Couple – Russ and Marion Rishell

As remembered by Bill Lembright.
Photos courtesy of Russ and Marion Rishell.

Years ago, Jan and I were exploring Jacoby Canyon when we came across an old mining couple, whose faces were so wrinkled they could have been models for Leanin' Tree coffee mug characters. They were prospecting for gold so we didn't ask many questions. As we drove on, the old man warned

Russ and Marion Rishell

that our two-wheel drive minivan was no match for the road ahead, and that if we got stuck, he wasn't going to pull us out. As he warned, the road got worse and I turned around.

Another day off, Jan and I were exploring the Ord Mountain mines, on foot, when I spotted what appeared to be, a couple of miners in the distance. We kept quiet until they left. The next day at

Russ and Marion Rischel

Lucerne Valley Market and Hardware, an old couple introduced themselves and said they had seen our vehicle parked below the gate to the Ord Mountain mines. We recognized them as the old mining couple we had met in Jacoby Canyon.

After that, we shared many adventures together, including our stories of meeting up with God. We treated them like adopted parents. Often Russ would point out unusually shaped rock formations, insisting they were not natural, but had been sculpted by the Spaniards in search of gold in earlier centuries.

On one adventure, the four of us were on our hands and knees in a mine tunnel, with Jan in the lead. She kept feeling something poke her and would say, "Stop it!" Finally she directed her flashlight to the rear and saw that the Rishell's dog, Taffy, was poking her with its long nose, trying to get around her in that narrow tunnel.

On a hike up Silver Creek above Buena Vista, Russ handed me a rope and pointed to a distant mine tailing up high and to the east of our trail. I asked, "Why the rope?" He said, "Just tie it to your waist when you enter the tunnel." That didn't make a lot of sense, but I tied the rope around my waist and crawled into the

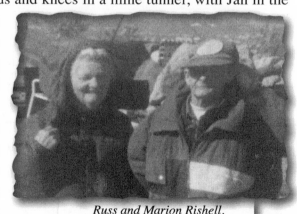

Russ and Marion Rishell,
passed 2003, 2012 respectively

tunnel. There was very little clearance, with cracked and sagging support timbers; so I turned back.

When I got back to Russ, I asked, "Do you think I'm suicidal?" To which he answered, "I just wanted to see how crazy you are."

Russ told us he used to mine coal deep underground in Pennsylvania. His fellow miners had hollowed out a cavernous glory hole. As was their custom, they would drill holes to blast free coal to load into ore cars. Immediately, after one seemingly innocuous blast, a section of a wall collapsed and a huge river of water rushed toward them. They scrambled for their lives to avoid drowning. Russ was so impressed, he gave up coal mining.

Victory Over Hardship – Robert (Bob) Penn

As told by Bill and Jan Lembright

Robert was born on January 14, 1937 in Los Angeles. His parents were George James Penn and Altisher Stovall Penn. His mother was soft spoken with a gentle nature; she was one of Lucerne Valley's characters.

He was only two years old when World War II broke out, but he remembers the planes overhead and seeing the searchlights.

In 1947 when he was 10 years old, and his father was in the service, his mother moved the family to beautiful Lucerne Valley. His mother, Altisher, was of Irish descent, her father was part Indian and she was born on a reservation in Oklahoma.

His father went to war because he was needed. His grandfather, James Robert Penn, was a Buffalo Soldier and a Lieutenant Colonel. He was among the first Buffalo Soldiers and is now buried in the Presidio in San Francisco. He served in World War I with Teddy Roosevelt and fought with him at San Juan Hill. Each Buffalo Soldier was given a section of land (640 acres) for their service. The first forest ranger was also a Buffalo Soldier.

Bob had many positive things to say about Lucerne Valley and credits his good character to Lucerne Valley. He remembered the Double J Ranch owned by Mary Costner, which was popular with many notable people. They also had many rodeos and the water was plentiful and sweet at Goulding's Box S Ranch. When he first came here, the valley was green and he said that it never froze at the Sky High Ranch. He remembers working for Mrs. Sloan. He also remembers that he saw orange trees growing here and that there were many dairy farms.

In 1947 he went to Midway School and was there with Don Fife. He recalled that one of the boys shot a teacher in the rear-end with a staple.

He remembers Patsy Ball and her husband, Slim. They did a lot to help Bob and his family. He and his family lived in a tent for 1 1/2 years with 6

Penn home. Photo courtesy of the Penn Family. B 5-7

brothers and sisters. Slim asked him who was going to build their house and Bob told him he and his mother would build the house. Slim told him that he and the American Legion would be out to help them build the house. The community came together and built their house in one weekend.

He spoke fondly of the Medici family and that when he graduated from high school, Mr. Medici was there. When Mr. Medici passed away he went to the memorial and the family warmly invited Bob to sit with them. Bob was deeply moved and never forgot them for their hospitality.

Bob's father passed away in 1962; they had nine children.

Mayor Charlie Parsons.

Charlie's Chats – Charlie Parsons
By Pat Judkins, 1994. Photos from the Lucerne Valley Phone Book.

The editor of South High School newspaper in Minneapolis, Minnesota won national honors for his work in 1934. Charlie Parsons, who was born in Minneapolis in 1916, first realized how much he enjoyed writing while undertaking this student endeavor.

During the Depression, journalistic positions were at a premium so Charlie began an apprenticeship program for typesetting and a career that pioneered the various transitions from hand-setting type in hot metal through photographic typesetting around 1960 and on to the 1990s computerized methods.

While working in newspaper and advertising typography, Charlie met a lovely copywriter named Genevieve. Gen became Mrs. Parsons on June 26, 1959. It was the second marriage for both of them.

Succumbing to his brother's pleas to leave Minneapolis and its minus 20 degree weather and enjoy the 70 degree average California had to offer, the newlyweds took a honeymoon trip to visit his brother in Monrovia. Charlie and Gen first bought a home in South Pasadena where they lived for many years. They are still honeymooning in California.

The Parsons first discovered Lucerne Valley when their son, Attorney Richard Stack of Barstow, purchased a cabin close to Johnson Valley. When they visited him, they used adjectives like "gorgeous!" and "magnificent!" They would sit in his yard, viewing the moon through the Joshua Trees and comment, "What a big front yard!" They drove to Lucerne Valley Market, then in the L.V. Shopping Center, to do their shopping. They remember Don and Marion Thrush who owned the meat department.

In 1976 they attended the July 4th Bicentennial Parade in Lucerne Valley. Charlie says, "It just got me!" The community spirit here and the friendly folks they met, helped them decide they wanted to be a part of this valley. They visited here part time from 1976 until Charlie retired two years later; then they moved here permanently.

In January of 1987 Charlie came full circle and assumed the position of editor of the *Lucerne Val-*

ley Leader newspaper. Prior to this job appointment he was a member of the *Leader* staff and wrote his popular column, "Charlie Chats."

Charlie and Gen are genuinely friendly, and soon took active roles in this community. He represented Lucerne Valley around the High Desert as L.V. Honorary Mayor in 1984-85. He has been a member of the MAC

The Chamber's Board of Directors includes: Seated from left to right, Ray Purkey, Charlie Parsons, F.M. Van Norman, Russ Jones; Standing, Angel Morales, Bob Chopp, Clarice Peterson, Bob Clark, Mark Vandenbroeke, Michelle Ege, Jack Jenkins; Not shown, Archer B. Hudson, Jr.

Board, a board member of the Chamber of Commerce, and member of the Lions Club, the Moose Lodge, the Museum Association and the American Association of Retired Persons. Gen is always at his side playing an active, supportive role on behalf of Lucerne Valley.

Charlie had only resided here for six years when he became aware this community truly needed a local telephone directory. In 1974 Gladys Nelson came up with the idea of a local phone book, and provided one for this community as a Chamber fundraiser while running for honorary mayor. Darlene and Jim Johnson put out a second phone book here as part of Jim's 1976 campaign for honorary mayor. It was called the Bicentennial Fone Finder, printed by Ralph Chamney of High Desert Printing, and they sought local business advertisements.

Charlie decided to commit to the Chamber and local residents to provide that much needed service as part of his honorary mayor campaign in 1984. This phone book was used for two years. In 1986 Charlie again undertook the responsibility as a service to the community. It was used for four years until everyone's copy was dog-earred or falling apart. The last phone book, and the one used by Lucerne Valley for the past four years was put together by Charlie in 1990. These three directories were monumental tasks, and Gen was his helpmate as they leafed through the huge Contel directory together, for the first two books, singularly picking out all the 248 numbers.

"The biggest pitfall about producing a community directory is making a mistake," Charlie said. "A telephone number is a very personal item to people, and it is important that it be correctly listed." Charlie always tried to keep the telephone directories a part of the Lucerne Valley Chamber of Commerce as a community service. In addition to telephone numbers; photographs, information about local organizations, and the history of the community were included. The community's response was positive; possibly ecstatic.

The phone books were a lot of hard work, but with Charlie's experience in typography, journalism, photography, ad design, and paste up; it all came together and a grateful community sang his praises. As Charlie would often say: "Keep 'em comin, kids."

True Assets of Lucerne Valley – Chuck and Julia Bell

By Millie Rader. This article was originally published in two parts in the "Town Characters" column of the Lucerne Valley Leader newspaper in March of 2009. Julia has since passed making this story even more important to capture here.

Chuck and Julia Bell Wedding. Photo courtesy of Chuck Bell.

The characters that I want to share with you this time have so many interesting facets that a once-a-week newspaper cannot afford enough column space. So, this will be part one of a two-part series. And just so that you don't miss out, their lives get more and more interesting as time goes on.

This week I have the pleasure of compiling the lives and accomplishments of a Lucerne Valley couple who, together have touched many generations of young and old alike within this valley. They don't look for a pat on the back, they just get things done. These two are very busy, very humble people. They are Chuck and Julia Bell.

It took some arm twisting before the Bells agreed to let me interview them for this column. They invited my husband, David, and I out to their home. This is important because David really needed to be there as he has a part in this story.

I was afraid in the beginning of our visit, that Chuck would spend more time telling me who I should be interviewing, rather than allowing me to drag out of him, the many important details surrounding the work that he and his wife have done to enrich this community. But I am persistent and we were finally able to get down to business.

Chuck and Julia do have a few hobbies, but most of their time and effort goes into the betterment of this community.

My husband and I have been bike riding and caught Chuck, out on his ancient 10-speed bike, in his old beat up straw hat. Other than that, Chuck really doesn't know the meaning of hobbies, unless you consider trapping gophers, or helping to maintain desert water sources for cattle and wildlife to be hobbies. I do know that much of their spare time is spent with their three granddaughters who live just a stone's throw away. Chuck has plenty of stories to share about his girls, each told with a twinkle in his eye and that wry grin that makes him look very much like a proud grandpa.

When Julia is not elbow deep in volunteer work, I have heard that she enjoys needlepoint, and gardening, and she is an avid reader. According to her daughter, Heather, she also does quite a bit of canning. (The last part sounds more like work to me.)

Let's talk about how they met. Chuck and Julia met and began dating while attending Knox College in Galesburg, Illinois in the mid-sixties. They continued their courtship long distance for three long years, while Julia finished school.

While Chuck was in school, he would come back to Lucerne Valley in the summer to work for Kaiser (now known as Mitsubishi Cement) bagging cement to earn his college tuition.

When I asked Julia how they managed to keep a relationship going back then without email and text messaging, she said, "I just adored Chuck and I wasn't about to let him go." After 41 years of

Chuck and Julia Bell, 2005.
Photo courtesy of Chuck Bell.

marriage, I think it must have been true love.

In 1968 they were married, and Chuck brought his city-girl bride out to live on the Lucerne Valley property that his grandparents had purchased in the mid 1940s. "I really didn't have too hard a time getting used to the change (Illinois to California,)" said Julia. "The hardest part was learning to cross a street without having to worry about getting hit every time."

Chuck went back to work for awhile at Kaiser, then moved on to work for the County of San Bernardino as an Environmental Analyst. He then worked in the Planning Department as a County Hearings Officer, where he dealt with land use issues.

His work for the county led San Bernardino County Supervisor John Joyner to appoint Chuck as his Field Representative for this area. He served in that capacity from 1986 to 1988, when Joyner left office after his third term. Chuck also served in that same position in 2004.

After his job with Joyner was done, incoming County Supervisor Marsha Turoci placed Chuck on the Planning Commission, again to help make land use decisions. Chuck then went to work for himself doing environmental consulting, and farming his land.

As we continued the journey through their lives, Chuck shifted the focus from himself and onto Julia, telling us that she started her work career as a "Kelly Girl," cleaning Chicago offices to raise her own college tuition.

After she and Chuck were married, Julia began her first teaching job at Lucerne Valley Elementary School. Julia's first class was fourth grade and one of her very first students was my husband, David who adored "Mrs. Bell" then, just as much as he does now.

Julia took the next year off from teaching to further her studies, and then came back to our local elementary school, this time to teach sixth grade; once again David was in her class. By this time she had gained a reputation as a "fun" teacher and the rest of us were quite envious. We all heard the stories of how much she enjoyed her students and how she motivated them to complete their work in a timely manner. As I remember, she rewarded those who had completed their work before Friday, by testing them in the morning and allowing them creative free time in the afternoon. She even had a rabbit in her classroom that she would allow the students to hold and play with. What I would have done to have had Mrs. Bell as my teacher. She went on to teach kindergarten, then sixth grade again, and then went back to school for her master's degree.

With her Master's in hand, Julia came back to the Lucerne Valley Elementary School as principal. This happened while our boys were in school; she served as their principal from 1995 to 1998. This made Julia the first local teacher, since my Aunt Alice Barnett, to also hold the title of principal. My aunt was principal when the district moved the school to its current site from what is now Midway Park.

When Julia retired, the school arranged a special surprise send-off with all the students and teachers present, and had my husband and two sons escort her to the stage, as a picture of her start to finish, having served two generations of the same family during her career.

The first portion of this story focused on the Bell's working life, the next part will be on their volunteer lives.

I have heard Chuck say many times, that Lucerne Valley has a higher percentage of volunteers, per capita than any other town. I think that he and Julia are partly to blame for that, but Chuck blames it on Julia. "Julia always got involved with a project and I then got sucked in along the way," said Chuck.

The Bells really got their start as volunteers through their children. Daughter, Heather, was into horses from a young age and in the early version of Equestrian Trails Inc. (ETI). known then as the Pony Express. Julia helped with running the club as Vice President, while Chuck would bring his tractor down to the Midway Park Arena and maintain it for the riders. I know that he even continued to do that for many years after his daughter was grown.

Their son, David, then got involved in Little League, and Chuck became a coach, and President of the organization. He again used his tractor to maintain the field, and once again stayed with it long after his son had moved on. "We did it for the kids," said a modest Chuck.

Since that time, Chuck has been involved with the Youth Accountability Board helping our young ones who have crossed over the legal line

Lucerne Valley Unified School District Board and Mitsubishi Cement Corporation Educational Foundation Board. Left to Right: Mike Davis, Jim Buckley, Tom Courtney, and Jean Morgan, Bud Biggs, Julia Bell, Bryn Risler and Teresa Reyes. Photo courtesy of Millie Rader, 2005.

complete their community service hours here in Lucerne Valley, fostering in them a sense of responsibility to their home town.

Chuck also helped start the Crossroads BMX Club, promoting in many of our children the love of bike riding. My sons were also involved in this endeavor, and not only improved their riding skills, but learned how to build and maintain a bike track as well.

Town clean-up has always been important to Chuck and in the late nineties, he was able to get four Adopt-a-Highway areas set up, covering eight miles of Highway 18. He did the footwork and helped, or coerced, four local organizations to participate; they are the Youth Accountability Board, the Lucerne Valley Chamber of Commerce, the Outriders, and R.W. Ranch. These organizations still maintain those roadways today.

I have personally worked with Chuck through the Chamber of Commerce, and Crossroads BMX. I also served on the Municipal Advisory Council (MAC) with him. I am pretty sure that he is the reason that I was appointed to that board in the first place.

Chuck's government service has served this valley well, as Chuck has served on the BLM California Desert Advisory Council for six years. He is on the Watermaster Advisory Committee for the Mojave Water Agency working to keep us from losing any more water rights. He is currently President of the Mojave Desert Resource Conservation District, with the primary project of eradicating non-native plants that consume tremendous amounts of water and displace native vegetation and habitat.

The Lucerne Valley Economic Development Association (LVEDA) was assisted by Chuck at its start up in the mid-nineties, where he now serves on the board. He is also on the MAC Land Use Advisory Committee.

Originally, through the Chamber of Commerce, and now through LVEDA, Chuck started the process, in the early eighties, to get the left turn pocket put in at Highway 18 at High Road. This project was just completed two weeks ago. He has worked on many other completed road projects with many more still pending.

Chuck attends all of the San Bernardino Association of Governments (SANBAG) meetings. This is the group that controls the budgets for Cal-Trans and the County Road Department.

"I have to keep on them," said Chuck. "I keep all of the records and history on these projects." He said the only way to finally get them (SANBAG) to do anything is to constantly remind them of their previous commitments.

Julia was "Citizen of the Year" in the late eighties. She was voted onto the school board in 1999, where she served as President. She is currently president of the Roadrunners, and serves as Secretary of the Mitsubishi Cement Corporation Educational Foundation, and she also sits on the Domestic Violence Board.

Whew, do these people ever sleep? No, Julia says that Chuck still gets calls all the time from people in the valley who need help with land issues.

When I asked Chuck and Julia why they devote so many volunteer hours to this town, they both gave me some insights into their core values and words to live by as well.

Julia said, "Our family has been liberally blessed with all the riches our beloved country has to offer…security, good health and opportunity. You have to pass it on, and give it back."

These two tend to think alike. Chuck's response to me at a different time was "Every U.S. Citizen, non-citizen residents, born here or not – has reaped the tremendous benefits provided by our founding fathers, and those who built, fought, and died for this great country, keeping it 'great,' starts at the community level."

Julia stepped down from the LVUSD school board in December 2012 due to health problems and passed away a month later at age 67. August 11, 2015, the new Early Childhood Academy on the Lucerne Valley Elementary School campus was dedicated in Julia's name.

"Julia was not about recognition," said Lucerne Valley Unified School District Superintendent Suzette Davis "Everything about her revolves around children and love. I can't separate the two things from her. This is the concept of the Early Childhood Academy … the time to reach young children is at the beginning."

Evelyn Carpenter in her studio 2004

Local Artist - Evelyn Carpenter
As told to Jan Lembright. Photos courtesy of Edith Carpenter.

Evelyn Carpenter, a talented local artist whose trade name is Eve Delight, is a quiet and unassuming lady and not one to brag on herself, but she had a delightful tale to tell once we talked her into sharing her story.

Evelyn's parents, whose last name was Delight, moved to Lucerne Valley in 1954 and bought 10 acres with a house at the corner of Post Office and Sunrise Roads and immediately started making improvements. They named their place the Delight Ranch.

Her father was an expert machinist by trade and made all his tools/laths by hand. He seldom bought anything. He made beautiful tables, with precise tooling and patterns, from rocks he found here or near Lucerne Valley, on a rock cutter which he made by hand. Evelyn attributes her artistic talent to him.

"My dad had recently retired from the National Supply Co. in Torrance," Evelyn said. "And like so many others, my parents thought it might be fun to try the chicken business." They came here to retire and found a new way of life. They loved the peaceful beauty of the valley away from the city hassle and traffic. They sold chickens to Zacky Farms, etc. but the chicken business never really worked out too well.

Evelyn and her husband, Herb, would come on weekends and summers, with their two children, Greg who was the age of eight and Susie who was two years old at the time.

Evelyn had served in the U.S. Coast Guard Women's Reserve, A.K.A SPARS during World War II. After serving her country, Evelyn decided to attend the noted Otis Art Institute in Los Angeles on the G.I. Bill. She took up painting and over the years showed and sold a number of her paintings. Many of her paintings are displayed around town, such as those in First Mountain Bank (now First Foundation Bank.) She also has a painting called "The Crossing" on display at the Eclipse Gallery on Bear Valley Road.

In the 1950s and 1960s, the Carpenter family spent almost every weekend with the grandparents, on the Delight Ranch in Lucerne Valley; they especially enjoyed the swimming pool. Their children loved Lucerne Valley so much that the couple purchased a lot on Emerald. In 1971 they lived in Lakewood and Herb was getting ready to retire from McDonald Douglas Aircraft. They had local contractor Bobby Delperdang, build a house for them, where they still live today. In time, their children purchased homes and moved here also.

Evelyn and Herb's daughter, Susie Smith, worked at the library for over 25 years. She would dress up in costumes to read to local children and won the title of Lucerne Valley's best story teller. All the children loved her. She passed away from cancer at the age of 54. She has a plaque with her name, by a tree in front of the library, which was planted in her honor by the County of San Bernardino.

On her website www.paintingdelight, Evelyn displays many of her artworks. She also gives more history on her artistry background and achievements. We borrowed her words written there in 2004 and condensed them.

She married her husband, Herb Carpenter, in 1945 and they had one son, Greg Carpenter,

Evelyn Carpenter's "Spanish Dagger" painting.

and their late daughter, Susan Carpenter Smith, four grandchildren, and six great-grandchildren.

She is a member of the National Watercolor Society, (Recording Secretary) Los Angeles Art Association, Whittier Art Club, Lakewood Art Association, Women Painters of the West, and Otis Alumni. She has exhibited in many well known art galleries among them are the Long Beach CA Museum of Art; Kramer Gallery, La Cienega Blvd, Los Angeles; Pacific Coast Club, Long Beach, CA.; Marble Arch Gallery-Gallery Petite, London; Paidea Gallery, La Cienega, Los Angeles; Las Vegas, Nevada; Laguna Beach, CA; Studio 5; Catalina; Palos Verdes, CA; Downey Museum of Art, Downey, CA; Traveling Art Shows by the National Water-Color Society; etc.

She has done numerous one-woman shows, winning over one hundred awards, and is represented in more than two hundred private and public collections.

From the mid-sixties to mid-seventies she changed mediums and devoted most of her time to pottery; she ended up with four kilns, two gas and two electric. The electric kilns were mostly used for bisque-firing, and experimenting with "found" desert clays, and glazes. Her 16-CU FT gas kiln was for high-fire glaze firing.

The last ten to fifteen years (in 2004) she had been delving into music, computers and genealogy. Shortly before 2004 she began devoting most of the day to painting again. She loves to do portraits, still life, non-objective abstracts from music, and of course the continuously changing mood of the desert is always an inspiration for a painting. She had a show of 27 paintings in June 2004 at the Victor Valley Museum, CA. That year she also completed a commissioned portrait of Janice Horst for the Janice Horst Lucerne Valley Branch Library.

When she moved to the high desert in 1971, it was the beginning of a new life-style. She resigned from all art organizations, mainly because of the driving distance, and began enjoying life here in beautiful Lucerne Valley with her husband, cats and dogs.

Evelyn now enjoys her grandchildren and continues to paint and enjoy her home here in the desert.

Final Resting Place – Thompson House

Compiled by Millie Rader. Photos courtesy of Tom Thompson.

Back in January 2014 I got a call from someone at the chamber who said there was a guy who was looking for the house on Hwy 18 below Mitsubishi where his dad grew up. The guy's name was Tom Thompson. So I figured he must be related to a guy here that I grew up with and lives in an old house on Hwy 18, by the name of Tommy. So I called Tommy and found out after all these years that his last name is actually Thomason not Thompson. But Tommy was curious about the old house. After calling

Tom he went up and found the house; it is the one across from Cushenbury Springs. Tommy then told me that Tom had some interesting LV history and I might want to talk with him. So I called him and the reason he was looking for the place was that his dad had just passed away and his final request was

Thompson house. B 5-8

that his ashes be buried near the house where he grew up, in Lucerne Valley.

Tom said he was planning a trip in February and asked if I would help him find the cabin. In February my husband, David, and I met him in town and led him up to the cabin and were asked to stay for the reunion of Tom's dad, Don Thompson, to the place that held his fondest memories.

One of the pictures included is of Tom's grandparents Claude and Marcella Thompson. There is one of Claude working on a bike pump with Tom's aunt Marcella in the foreground. She was named for her mother. Another picture is of kids riding donkeys, again Marcella and Don and another brother.

Tom's dad never talked about his past much so he didn't have many details, only that his dad had enjoyed his time here. Tom thinks that the house was built in the early twenties. He knows that his grandfather built it of rocks found in the area. That it had a well, but before the well was drilled the family depended on Cushenbury Springs for water. Tom does not know why the family came there or why they left. He said that his father knew that his dad had a still and that he was usually on the

Thompson house with Claude and daughter. B 5-8

wrong side of the law so they probably left in a hurry. I have also included a picture of Tom's dad, Donald Claude Thompson, taken at the house in the late 1980s.

Thompson, Tom and family Feb. 4, 2014.
Photo courtesy of David Rader. B 5-8

Claude Thompson Final Resting Place.
Photo courtesy of Tom Thompson. B 5-8

CHAPTER 6

Fighting Fire and Outlaws

Compiled by Millie Rader

Fire Department

The August 18, 1958 edition of the *Los Angeles Times* carried a picture of this fire truck with the caption "A 1922 Ahrens Fox pumper rig with American-LaFrance Power is the latest addition to the Lucerne Valley Volunteer Fire Department. A gift from

1922 Ahrens Fox pumper. Photo courtesy of Lucerne Valley Museum Association.

Mrs. Glenford Alton of Whittier, it was one of a collection her husband kept as a hobby. It pumps 5000 gallons an hour. Local pastor and retired Los Angeles Fire Department Captain, E.C. Spruill used his fire fighting contacts to help make this donation happen."

Early Volunteer Fire Crew. Photo courtesy of Lucerne Valley Museum Association.

This picture was taken by Marge Wilson in front of the first Union Service Station just west of what is now the China House on Highway 18. The volunteers pictured here are Rene Belbenoit, Bob Coavin, Lew Cowan, Bob Robinson, Buck Jones, Fire Chief Dale Wilson, and Dick Grobaty. There is no date on the photo, but it was most likely before 1955.

1959 Volunteer Fire Department. Photo courtesy of Lucerne Valley Museum Association. A 6-1

This photograph of volunteer fire fighters was taken in front of an early fire station located on the south side of Highway 18 near the "Y" Intersection where the Valero Mini-Mart is currently located. This *Lucerne Valley Leader* newspaper photo caption read "Volunteer Firemen and equipment at a recent special training session." In the photo are Verne Ely, Pete Racobs, Gene Jones, Frank Matteson, Jim Goulding, Jr., Bob Rose, Chief Bud Briscoe, Don Pinard, Captain Bill Hoffman, Mike Callahan, Assistant Chief Francis (Mac) McDougall, Dennis Medici, Harley Van Zee and Jack Pinard. Other members not available for the picture are Robert Clark, Frank Crawford, Bob Corbin, David Fry, Scotty Calkins, Dick Grobaty, Bob Ely and Honorary Captain Edward Spruill. An estimate of property value saved by the unit during 1959 was $90,909.

Flash Flood clean-up. Photo by the Leader Newspaper. A 6-2

Following a September 1971 flash flood that washed mud and debris through the center of town, the Fire Department's Chief Reyes brought a broom, a fire truck and crew to help clean up the mess.

This 1976 photo shows the Fire Station at its current location just east of Pioneer Park. At the time of this photo, the unit had three fire trucks, of slightly newer vintage, a rescue wagon, and the old Cadillac ambulance donated by Kaiser Cement.

1976 Fire Station and Equipment. Photo by Lucerne Valley Leader.

Firemen Jim Pettigrew and Mike Estrada were out updating information on water supplies and reevaluating high-hazard target areas. They multitasked by selling tickets to the Zogi Variety Show sponsored by the Fireman's Association to raise money for the 1976 Bicentennial Independence Day Fireworks display. This 1949 Ford F4 Pumper was a hand-me-down from the Apple Valley Fire Station and added to the Lucerne Valley Fleet sometime in the 1950s. Sometime in the 1970s it was modified for medical aid.

1949 Ford F4 Pumper. Photo courtesy of Lucerne Valley Leader.

Ben Van Wyk with pumper truck turned dump truck. Photo courtesy of Millie Rader.

San Bernardino County Fire Captain Ben Van Wyk holds the longevity record of 36 years with Lucerne Valley Fire Station 8. Captain Van Wyk began fighting fires in Lucerne Valley in 1978 as a 14-year-old Fire Explorer Scout. At the age of 18, he hired as a Paid Call Fire Fighter, and in 1984 he was hired full-time. He moved up through the ranks as an engineer, then engineer/EMT2 and then to his current rank of Captain. Captain Van Wyk has fond memories of driving the 1949 Ford Pumper, pictured here, to fires with Chief Art Bishop sitting beside him telling him to "drive faster." Van Wyk also acquired many of his mechanic skills working on this truck. The pumper truck was later outfitted with a dump bed and is still used by the Lucerne Valley park department employees. Van Wyk also supported the new county civilian training for Community Emergency Response Teams.

The caption beneath this undated photograph from the Lucerne Valley Leader newspaper stated that this car fire was on Highway 18 near Sky High Road. None of the volunteer firefighters pictured here were named. Note that they were all in street clothes.

Car Fire. Photo courtesy of Lucerne Valley Leader Newspaper.

State and County Firehouses 2018. Photo courtesy of Millie Rader. A 6-2

Sheriff's Posse

Posse circa 1962. Photo courtesy of Lucerne Valley Museum Association.

The Lucerne Valley Posse was active, not only in search and rescue, but also in representing the town of Lucerne Valley in numerous parades and other activities. Here twelve Posse members are gathered before riding in what appears to be a Big Bear parade circa 1962. On the horses from left to right are Web Betz, Don (last name not recorded) and Bill Barnett. In front of the Posse Search and Rescue trailer are Noel Shriner, Ray Bonin, Art Bristol, Mel Olin, Deputy Red Stillwell, Bert Eberly, Dennis Medici, Bob Heines, and Chief Gardis (standing.)

Sheriff's Posse Circa 1950's. Photo courtesy of Lucerne Valley Museum Association.

This early picture of the Lucerne Valley Posse, circa 1950s, was discovered by Lucerne Valley Sheriff Sergeant Van Putnum on the wall of the San Bernardino Sheriff's Historical Society. These posse members were most likely out on a training mission. The names of these men are unavailable.

Later Posse. Photo courtesy of Chuck Rader.

The Lucerne Valley Posse was still going strong in the 1990s. At the time of this writing only five names are available: Bill Oliver, Betty Stevens, Bob McWhorter, Art Bristol and Charles Rader. This photo belongs to Art Bristol who joined the Posse in 1960, then later trained to become a Level 3 Sheriff's Reserve member. He retired in 1992 after 32 years of service. The Sheriff's Department presented him with his original badge at retirement.

Charles (Chuck) F. Rader Historian, Sheriff's Deputy, and Firefighter

Chuck preserved Lucerne Valley History, in writing, for at least the last 30 years and before that he was creating it. He was also published in the Mohahve Historical Society's "Mohahve VI, A Collection of Histories."

Moving from Oregon to Lucerne Valley in 1953, Chuck became very active in the local economy as well as in the preservation of the community. He was part of the San Bernardino Sheriff's Department, as both a paid Deputy, and as a volunteer for 60 years.

The Lion's Club members put in many years and funds toward starting a local fire department, tried to turn it over to the county with no response, and had to let it go, knowing that as long as they continued to man and fund it, the county would not. During the few years that it took for the county to come up to speed, three men made up the vol-

Chuck Rader. Courtesy of Chuck Rader.

unteer fire department; Dick Owen, Dick Grobaty and Chuck Rader.

Chuck and his wife, Martha, were married 59 years and raised four boys, with two still living and raising families in Lucerne Valley.

The Lucerne Valley Museum Association was also one of Chuck's passions. Orville Green was in charge of the Museum when Chuck joined. When Orville passed away, Chuck and Martha kept the Museum Association going. Chuck served as President of that organization for many years. Lucerne Valley is known for its volunteer spirit and Chuck Rader had a strong streak of it in his makeup.

"He epitomizes the individual character and characteristics that made this country so great, the attributes and values of so many past generations. They did everything they should and much more. Chuck was Americana all the way," said Chuck Bell, President of the Lucerne Valley Economic Development Association, who, along with Chuck Rader was part of the team that brought this book into existence.

Deputy Chief Robert Wickum, left, presents a plaque to Charles (Chuck) Rader for 60 years of service to the department and the Lucerne Valley community. Photo courtesy of Lucerne Valley Leader Newspaper.

CHAPTER 7

Need a Job?

Desert Hills Guest Ranch
Joe and Janice Horst

Written by Granddaughter Karen Horst
Photos courtesy of Karen Horst

Joseph Raymond Horst, born May 16, 1903, grew up in Lebanon, Pennsylvania. Janice Olive Haynie, born September 22, 1909, grew up 25 miles away in Lancaster, Pennsylvania. They met in Lancaster in 1927 and married in 1928. That same year, they moved to Los Angeles so Joe could take an engineering job at Douglas Aircraft Company. Their two sons, Robert, and his younger brother, Richard, were born at Centinela Hospital in Inglewood.

Then the Great Depression hit the aircraft industry leaving Joe out of work, so the family of four returned to Lebanon, PA in 1931, to live on the Horst family farm. Douglas Aircraft rehired Joe in 1933, the family returned to California and bought a home in Santa Monica. Janice ran the household and volunteered in civic organizations

Young Janice and Joe 1928.

including the YWCA and the PTA at her son's schools. Throughout World War II she volunteered for the Red Cross Blood Bank.

"She became President of every group she joined," her son Richard said. A member of a woman's choral group in Santa Monica, she also sang on a local radio program and enjoyed performing at various community venues throughout her life. Her signature song was "A Bird in a Gilded Cage." Both Janice and Joe were always active members in their church.

During World War II, gas rationing limited cross-country road trips and family vacations. Joe and Janice started visiting the guest ranches sprouting up in the high desert outside of Los Angeles, including the C-Bar-H and Rancho El Sueno in Lucerne Valley. By the 1950s, Joe was working for Northrop Aircraft Corporation and approaching retirement. Empty nesters, with their children both adults

Janice and Joe early 1950s

and out of the house, Joe and Janice decided to start their own guest ranch. In 1954 they bought the Wickware Ranch, a home with 40 acres off Crystal Creek Road south of Hwy 18. They added onto the home, including a large dining room for guests, built a swimming pool and several cottages for twelve guest lodgings. There was a barn and stable for their burros, Sweetie Pie and Cutie Pie. They opened for business the following year as the Desert Hills Guest Ranch. Janice did all the cooking and cleaning with the help of Edna, (last name lost to memory), her faithful friend and employee of many years. Joe commuted to work in Hawthorne for several years before retiring full-time to serve as the ranch manager and handyman.

Brochure photo of Office. A 7-1

Brochure photo of Pool. A 7-1

The Desert Hills Guest Ranch hosted hundreds of visitors. The actor Steve McQueen stayed for a week with his crew while shooting the movie, *On Any Sunday*, a 1971 documentary on motorcycle racing.

Once while cleaning a guest cabin, Janice discovered a trio of desert tortoises stowed inside the car of one of her guests. Upon hearing the frantic creatures trying to escape, Janice freed the tortoises and vehemently scolded her guests for trying to abduct the wild creatures.

Preparing hot racing bikes for documentary film are riders, (left to right) Malcolm Smith, Steve McQueen, Mert Lawwill, who huddle at Desert Hills Guest Ranch, their headquarters for desert filming April, 1971. Photo by Bruce Brown

In 1956 Joe appeared as the first witness for the prosecution in the murder trial of his neighbor, Norma C. Hallock, who was accused of killing her husband, Robert. Joe testified that she drove up to the guest ranch to speak with Joe, saying "Oh, Mr. Horst. What should I do? I've shot my husband." The jury convicted her of involuntary manslaughter.

In 1973 or 1974 they sold the ranch in order to truly retire. They bought a house on a two and a half-acre property off Blackhawk Road, in the Russell Tract, and continued to serve the Lucerne Valley community. Even while running the ranch, Janice and Joe were active in establishing vital services to the community, including water and fire protection and both served on multiple community boards. A member of the Airport Commission, Joe helped create the Apple Valley Airport. Janice frequently traveled to Sacramento and San Bernardino to give legislators and bureaucrats a piece of her mind.

Joe passed in January 28, 1983, but Janice stayed busy with community service. She was a member of the

Janice and Dad Goulding 1955.

Chamber of Commerce, the Roadrunners, and the Women's Club. She was instrumental in the establishment of County Service Area 29. Her work with the Friends of the Library included raising funds and pushing through the construction of the current library building, and expansion that was named in her honor in 2003. She was recognized as Volunteer of the Year by San Bernardino County in 2003. She lived fiercely independent, in her own home until passing November 26, 2003. Joe and Janice are now buried together at Lucerne Valley Memorial Park in the Pioneer Section.

(Karen Horst is the daughter of Joe and Janice's son, Richard, who is still alive and well. She was born in 1963 and spent a lot of time at her grandparent's ranch while growing up. Her best memories are of swimming in the pool, watching out for black widows, and eating Grandma's fried chicken on "those cowboy plates.")

Producing Eggs and Entertaining Guests – The Gross Ranch
by Millie Rader as told by Gennine (Gross) Walker
Photos courtesy of Gennine (Gross) Walker

Mr. Gross.

Geninne and her husband, Jim Walker, now live in Apple Valley, but she lived in Lucerne Valley as a girl with her mother, Genevieve, and her father, Henry Gross, who was an entrepreneur.

Henry raised chickens in El Monte in the early 1940s but the weather was too damp and caused health problems for his wife. The Gross family then moved to Lucerne Valley in 1948. Geninne said that before he had even finished the house, he moved his family to the valley and then started building a chicken barn. The house was built of wood but then her dad bought a block form and they began making all of their own cement blocks. The rest of the buildings were made with homemade Gross block. The ranch was located on Valley View Road, but somewhere along the way the name was changed to Laramie Road. They were about a quarter mile east of Mesa Road.

Geninne said that her grandparents came to visit with their trailer a year after they had moved to Lucerne Valley and were there for the famous snow of 1949. This snow has been mentioned in other stories. Local residents were snowed in for a week or more, but those who lived here at the

Snow of 1949 Lynn, Diana, grandparents and Geninne.

Egg handling building. A 7-2

time were hardy pioneers and had plenty of food and firewood to see them through.

Henry supported his family with the chicken ranch until around 1956, when he built three cabins and created a guest ranch for vacationers wanting to get out of the city. He also housed some of the construction workers building the Kaiser Permanente plant (now Mitsubishi Cement Corporation) at Cushenbury.

The cabins were a single room with sitting room, bedroom and kitchenette and an attached bathroom. Two of the cabins have now been renovated and combined into one to form the Chiropractic offices of Rice Chiropractic. Chiropractor Valerie Rice is the daughter of Allen and the late Roberta Stanfield who now own the old Gross Ranch.

Gross built an in-ground pool and a shuffle board and had games and campfires.

The Ranch has had several owners since it was the Gross Ranch. Roberta Stanfield's parents Milo and Goldia Richards purchased the property, with all of its original buildings still intact in

Front porch. A 7-2

1997. They soon moved out from Hesperia, and lived the rest of their days here. Valerie also opened her chiropractor office on the ranch at that time.

The Richards have both since passed and Allen and Valerie have turned the place into a gentleman's farm with cows, goats, chickens, turkeys and even a miniature donkey named Shorty.

In-ground pool. A 7-2

Gennine's parents divorced in the late 1950s and her mother later married Kenny Gobar and continued living the life of a desert rancher's wife. Dad, Henry, went on to start Desert Stationers store in Victorville where he was quite successful.

Henry Gross, Desert Stationery.

Ewing's Trading Post and More

Compiled by Millie Rader. Photos courtesy of Jack Ewing.

The Ewings were business people with big ideas. The first generation of Ewings to come to the valley were Arthur C. and his wife, Ethel. They built the rock building (A 7-3) on the southwest corner of Trade Post Road and Highway 18, where Hi-Country Realty is now. If you didn't know, that is how the road got its name.

They also built the Dome building, west of the rock building, where they held dances and roller skated for many years. According to Barbara Veale, servicemen came all the way from George Airbase, now SCLA, in Victorville, to dance with Lucerne Valley girls. The men were charged $.50, but the girls only paid $.25. (You are free to draw your own conclusions.)

The exact dates when those buildings were erected are unknown, but we do know from Arthur C. and Ethel Ewing's grandson, Jack, that his grandparents moved from Torrance to Lucerne Valley in 1929. They first worked for the original owners of the Jackrabbit Café and Service Station, and then decided to build Ewings Trading Post and Ethel's Café. We know according to an ad found in the April, 1947 edition of the *Desert Grapevine* newspaper, both the Trading Post and the Ballroom were in full swing at that time.

Jack, his sister, Charlene, and their parents, Arthur N. (Jack) Ewing and Nell, moved to the valley sometime later and conducted business in the buildings on the northeast corner of Trade Post Road, across from the Ewing Trading Post. To make things confusing, Jack's dad, Arthur N., was also called Jack.

Ethel and Arthur Ewing.

Also in the April, 1947 newspaper, there was an ad for Ewing Real Estate and Insurance with Notary and Business service. It lists the names, Arthur C., Nell K., and Arthur N. (Jack) Ewing as those providing these services.

The younger Jack also provided an ear-

Ewing's Ballroom. A 7-4

Jack Ewing.

ly newspaper clipping that tells of a meeting of the newly created Mojave Realty Board, which met at the Victorville Café to vote in the by-laws. Among those present were listed Jack and Nell Ewing. The photo included two Lucerne Valley Realtors, Jack Ewing and C. Clark Battelle. Though the old clipping was not dated, the website for the High Desert Association of Realtors lists the original name as Mojave Realty Board and states that it was formed May 22, 1948; and the same gavel that was used in that first meeting is still used in their board of directors meetings today.

Jack also wrote a letter to his old pal, Allen Stanfield, August 28, 2013, about his memories as a young lad in the valley.

'Dear Allen and Others, he wrote. We were very lucky to have lived in Lucerne Valley. Where else could you sleep in a cave like Strawberry Peak; go in a mine in the Buttes; walk, hop and skip on hot pavement from Trading Post Road to the Post Office and back barefooted; witness an Easter Sunrise Service at the cross on the Buttes; see movies at the Women's Club House; witness the great people of Lucerne Valley; just unreal; hardworkers; tough as nails; artistic;

Jack Ewing Sr. (top left) Real Estate Board.

nothing phony; Rene (Devil's Island) Belbenoit; Rev. Coons (just great); Mrs Hempfield Goulding's books *Range One East* and *Raising the Dust*; find a yard like Wheeler's place for everything you'd need; and have a bus driver like Mr. Ball.

Marty's Trading Post, 1963. Photo courtesy of Lucerne Valley Leader. A 7-3

'We are lucky, Allen, that's all I can say. Just great people, memories, it was a different time and place.

'Today we have good kids coming up. Different ways, very tech savvy, but they'll never know what we did growing up.

'If you would put some names to the pictures I sent let me know "ASAP." ASAP means "Always Say A Prayer." ~A Friend, Jack Ewing.'

Jack sent a whole packet of pictures, many of the ones scattered through this book.

Though no Ewings from this family live in Lucerne Valley today, younger Jack's son, Arthur, and his wife, Denise live in Apple Valley and they were kind enough to get us in touch with his dad.

Rene's new store. Photo courtesy of the Leader Newspaper. A 7-5

Rene Belbenoit Ranch Store

Compiled by Jan Lembright

The long journey that led Rene Belbenoit to Lucerne Valley began in France shortly after World War I. Rene, a French infantry veteran, was a servant for a countess, while trying to save money to marry a nurse. Impatient, he stole $300 worth of the countess's jewelry. He deserved a jail term: he got eight years at hard labor in the penal colony on the northeast coast of South America. He was shackled and forced to work 12-hour days of hard labor in mosquito infested swamps on a starvation diet. Determined to live, he organized four escape attempts, each one a disaster. Each time, he was thrown into solitary confinement where the sun and rain beat into roofless cells and men died or went mad, and his sentence was doubled.

In 1936, he escaped to Trinidad in a boat with five other convicts. He was toothless, weighed 97 pounds, and lugged a 40-pound, handwritten manuscript, wrapped in oilcloth. It was titled *Dry Guillotine*, the convict's name for French Guiana, and told of the horrors in stark detail.

His adventures took him to Costa Rica, Nicaragua, Honduras and El Salvador. He stowed away on a Los Angeles bound freighter. Posing as a seaman, he walked onto the dock past two customs officials. Through many ordeals and a fight to become an American citizen, he finally came to Lucerne Valley.

In 1949 doctors told Rene to seek tranquility and clean air for his health; since he had a bad heart as a result of his turbulent years. He found peace in Lucerne Valley, where he opened a store and sold men's work clothes, shoes and yardage.

Rene Belbenoit, voting for the first time in the United States, after receiving citizenship papers 1956. Photo courtesy of Lucerne Valley Leader Newspaper.

Rene was a small man; only 5-foot tall and weighed 120 pounds. He was well educated and had very nice manners. He had a wife, whose name was Lee Gumper, an attractive widow and businesswoman. He had it all, except what he wanted most of all -- citizenship.

With much determination; he came through hardship, terror, and adventure enough for a dozen men. He was a native of France and an escaped prisoner, but to the people of Lucerne Valley he was a friend, neighbor and patriot. He was also an international celebrity – the man who had done more than any other to close the infamous

French Guiana prison colony commonly called, " Devil's Island." He wrote of the deplorable conditions of prison life and several books, including *I Was a Convict on Devil's Island*.

After several years of struggle to become an American citizen, he won his victory and became an American; he had been one in spirit for years. He wrote against French injustice although the penal colony had been closed. When he died on February 26, 1959, Deputy Stillwell found a manuscript on the table in front of his body – another testimony to his unconquered spirit.

Rene came to love the far vistas, changing colors, and hard, clear lights of the desert. He couldn't drive, but Marjorie Wilson, who operated a Lucerne Valley service station with her husband Dale, recalled taking Rene on trips into the desert. He would linger to marvel at plants and rock formations.

Excerpts of this article were taken from Lucerne Valley reporter Don Roberge who was editor, public relations specialist and journalism professor. His sources for this article include the *New York*

Times, Lucerne Valley Leader, Newsweek, Saturday Review Fortnight, and *Range One East*. It also includes accounts from people who knew Rene Belbenoit, and his books.

Rene's building in 2017 a promised pharmacy. Photo by Millie Rader. A 7-5

Dick Grobaty aka "Mister Lucerne Valley"

Excerpts from an interview by Pat Judkins in the Lucerne Valley Leader newspaper of April 19, 1989 with additional information added by Jan Lembright.

Dick was born in Chicago, Illinois on September 3, 1902. His true name was John. He was married in Los Angeles in 1925. His son was John Herbert Grobaty Jr.

Dick first saw Lucerne Valley in 1928 when he was driving a Model T Ford to Big Bear. He stopped at the original Box S Ranch. He thought, *If I never come through here again it will be too soon for me! The roads were dirt. We got half way to Big Bear and here came a herd of 30 to 40 cattle.*

Dick spent nearly 30 years in Hollywood where he sang on *"The Milton Berle Show"* and with John Charles Thomas on Sunday morning's *"Westinghouse Hour."*

Dick Grobaty in his store. Photo courtesy of L.V. Leader Newspaper.

From 1945-1950, Dick was business manager for Erle Stanley Gardner of Perry Mason fame. Dick met his second wife while visiting Erle at his ranch in Temecula, referred to as the 'Fiction Factory.' Dick married her in 1950, and they came to Victorville to visit her daughter, who was quite ill. The daughter leased a restaurant in Lucerne Valley that would soon become The Malt Shop, located where the China House's east dining room is now. Dick soon took over The Malt Shop and said he was selling 150 gallons of ice cream per week, with a choice of 20 flavors; they sold bulk ice cream at ninety cents a quart. (Rose was the mother of son John, but the names of Dick's other wives could not be

Rose, John, and Dick. Photo courtesy of Lucerne Valley Museum Association.

found in any accounts of Dick's life, including his own.)

After the death of Rene Belbenoit in 1959, Dick moved from The Malt Shop to Rene's store location and opened Dick's Center Store. Reverend Charles Coon and his wife, Lucille, leased the building The Malt Shop had been in (from Roy Clark), and opened the Country Kitchen.

Dick was a volunteer fireman. In the early 1950s a firehouse was built with donated material and volunteer labor. The block structure was located approximately where the Sinclair Gas Station currently may be found. To report a fire, people called Dick. He would press a button on his wall that activated a siren on top of the firehouse to summon the volunteer firemen.

Explaining the unique manner in which our volunteer firefighters were summoned in the 1950s, Dick said, "McDougall's owned the corner (near where the Sinclair Station is now). They donated the property and the Lucerne Valley Lions constructed the building for the volunteer fire department, which included a one-hose cart. There was a wire from this building to my store. If someone phoned me to tell me a fire broke out, I pushed a button to set off a big alarm system on the roof of the building. It could be heard all over the valley. At that time, I lived at the Lucerne Valley Motel, with a similar set up, so that I could answer fire calls at night. Later I moved to the Muffin Mountain Motel, which in now the Ace Motel."

Dick said the Jackrabbit Cafe was where Halleck's (Valero Gas Station) is now, the Sand Bar was where Patricia's Restaurant was at the time Pat wrote this, which is now Adelita's and the first Moose Lodge was at Pop Ewing's building, now the Family Outlet. He said, "A lot of movie pictures were made here. Roy Rogers liked to go to our Lions Club Gun Range. He would be asked to shoot. He couldn't shoot any better than anyone else, but they thought he could because of his name. The Russell brothers built the downtown shopping center, the building I was in and many, many houses. John Russell constructed the building where Dick's Center Store was for $3.25 a square foot; and nobody builds them today like he did. The Regensbergs owned a market where Mark Riddle's Auto Restoration business is now. Danny was away at college then. The original Y Café (currently Kallan's) was a little white building behind the current one; it burned down."

Thus, began the life with the people and community Dick would learn to love. He has been called "Mr. Lucerne Valley", Grobaty Little League Field at Pioneer Park was named after him. He was an emcee for hun-

Dick running for honorary mayor 1966. Photo courtesy of Lucerne Valley Leader Newspaper.

dreds of community events, and contributed endless volunteer hours to this valley.

He was invited to join the Lions in 1951. He was their president in 1952, when there were about 15 members; he was active for 39 years.

For 35 years and until quite recently, United Parcel Service delivered packages for valley residents to Dick's store, because they couldn't find half the people who lived here.

"The greatest event in my life was moving to Lucerne Valley in 1950," said Dick. He passed away September 27, 1990. He was an active member of Lucerne Valley for over 40 years.

McDougall's Well Drilling

As told to Jan Lembright, February 2016.
Photos courtesy of Fran (McDougall) Jones.

McDougall's office building. A 7-6

Bob was born in 1922 in New Castle, Colorado to Mac and Beryl McDougall. Although they were very poor, he said it was the way of life, as they knew it, and he was happy with his surroundings. He was 16 when he started working in the zinc mine with his dad, where they worked 10-hour days for 50 cents an hour. He worked there until WW II started, when he went into the marines.

When the war was over, Bob went to Hawthorne, California, where his mother was then living and where he met his future wife, Gert. Gert had moved to Colorado from Nebraska when the war broke out. There she went to school to learn how to weld, and while there, she met Bob's mother, Beryl. After they completed their schooling, they both went to California to work in the ship-yards and were part of the group known as "Rosie the Riveters."

Around that time Bob, his father and a partner, decided to go into the well drilling business. They found a drilling rig, with a missing part, and were told the part could be found in Lucerne Valley. They located Lucerne Valley, where they found an old wooden drilling rig for sale, and

Bob and Gert, early days.

Beryl McDougall

there they stayed. After they came to the valley, they often had to go long distances to find equipment and parts and it took months to order and receive them. In those days the other well drillers were Junie Gobar and Cliff Steel.

Bob and Gert's wedding photo.

Bob in cockpit.

Bob said he and Gert missed each other. To solve that problem they married and returned to live in Lucerne Valley. When asked her reaction to the area, Gert said, "I grew up in a small town in Nebraska so this didn't bother me." They moved into their first home in December, 1948. It was a one-room cabin, with no utilities, on Baker Road. The night they moved in, snow began to fall. By the time it stopped, there was 3-4 feet of snow on the ground; Lucerne Valley was snowed in. Bob said he built a snow plow to go on the front of his one-ton GI truck and drove around to clear driveways and streets so people could get out. The county cleared only the main highways and everyone else was on their own.

Not long after that incident, Bob and Gert, and Bob's Mother and Father went in together to purchase the land on Highway 18, where

Bob in uniform with Dad.

their well drilling shop is still located. That land included, at the time, the property where the Bank of America used to be just south of what is now the Sinclair Fuel Station. It also had the little house that still sits between the Sinclair and the Valero Gas Stations. Bob and Gert moved into that place. Bob said that while they lived there, James "Dad" Goulding would stop by and visit with his dad and mom. Goulding was also from Colorado and they had a lot in common.

McDougall family: Gert, Fran, Sharon, Bob, Carol, and Bobby.

In 1950 Bob and Gert created the ranch on Cody Road, that they have called home ever since. On this property they have raised many head of cattle, fruit trees, and large vegetable gardens. They will both be 96 years old this year (2018) and still maintain their fruit trees and have a very large vegetable garden.

Bob said Mr. Lewis, the man they bought the business property from, was a welder. He showed Bob how to weld one time, the rest he learned by trial and error. Bob has put pipelines in between Lucerne Valley and Big Bear and put in the water lines at the former Lucerne Springs, now called Jubilee Water Company, in the Russell Tract. He also laid many gas lines around the valley.

The McDougalls were in the well drilling business here for over 50 years. The company employed 5 or 6 people at a time. Gert handled the office business, while

New well rig.

raising four children. "The best secretary I could ever have," said Bob. Their daughter Fran (McDougall) Jones and her husband, Dave, worked for the company Morgan Daniels was the bookkeeper and Gert's brother, Bill Hoffman worked for him for 38 years. There were also Dan Quinones who helped

Grand Marshalls, July 4, 2012.

drill wells, and Dennis Medici, who was fresh out of high school and starting his first job, who learned to weld from Bob. Medici, who later went on to run his own welding and fabrication business here for many years, said that "McDougall was the best welding teacher I ever had. I appreciate what Bob taught me and I still use it to this day." Cliff Reed also worked for Bob for many years.

Bob and Gert have three daughters; Sharon, Carol and Fran. They had a son, Bobby, who has since passed, who worked in the business after college. Bobbie also had a ranch on Rabbit Springs Road known as The Range Shadow, where

he raised cattle, planted barley and had a garden. Bob said the biggest squash Bobbie grew was 6 feet long and weighed 75 pounds. It ended up as cattle feed.

Sharon and Carol both moved out of town after they were grown, but Fran and Dave stayed to raise their two boys in Lucerne Valley.

Bob and Gert, and Bob's parents, were very active in the community. Bob and his dad were charter members of the Lucerne Valley Lions Club, which was founded in 1947. In 1978, the Lions Club bought the land where it is currently located, adjacent to Rabbit Dry Lake. Bob installed the well there. He is very proud to be a part of the Lions and of all the work done within this valley by its members. Bob's dad was also part of the Lions Volunteer Fire Department and his mother was Lucerne Valley's very first Honorary Mayor.

Bob McDougall

Drive-In and Driving – Herts and LaScalas

By Scott and Kathy Hert

(These two were hounded by the editors of this book to provide their story, as it is tightly woven into the fabric of this valley. Thank you Scott and Kathy! ~ The Editors)

Scott's side of the story:

My family (Pete and Norma Hert and children) moved from Orange County to Adelanto, CA when I was in kindergarten (1959). We lived in a makeshift house, in the middle of the desert, three miles west of where the Mavericks' Stadium is now. We had no electricity, running

Herts take over Papa Joes January, 1976. A 7-7

water, or phone and had to haul in our own water. We ran our refrigerator and lights off propane.

My dad worked for Pfizer's Victorville plant at the Narrows, off Highway 18. He worked the night shift, and when his shift was done, he would pick up hay for the farmers out of the hay fields in Apple Valley and Lucerne Valley. I was too young to drive or pick up the hay, but I helped by rolling bales from two rows into one row, which made it easier for him to pick up the bales.

When I was in 5th grade (1964), my dad was offered a job in Lucerne Valley for La Habra Products, which is now OMYA. This was a promotion for him, and that is when we moved to Lucerne Valley. This was the first time we had electricity, running water and a television. When he went to work for La Habra Products, there were only 4 employees running the plant and quarry.

When we moved into our house on Mesa Road, the Chamber of Commerce had a program called The Welcome Wagon. Ladies from the community would come out and greet new residents to Lucerne Valley. I remember that when they came over, my mother asked me to make some iced tea for the ladies. I made it just how I liked it, with a lot of sugar. Needless to say, they drank very little of the iced tea.

Later we moved into our house on Foothill Road, where we lived until the county built us a new house, in front of our old house, because they needed to put a flood control ditch right next to our house. Things were different back then. When we were little kids, we could ride our bikes down to the highway and go to Dick's Center Store to buy candy and toys. Dick was the last to sell penny candy in town. There was never a problem with us kids riding around town on our bikes.

After a few years of working at the plant, my dad purchased the Richfield Gas Station from the Blair's. (I think I was in Junior High School then. Lucerne Valley only had an elementary school, so from junior high through high school, all kids had to be bussed to school in Apple Valley.) Dad worked there and my mom did the books at night, at home on the kitchen table, with an old hand-cranked adding machine. My dad gave credit to a lot of folks until they got their Social Security checks each month. I worked there all through high school pumping gas, washing windows, and changing tires. Somewhere along the way, the Richfield Oil Company changed the name of the gas stations to ARCO. (Atlantic Richfield Company). My sister, Debbie, also worked there. My other siblings were too young to help out. Sometimes, Hollywood filmed parts of movies at the station. That was always exciting.

Some of my dad's friends, who would come by the gas station were Pete Racobs and Johnnie Herman. They were partners in the local ready-mix plant in town, where Hi-Grade Materials is located now. Don Poe was also a friend that came by the station, and eventually married my sister, Debbie, two weeks before Kathy and I were married in 1975.

I remember I also worked, off and on, for other people in town. After I got my driver's license (about 1970), I would help Dale Burkes deliver water, with his water truck, to the cabins around town that did not have running water. I worked for a time at Leo's Market, while still helping my dad pick up hay at the Katy Ranch in North Valley. It was a beautiful 500 acre Alfalfa/Cattle Ranch.

Scott and Kathy Hert in front of their Trucking business 2018. Photo courtesy of Millie Rader. A 7-8

After I graduated from high school, I moved to Long Beach to work in the oil fields. It was very hard work and included long hours on the offshore rigs. I then worked for Ralph's Grocery Company driving a truck; they helped me get my commercial driver's license.

After awhile, I got homesick for the desert and moved back to Lucerne Valley. That is when I met "Papa" Joe La Scala. He would drive between his grocery store in Lynwood and the Papa Joe's Restaurant in Lucerne Valley. One day his pickup truck broke down and I stopped to help him get it started I declined to take the money he offered, so he asked me to come to the restaurant for a hamburger. That is where I met his daughter, my wife-to-be Kathy. He offered me a job driving his produce truck for the grocery store in Lynwood, which I gladly took, as I was out of work at that time. The Lynwood store is where Kathy and I started working together, and we haven't stopped yet.

Kathy's side of the story:

Joe and Mae (Helmi) La Scala opened the Papa Joe's Fast Food Restaurant in Lucerne Valley, in front of the Pueblo Plaza on Highway 18, across from the Dome building, just west of Tradepost Road. Joe and Mae ran it and Kathy worked there on her summer vacation from college. That is where Kathy met Scott S. Hert; while taking orders and cooking with her father, Papa Joe. Joe and Mae lived in Apple Valley and ran a grocery store in Lynwood and the restaurant in Lucerne Valley. They made a big circle every day from Apple Valley to Lynwood, and then to Lucerne Valley, running and checking on both businesses, and then returning home to Apple Valley at night.

After Kathy worked there for part of the summer, she also went to work at the grocery store (Joe's Food Spot) in Lynwood. After a week or two, Scott started working there, driving the produce truck from the LA produce market to bring produce to the store in Lynwood. He also did everything else at the store, alongside Joe, since he had experience in the grocery business, working at Leo's Market when he was in high school. Scott and Kathy hit it off, became engaged, and Kathy did not go back to college. They were married in December of 1975 and worked, at the market in Lynwood, until it was sold by Joe after Mae became ill. Joe also leased the Papa Joe's Restaurant to a couple with the last name of Johnson. When the Johnsons were unable to make a go of the restaurant, Joe asked Scott and Kathy if they would like to run it for him and move to Lucerne Valley. At the time Scott and Kathy were living in Lynwood, in a house behind the Joe's Food Spot Store. So, they moved to Lucerne Valley and ran the Papa Joe's Restaurant until Joe's lease was up, and he closed the restaurant. Scott and Kathy had an option to keep the restaurant open and sign a new lease, but, they decided not to continue due to the increase in the lease amount. Joe and Mae sold both their businesses and lived in Apple Valley, until Joe became sick. He passed away in October of 2003. Mae still lives with Kathy's sister, Linda, in Oak Hills, CA. She is 84 years old.

Scott and Kathy found work at an alfalfa/horse farm between Lucerne Valley and Apple Valley, south of Highway 18, where they lived, while Scott also worked part time for Lucerne Valley Market.

They then moved back to Lucerne Valley, lived and worked for Merrill Hart (Woody Hart's father) at his hydroponic farm, raising cucumbers. They lived there when daughter Carolyn Hert was born. At this time, Scott also worked at McDougall's Well Drilling, with Bob and Bobby McDougall. When Merrill Hart sold his hydroponic farm, Scott and Kathy moved and worked at Merrill's alfalfa farm on Lincoln Road. They lived there until Scott started driving trucks for R&K Trucking. Woody Hart also worked for R&K Trucking. Scott would make a big circle from Kaiser Cement (Mitsubishi) to ready-mix plants owned by A&A Ready Mix and back twice a day.

After some time, Scott started working for R&K Trucking out of Gardena, so Scott and Kathy moved and lived in Long Beach, CA for about a year. They moved back to Lucerne Valley when able to do so and bought a house on Midway Ave, where they lived when their three boys were born. They also started Hert's Diesel Service on an adjacent lot. R&K Trucking needed parking for their trucks, and someone to work on those trucks, which is why Hert's Diesel Service was started in 1978.

Scott worked for R&K Trucking, until he bought his own truck in 1983 and had one customer, Burton's Ready Mix, Inc. in Big Bear Lake, CA. As time went by, Mitsubishi Cement asked him to haul more and more loads. S S Hert Trucking expanded, bought a second truck and hired Jim Marshall Sr. as the first employee.

With continued expansion, the company moved the truck yard from Midway Road to Highway 247 (Old Woman Springs Road.) Their efforts to relocate were supported by the area and a county; zone change for the property was approved. The move to the current location was on March 31, 1996. The company has been there for 21 years and has 68 employees. The three Hert boys, Steven, Chris and Scott are actively involved in the company and are being prepared to take the reins, when Scott and Kathy decide to retire.

Scott still farms alfalfa and barley hay and, raises a few head of cattle on the farm, where he and Kathy live. They have 12 grandkids.

George Halleck's 25th wedding anniversary, 1972.

Hallecks Market

Jan Lembright, as told by Bob Halleck Jr.
Photos courtesy of Gladys and son Bob Halleck.

Bob Halleck Jr. was 15 years old when his family moved to Lucerne Valley from Los Angeles in 1963. He was born in Los Angeles and has a sister named Genève. His parents were George and Gladys. George was in business in Los Angeles, tired of the city and wanted a change. He was in the grocery business at the time, which he sold and moved to Lucerne Valley.

He had learned about Lucerne Valley from Gladys' brother, Jim Nasif. Jim had moved to Lucerne Valley in the early 1960s and started a dude ranch called Tall Trees. It had animals and garden cottages, and a swimming pool. Bob remembers a two lane road from the freeway to Lucerne Valley, with only 3 stop signs.

At first George came by himself, got acquainted with the residents and a feel of the valley; which he liked. and brought the family to Lucerne Valley. Bob remembers one day his father and grandmother, Gladys' mother, drove out to the cove. Bob said it was as far out as anyone could get from civilization. Bob hated it, but George loved it. He found a house with 10 acres, electricity, and water. There was a reservoir that became a swimming pool and within 72 hours they bought it. Bob said he couldn't believe it. They lived there for ten years, then moved to their present house east of town. At the time, there was only a party line so if you needed to make a call, you had to ask the person on the line to hang up so you could make your call. When the Doctor came that all changed because he needed a private line.

Bob Delperdang Sr and Leola Burkes building Halleck's Market 1973

Aerial shot of Halleck's Market. A 6-1

When George arrived he was semi-retired and focused on developing a ranch with animals. The only problem was that Bob and Gen fell in love with the cows and would not let George butcher them, so that idea was short lived.

George went to work for Leo's Market and worked for the owner, Danny Regensberg for 10 years. Bob and Gladys said they were allowed to charge all their groceries, but by the end of the week, they had spent most of George's paycheck to pay it back. Gladys said they had a policy to support all the local businesses, so they rarely went out of town for anything. At that time George made $60 a week.

The businesses in town were: Western Auto, Dick Grobaty's Center Store, a liquor store, a doctor and a clinic with a nurse, Bauer Electric, Papa Joes Cafe, Jackrabbit Cafe, West End Market, an escrow office where June Miller worked, her husband Bud Miller was the barber and Filippi's Coun-

George Halleck receiving award from Bob Kumley in the Hitchin Post Restaurant, 1960s what is now El Coyote Loco

try Kitchen. George wanted his own store and in 1973 he received financing to build Halleck's Market; in 1978 he added gas pumps. George hired Bobby Delperdang, Jr. to build Halleck's Market and Bobby, in turn, became the youngest general contractor in the history of San Bernardino County. This was the first new building to be built in Lucerne Valley in 30 years.

George was involved in many activities; he ran for honorary mayor against Beryl McDougall and John Chop. He was a member of the Moose and owned the *Leader* newspaper for a short time. In 1983 George sold the business to Mr. Park, and it is now the Valero Gas Station.

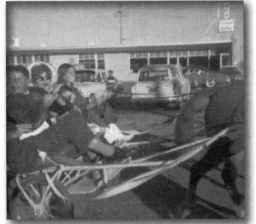
George Halleck Independence Day Parade Grand Marshall, 1960s, with Gladys Halleck

Lucerne Valley Leader Newspaper

By Barbara "Rusty" LaGrange & Millie Rader

When I (Barbara LaGrange) hired on in the winter of 1985, Charlie Parsons was the editor. Bob Clark was owner and publisher. His wife Pauline was a silent partner except for an entertainment column called "Pearls of Pauline." Our staff was a well-oiled machine with most of us doing double-duty in some capacity.

As I had history of writing for weekly news in northern California right out of college I also spent some time with Hi-Desert Star in Yucca Valley when I first arrived in the High Desert in 1975, so training me as the new cub reporter was easy. I soon got more responsibilities and helped Charlie make a graceful exit as a retiring editor.

Keeping up with the community was a new task as managing editor. Not only did I cover as many civic meetings as possible, I often wrote seven articles a week. Weather became its own celebrity, one year we suffered high winds that closed the highway. One storm caused an 8-car and semi truck pile-up on Rabbit Dry Lake. I raced out to capture the accident. The sand blew so hard I could barely get out of the car. I opted to shoot from my doorway. When I was done my windshield was pitted, my camera was full of silt, I was spitting grit most of the day, and when I got home I had sand patterns pressed into my skin that burrowed through three layers of clothes. That was sandblaster weather.

As I offered a new perspective to covering news in the area, many readers asked me to cover topics that others had not. One was the low-life news where local citizens wanted to know who to keep an eye on. Petty thieves were rampant then. People were angry -- an outrage to a small, quiet community.

I checked with the local sheriff's department and found that they seemed shocked that I would meddle in their records. It took a while, but I christened my column "Crime Log" and included actions taken to clear crime from our streets from the sheriff's public log. It was a big hit. Suddenly, people knew exactly who their local criminals were. That opened the door to better crime stories.

I never considered myself a crime reporter, although the deputies thought I could handle it. One time I got a call to come to a dead body crime scene near the railroad tracks and take specific photos, but leave out three key details. I jumped at the chance. They also offered me a scoop

on the Daily Press – unheard of for a small weekly. That was my coup. The photos hit *The Leader* the next day due to some fancy timing at the printer's shop. I beat the Daily Press by a day, kept my three clues quiet, -- close to the vest – and earned more insider information.

I'll share one more tidbit. I received another phone call to jump on a sheriff's helicopter to view a huge marijuana farm raid. Units from three government agencies aimed to jump in, round-up the growers, and burn the fields. I was itching to go but one thing stopped me – I was pregnant with my first child. I had to back away from that wild ride. Besides they said then, as they say today, that second-hand smoke could be deadly. I just couldn't take that chance. But believe me, I was honored to be called. My camera was always ready.

The Early Owners -- John Hudson started the Lucerne Valley *Leader* in 1955. We know from *Leader* articles that Danny and Ginger Regensberg, in partnership with Bob Halleck Sr., owned it in 1965-1973. Greg Churchman took it over in 1973, and Dan and Nita Webster began publishing it in 1974. The Websters owned it for quite awhile before Bob and Pauline Clark took it over. Bob and Pauline probably bought the paper in the early 1980s, but didn't come to Lucerne Valley full-time until Bob retired from another business. He hired a few young editors in the beginning, one who didn't want to do anything but investigative reporting. In a small desert town? Others drifted through.

The Staff -- Pat Judkins – typed the news releases into format, and created the "My Word!" column. Pat was known for having her ear to the rails. She developed a strong following of readers, who either lived in town, with relatives being out-of-town, or local citizens, who had just moved away and wanted to keep in touch. Her specialty was asking history questions pertaining to memories of Old Town Victorville and Hesperia, wondering about folks who remembered Apple Valley's celebrity population. She even wrote about Long Beach and other Southern California destinations in order to prompt early memories of her readers. Even if you didn't know the folks she referred to, she made each column interesting and linked them back to people known in town. Someone always had a history tidbit to share.

Don Judkins – freelance photos. Don was Pat's husband, so he naturally had quick access to the news. He was often out covering emerging news like an auto accident, wildfire, or sandstorm. Eventually he was the photographer for civic groups and special events through the years. He still lives in town.

Maureen Pederson – typist. Maureen was a quiet, petite gray-haired lady who was a recent widow but loved to stay busy in the newsroom. She came from Nogales, Arizona, and was our lead typist hammering out the Legals and Classifieds each week. She was also known to cover Pat's typing assignments, and helped print the headlines. We used a headline writing machine then that spaced the letters and changed the fonts to meet the space we needed. It printed out in a sheet like photo paper, then had to be trimmed with a paper cutter.

Editor Charlie Parsons was a gray-haired, retired newsman who liked the idea of spending his last years in a quiet town with a weekly edition. At that time, 20-page editions were more common. We had a lot of civic groups and church organizations – 22 of them if I recall -- that needed coverage. Everyone was busy with some social activity. Food banks made sure that low-income families had a turkey and all the trimming for the holidays and children had warm coats. Charlie was known for ending his editorials with "Keep them coming, kids." That was in reference to keeping in touch with letters to the editor. He loved the interaction with the community.

Putting the "Paper to Bed" -- As I mentioned earlier, the elements of the paper were typed up and then cut and pasted – not into a document – but into "galley sheets." Galleys were spread out across several light tables so the ease of aligning the printed columns to the sheets was faster. Each paper column was hand-cut with scissors and run through a small waxing machine. The wax adhered the paper to the sheets. The wax also allowed us to move the pieces as needed.

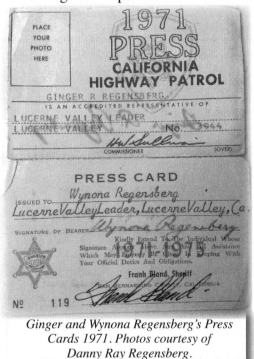

Ginger and Wynona Regensberg's Press Cards 1971. Photos courtesy of Danny Ray Regensberg.

Many nights our paste-up staff would be cutting, waxing, and arranging a page only to see that something had to be rearranged. Our team was Bob, Charlie, me and sometimes Pat or Maureen Pederson.

Photos were handled the same way. I developed the film in the darkroom, selected the prints I liked, processed them, and once dry, brought them out for trimming and waxing. All of the pieces for each page was painstakingly placed and set with a hand roller to make sure nothing moved.

Don Judkins was often the driver to deliver the galleys to

Hi-Desert Star in Yucca Valley, a 45-minute drive east of town to their press, and out early to deliver our news "hot off the press." Those were the days that satisfied my journalism adrenaline needs.

Pagination and the Tech Era -- As the newspaper industry changed, and our little paper was bought up by larger companies, we said goodbye to the Clarks, who retired to the coast, and hello to pagination and computer uploads.

Gone were the days of paste-up, although we still "cut and pasted" electronically on the computer screen… it just wasn't the same. I was working on the computer now more than in the darkroom. Folks at the *Big Bear Grizzly*, our most recent buyer/owner, already had the content for the classifieds and legals, and the ads were designed there as well. Pagination was here to stay.

The Morgue -- In newspaper jargon, all old files and photos are sent to the Morgue, not abandoned. We had lost some of our Morgue due to a leaky office roof. We also had young editors who didn't really know what happened to the "old stuff." That was sad to hear.

In a recent change of hands, I had no idea that the Morgue was in storage. Last I heard, the contents had been tossed and all the photos were stuck together from the waxing process we used. But recently I found out that the old papers are stored safely.

Thanks to Mitsubishi Cement and perhaps its education foundation, the Morgue is being resurrected into indexed files that soon will be accessed by computer. Newspapers across the nation are now embracing their Morgues and allowing more research and sharing of information more than ever before. I'm glad to hear that. It's our history that keeps us grounded and our heritage that defines our pride of Lucerne Valley.

As things change, and we lose our routines to new ones, I often think of a quote I received during a history interview with a woman who, in the 1920s, was one of the first single women to come out west to teach. She wasn't sure at first about this desert life, but once she became accepted by her new family of students, she didn't really want to leave, and she lived here for many years. Her name was Ethel Windchantz and she claimed that High Desert children developed a unique perspective of life because "out in the vastness of the desert, there is no obstruction, no borders, no limits but their own imaginations. They take that with them no matter where they go."

Newshounds – Don and Pat Judkins

Compiled by Millie Rader, As told by Don, Wayne and Tonya Judkins.

Wayne Judkins was still a teenager when his parents, Don and Pat, started working for the *Lucerne Valley Leader* newspaper in the early 1980s. He said his mom would stick her head into his bedroom door, say they were off to get a story, and he would yell "bye Jimmy Olson and Lois Lane." His dad, with a ball cap and camera strapped around his neck, and his mom with reporter's notebook in hand, would be off in search of a good story.

Pat had worked for the *Advisor* and *Penny Saver* papers in Bellflower before the family moved to Lucerne Valley in 1981. She could type 175 words a minute.

Wayne said the reason they moved to the desert, was because his dad was tired of the city and found that the owner of the Muffin Mountain Motel, now called the Ace Motel in Lucerne Valley, was

Don and Pat Judkins. Photo courtesy of Don Judkins.

tired of the desert. They swapped the Judkins city residence for the motel. His dad was attracted to Lucerne Valley because it would be the perfect place to fly his model airplanes. Don is still into model planes.

In the 1980s, the Leader was owned by Bob and Pauline Clark and was quite a large operation, employing 5 or 6 people at a time. Don remembers it all started when Bob Clark asked Pat to write an article for the paper; when finished she didn't know what to call it. Don's parents were visiting at the time; his mother suggested the title, "My Word." The story was such a big hit that Clark asked Pat to write a column each week called "My Word," which she continued to write until she retired in 2006. Wayne said the downside to his mother's column was that the entire town always knew what he was up to.

Soon after Pat began writing her column, Clark asked if she knew anyone with a camera. She told him that her husband had eight of them. That started a 25-year newspaper career for "Jimmy Olson and Lois Lane."

After Brehm Communications, who owned the *Big Bear Grizzly* newspaper, purchased the Leader sometime in the early 1990s, Don and Pat would drive the galleys to Yucca Valley each Tuesday for printing and pick up the papers the next day. During their time with the Leader, they also worked with Leader editors Bill Ewing, Ellen Porter, and Bill Homer.

Besides keeping up with current affairs in her "My Word" column, Pat wrote numerous articles on the history of this town and its quirky brand of characters. Much of her research was done talking with people all over town. Many of her stories can be found in this book.

Pat and Don sold the Ace Motel in 2006, and they retired from the newspaper business soon after. Before they sold the motel, Pat and Don purchased the Granite Mountain Ranch, near Rabbit Dry Lake from Margie Valenzuela. Don and Chuck Valenzuela (Margie's deceased husband) had been good friends. Don told Margie she could live in her home there for the rest of her life, which she did. Don still lives there along with his son, Wayne, daughter-in-law, Tonya, and grandson Alex.

In the 1980s, Don and Chuck Valenzuela started the Antique Power Association, an antique tractor and engine club. They entered their tractors in the Lucerne Valley Independence Day Parade and displayed them at the San Bernardino County Fair every year. Pat was actively involved with the Roadrunners who put on events for the local children. Her hobbies were creating ceramics and spending time with Alex, her only grandchild. Pat's daughter-in-law, Tonya said Pat learned to play Super Nintendo and ride motorcycles just to hang out with Alex.

Pat passed away on Valentine's day, 2008, at the age of 76.

Dick Grobaty, interviewed by Pat Judkins. Photo courtesy of Lucerne Valley Leader.

Barbara's Answering Service

By Millie Rader. Photo courtesy of the Veale Family Trust.

When Henry J. Kaiser built the Kaiser Permanente Cement plant (now owned by Mitsubishi Cement Corporation) in Lucerne Valley in 1957, he brought part of the Kaiser truck fleet from his cement plant in Cupertino near San Jose, California. This also brought the relocation of the drivers and their families to Lucerne Valley and the surrounding communities.

But Kaiser had a communication problem. He was able to get phone service brought into the plant, and a line was run out Rabbit Springs Road, but most of his drivers lived farther out and had no phones; so he was unable to let his drivers know when they had a load to run.

Young Barbara (Barnett) Veale was just out of high school and her family lived on Rabbit Springs Road and had one of the first phones in the valley. She decided that she could help Kaiser reach his drivers, and make some money at the same time, when she started Barbara's Answering Service.

According to Barbara, she would get calls any time of the day or night and go out sometimes, as far as Adelanto at 3:00 am, to rouse a driver for work.

This writer, while working on a story for the business section of the book, found an October 23, 1958 *Leader* newspaper article on the grand open-

Barbara Barnett with brother Charles a few years before starting her business.

ing of the A&W Restaurant. Knowing that many of the friends I grew up with in Lucerne Valley had worked at this little eatery, I posted the front page of that newspaper on Facebook. My sister, who lives in Texas, noticed my post and in it recognized an announcement, next to the A&W article titled, "Barbara To Answer." According to the small announcement, the newspaper was one of the newest subscribers to Barbara's Answering Service. They wanted to give their subscribers and advertisers the best in up-to-date service, allowing anyone with something important to tell them, even if it were at midnight or on Sunday. It stated that Barbara would be only too happy to deliver the message.

Barbara also delivered messages for the local doctor and several other businesses, but Kaiser was her biggest customer, and it wasn't long before that company hired her to work at the plant. Barbara then handed her business over to her mother, Lena Barnett.

The front page of the January 28, 1960 *Leader* newspaper ran the headline "PHONE EXCHANGE FOR VALLEY." The article stated that the California Interstate Telephone Company was to spend $480,000 on local installation. It said that the day of the eight- party telephone lines in Lucerne Valley would be a thing of the past. One and two-party business and one, two and four-party residential connections would soon be available. The minimum day rate charge of 30 cents would be made to call Apple Valley and Victorville and the cost of the party lines would be less than what current subscribers paid for the eight-party lines. It was at this time that the phone company building was placed on Highland Road, where it is now, and 852 new telephones were to be installed in the valley. Completion was forecast for late in 1961.

With the expansion of phone service to the valley, Barbara's Answering Service was no longer needed and soon after closing the business down, Lena went to work for the Lucerne Valley School District, where she worked as a gardener/custodian/bus driver until she retired. Barbara married and worked for Kaiser until she had her first child, who is the writer of this little tale. Once Barbara's youngest child was in school, she, too, went to work for the school district. She later went back to college to get her degree in Real Estate, and joined her husband, George, selling Real Estate for United Farm Real Estate. They, along with partner Danny Regensberg had two offices. One was in Lucerne Valley just west of Cafe 247, in the building currently owned and occupied by Blue Mountain Firewood. Barbara worked out of the Victorville office located near the freeway on Bear Valley Road. When George passed away in December 1989, Barbara closed both offices and went to work for Omya Limestone until she retired. At 75 years of age, she opened a little shop in town called the "County Cottage Boutique." There she sold items handcrafted by local artists; she closed that business shortly before she passed away in 2016.

Air Service to Lucerne Valley

Compiled by Millie Rader. Photo courtesy of L.V. Museum Assoc.

According to the July, 1946 *Desert Grapevine*, an Air Service had been inaugurated between Lucerne Valley and the Grand Central Air Terminal in Glendale. This was a call service; we assume reservations had to be made ahead of time. The phone number given was for Myron B. Baldwin, a pilot of wide experience, the article states. It goes on to say that for the present, he is landing on the dry lake near Barstow Road, and that this service will be a convenience to the residents and guests of the valley. The fare was $7 one way and $13 round trip.

Grand Central Air Terminal was an important facility for the growing Los Angeles suburb of Glendale in the 1920s. It was also a key element in the development of United States aviation. The terminal, located at 1310 Air Way, was built in 1928 and still exists, owned since 1997 by The Walt Disney Company, as a part of its Grand Central Creative Campus. Three hangars remain standing. The location of the single concrete 3,800-foot runway has been preserved, but is now a public street known as Grand Central Avenue.

The plane pictured above is probably pretty close, in year, to the plane Baldwin used to carry passengers from Lucerne Valley to Glendale.

Lucerne Valley Shopping Center

Compiled by Millie Rader.
Photos courtesy of Lucerne Valley Leader Newspaper

The first shopping center in Lucerne Valley is located on, what was then known as the 29 Palms Highway, now known as Old Woman Springs Road. It was built by the Russell Brothers Desert Builders who broke ground April 13, 1956. According to the April 19, 1956 *Leader* newspaper, they planned to have a half-acre black topped parking lot bordered on the west by Leo's Market and on the east by Coleman Driver Mesa Drugs. All the buildings in the center would be air-conditioned.

Leo's Market was first opened in 1950, when Leo Regensberg and his wife Elma sold their market in Los Angeles and with son, Danny, moved to Lucerne Valley. They purchased a building from Dan Stewart, where for many years he ran Stewart's General Store and opened, what was then,

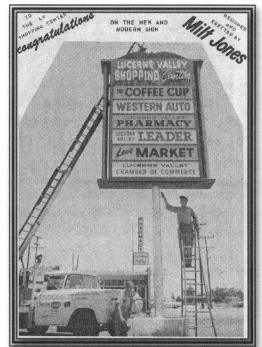

New Sign, 1967. A 7-9

Leo's Market Opens, 1956. A 7-9

the largest market in Lucerne Valley. Mark Riddle's Auto Restoration business is at that site now.

Three years later Leo passed away leaving his wife and son, who was in college, to run the business.

According to the *Lucerne Valley Leader,* Leo's Market opened it's brand new 5,000 square foot, air-conditioned store on September 27, 1956. Don and Marion Thrush were the owner/operators of the meat department.

They had many employees, but a special young lady came to work for them in February, 1956. Her name was Ginger Pittman and five years later, on April fool's day, she married Danny Regensberg. They have two boys, Danny Ray and Jon Mark.

They enlarged the market in 1960, and then in March of 1975, sold the market business to Ernest, Barbara and Linda Gommel, who renamed the business Lucerne Valley Market. The Gommels later constructed the new Lucerne Valley Market in its current location, at the corner of Highway 18 and Crystal Creek roads.

Lucerne Valley Shopping Center, 1956. A 7-9

According to Danny Ray, his dad and grandmother owned the Market building outright, and owned the rest of the shopping center, in partnership with the Russell brothers. In 1985 Elma and Danny opened Lucerne Valley Liquor, and Ginger continued to run that store after Danny passed away in 1989. Danny Ray and Jon purchased the remainder of the Lucerne Valley Shopping Center in 1992. Ginger later sold the liquor store and bought Starlight Video in 1998, which she managed until 2014. Son, Danny Ray, then came back to Lucerne Valley, from his home in Las Vegas, to run the shopping center for his mom. She passed away in 2015 and the shopping center was sold in 2017 to Dr. Hoang Nguyen who plans to open a medical clinic and pharmacy.

Regensbergs Sell 25 Year Old Business

REGENSBERGS SAY FAREWELL — Elma and Danny Regensberg have sold Leo's Market after owning and operating it for the past 25 years. Elma and her husband, Leo, since deceased, opened Leo's Market in 1950 in the building which now houses Hawley's Hardware. They moved to the present market site in 1956. Ginger joined the crew in 1961 when she and Danny wed. The little Regensbergs are Danny Ray and Jon Mark. New owners Ernest and Barbara Gommel will take over Sunday, running the market under the new name of Lucerne Valley Market. See inside for more pictures and story.

The Lucerne Valley Shopping Center currently supports 11 businesses: Rock's Pizza, The Style Shop, His Closet, Quality Treasures, Lucerne Valley Leader, The Clubhouse, Cheryl's Clay Play, Center Water Company, and Lucerne Valley Liquor.

Douglas Service Station

Compiled by Millie Rader

In 1968, a series of letters were written by the Lucerne Valley Chamber of Commerce to the First District Supervisor, asking that the old Douglas/Shell Gas Station either be torn down or made secure. At that time it was part of the Dolley Trust, and they obviously must have agreed to secure it, as the building still stands today on the northeast corner of Highway 18 and Trade Post Road.

Here is the description written about the old station at that time (1968.)

Old Service Station, 1968. Photo courtesy of Lucerne Valley Leader Newspaper. A 7-10

So-called Lucerne Valley "Old-Timers" remember way back when Bill Johnson owned the gas station at the northeast corner of Highway 18 and Trade Post Road. They sold Douglas Fuel. Several years ago, Johnson sold out to Del Gates and moved to Yucca, Arizona.

Gates changed it from Douglas to Shell Gas, then moved out when he built the new station, later owned by Don Chase, which is now the Sinclair Gas Station. For a short period of time, John Corrigan operated the old station as a Powerine dealer.

(The property, with the old gas station still in place, has been used since that time as, among other things, a heavy equipment rental yard, auto repair shop, recycling yard and now as a wood yard. – Editor)

Service Station building 2018. Photo by Bill Lembright. A 7-10

Photo courtesy of Lucerne Valley Leader Newspaper.

McBride's Hardware

In this 1983 photo Earleen and Kaarman McBride and their assistant Bru Reynolds are shown during the Grand Opening of their new hardware building in the Lucerne Valley Shopping Center. The McBrides purchased Lucerne Valley Hardware from Rig Crawford in January, 1960. At that time it was located, in what is now, the dining room of the China House. The McBride's store became a full-fledged Western Auto Agency on September, 1962. They completed the new 25 by 40 foot block building one week before their grand opening. At the same time Western Auto launched a new nationwide catalog program for its 438 company stores.

The Family Businesses – Delperdangs, Archers and Riddles

Compiled by Millie Rader. Photo courtesy of Lucerne Valley Leader Newspaper.

Master Bobby Delperdang and partner, Miss Pat McCall, "tripping the light fantastic" at the weekly Saturday night dance.

Community involvement depicts the following three families. The Delperdangs, Archers, and Riddles, who are connected by marriage and have all been influential within the community. Robert (Bobby) Delperdang's parents, Bob Sr. and Cyrilla (Sally) Margaret Schiltz, moved from Los Angeles to Lucerne Valley in 1948 for health reasons. They brought with them their four children: Marjorie (Margie), Elizabeth (Betty), Bob (Bobby) Jr. and Sharon. They purchased a property on Highway 18, less than a quarter mile east of Trade Post Road. There Bob Sr., a general contractor, earned a living building chicken barns and operating a feed store.

Not long after moving to the valley, they also purchased the Y Café, where Sally ran the kitchen. They hadn't owned the Café long, when it burned down in an unfortunate electrical fire, but they had it quickly rebuilt and operated it until they sold it in the late 1960s. Under different ownership, the business continued on in that location with the same

Bobby Delperdang building Hallecks Market. Photo courtesy of Linda Riddle.

*Bob Sr. and Sally Delperdang in the Y Cafe.
Photo courtesy of Linda Riddle.*

name until 2016, when Shadi Haddad, who owns several other High Desert restaurants, purchased the property and renovated the building inside and out and renamed it Kallan's Bar and Grill.

Bobby said his parents had to overcome a lot of adversity in the beginning, from the Café burning down, to the local chicken businesses going under, to a hot water heater that blew up, and burned most of Bob Sr.'s body, but they always came back stronger than before.

Bobby started first grade at Midway School soon after they moved here. Miss Barnett was his teacher. While still in high school, he began to follow in his father's footsteps in the construction business.

Before he even had his contractor's license, Bobby was hired by Lucerne Valley Lime-Rock Products, the first company to process limestone on Crystal Creek Road, where Omya (CA) does business today. The company hired him to frame a silo foundation.. He said that he lay awake for several nights working through how to position the anchor bolts that would hold the huge silo in place. When the engineers set the silo in place, they said everything lined up perfectly. The engineer was happy, but other local contractors grumbled that Bobby had gotten the job without having a contractor's license. This prompted Bobby to get his license, and at age 25, he became the youngest licensed contractor in San Bernardino County.

Bobby's future wife, Sara Archer, moved to town in July 1958, when she was 13 years old. Her parents were Lyndall Johnston Archer and Altus Franklin Archer. They had owned a home in Glendora when her father decided he needed a change in pace and traded the family home for a piece of property on Highway 18, where he opened the first auto parts store in Lucerne Valley. This store later became the first Napa Auto Parts store in the valley. Her family lived in a small house on the property behind the business.

Sara met Bobby, as a young teenager when she was at her father's business and Bobby rode up on his motorcycle. They grew up together and started dating the summer between Sara's junior and senior year of high school. They were married December 27, 1963.

Pretty Mrs. Bob Delperdang, Jr. takes a bow, earns kudos from Lions on her aid.

Bobby worked many years for another local contractor, John Russell, and helped build all of the Lucerne Valley Shopping Center on Old Woman Springs Road. He and his dad also built over 200 cabins in Big Bear.

Bobby was the youngest past president of the Lucerne Valley Lions Club. As such, he pushed Edison to bring electricity to the Lion's gun range. Other Lions had tried but were told it would cost $70,000. Bobby made an arrangement with Edison that the Lions would get all of the easements, purchase the power poles, and pay for street lights for seven years, and Edison would not charge them to run the power lines. Many of the property owners along the easement agreed to help purchase the power poles.

Al Archer shows where bottle shattered window of his Shell Service Station. 1963.

In 1977 Bobby was building poultry barns throughout San Bernardino County and needed a local source of materials, so he and Sara purchased the local hardware company, Hawley's Hardware. Changing the name to Valley Hardware, they began building trusses and their business exploded.

"The one who really helped our hardware business grow was John Russell," said Bobby. "Back then, local contractors had no place to buy lumber or trusses. John told me that anything I stocked he would buy. This saved him a trip to Apple Valley every time he needed supplies."

The business finally outgrew the first building, and they began to look for another. Years earlier, Bob Sr. had built a storefront on Highway 18, east of Baker Road, for Lew and Bess Cowan for their Hotpoint Appliance business. There wasn't enough volume with the appliance sales, so they put in groceries and called it West End Market. By 1980, West End Market had closed and the Delperdang's bought the property. They remodeled the building and moved their business there. A year or two later, they built the warehouse in the back. In 1990 they had again outgrown their existing building, so they added a larger building on the neighboring property, where they continued to operate Valley Hardware, until selling to Butcher Block Hardware in 2006.

Now that you have a sketch of the Delperdang/Archer connection, here comes Bob Riddle, who started working for the Delperdangs selling hardware, in 1977, when he was just 14 years old.

Now we have three Bobs in the mix, so try to keep up. The Delperdang's daughter, Linda, also worked at the hardware store. "Bob and I pretty much grew up together, working at all of the hardware store locations," said Linda. She and Bob Riddle were married in 1983.

In 1984 Bob and Linda Riddle bought the LV Auto Parts Store, in the same location where Linda's grandparent's auto parts store had been. Her grandparents had sold the property to Bobby's brother-in-law, Jim Broadhead, who then sold it to Bob and Linda. Bob and Linda acquired the Napa brand, and hired Bob's brother, Mark, who worked for them there for a few years. Mark now runs his own business on Highway 18, where the Delperdangs first hardware store was once located. He restores and sells vintage cars and military equipment.

In 1990 Bob Riddle got his contractor's license and starting doing work for the mines. It wasn't long before he started his own business, Robert Riddle Construction, which he operates to this day.

The Delperdangs and Riddles built Lucerne Valley Storage on the north side of Highway 18 just east of Custer Road in 2007. They expanded it later to include RV and equipment storage. They then sold it in 2018.

Ken Riddle, Bob Riddle's dad, brokered his own real estate business, called Lucerne Valley Realty from 1982 to 1995, in the building on Highway 18 across the street from both the hardware store and the current Lucerne Valley Realty, owned by the Lynns on Highway 18. His daughter, Teresa (Riddle) Reyes is a realtor for Lucerne Valley Realty to this day.

Between these three families, many of the community's business needs are supplied.

Carol LaCroix, 1967.
Photo courtesy of Lucerne
Valley Leader Newspaper.

Longest Active Business in Town – Style Shop

Compiled by Millie Rader

The Style Shop now located in the Lucerne Valley Shopping Center, near Rock's Pizza, has to be the longest established business in town. A 1967 Leader Newspaper article ran the heading, "New beauty shop open here. A localite completed her cosmetology course and brings high fashion to Lucerne Valley this month in the form of a beauty shop. Carol LaCroix, owner-operator opens "The Style Shop" on Monday April 17. It is located in the Multi-Building on Old Woman Springs Road. Doors open at 9:00 am. (This where Little Joe's restaurant is now.)

The article continued – "The new business operator has been a Lucerne Valleyite for the past 12 years and is the daughter of Sue and Walt Richards of North Valley. She is also the wife of Phil and mother of two, Sharon who is three years old and George age six and a half."

Carol later renamed her business "Carol's Style Shop," and could be found there 5-6 days a week cutting hair for men, women and children. In 1980, Carol's daughter-in-law, Denise, joined her and they worked together until Carol's retirement in 2006.

After Carol's retirement, Denise changed the name of the business back to the original "Style Shop." The business is still running strong and will soon celebrate its 50th anniversary.

When asked, Denise said she enjoyed the freedom to set her own hours and the ability to attend her son and grandson's baseball games. What she liked best was how close she was with her clients. "One of my clients, Joyce Burns, has been with me for 36 years. She is like a second mom. Many are like family to me."

Joyce Burns and her husband, Bob moved to Lucerne Valley in 1952 to grow alfalfa on their 170 acre ranch, at the north end of Midway Road. She said Carol started styling her hair shortly after opening her shop on Old Woman Springs Road and then Denise took over soon after Denise's son, Phillip, was born. Joyce now lives in Apple Valley but still drives to Lucerne Valley every week to get her hair done.

Denise LaCroix and Joyce Burns. Photo by Millie Rader.

Post Office – From 1912 to Present

Photos courtesy of George Knowlton

Koehly Ranch and Post Office, 1916. A 7-11

The first government sanctioned Lucerne Valley Post Office was established in 1912 on the southeast corner of Rabbit Springs and Post Office Roads in the home of John and Rosa Koehly, who moved to Lucerne Valley in 1909. Rosa Koehly was appointed the first Postmaster. Some days only 8¢ worth of stamps were cancelled, which was her salary for the day.

Sam Wood was the first official mail carrier. He is pictured delivering the mail to the Koehly Ranch. The woman and child with him are not named. In the early years, the mail was dropped off at the Rabbit Springs Way Station by whoever was passing through. After James Goulding established Box S Ranch, the mail was dropped off there and piled into a washtub, where the early pioneers would fish through to find anything with their name on it. No formal address was required. Even in the 1950s, Chuck Rader remembers receiving a piece of mail with his nickname "Snarky" and Lucerne Valley, California as the only address.

Emma Campbell, 1916. A 7-11

Sam Wood, First Mail Carrier. A 7-11

Here, Emma Campbell is photographed in 1916 entering the post office located at the Koehly home. The Koehlys also sold groceries, it was called the Koehly Swiss Ranch Grocery and many people used their visits to the post office/store to visit with friends and catch up on the latest news.

Rosa Koehly and Family. A 7-11

This photo was featured in a historical segment of the December 2, 1965 *Leader* Newspaper. It is taken from an album of Rosa Koehly. The caption reads, "This picture, taken in 1915, shows the Lucerne Valley Post Office on Post Office Road. Shown in the picture is Rosa Koehly holding her daughter, Lorraine, with Emil and Betrix standing and Mary in the buggy with her Pa." (John Koehly)

In 1935 the post office moved to a one-room building on the highway, west of the Homestead Bakery at Box S Ranch, with Ed Smith as postmaster. Ed Smith was also a licensed electrician and scoutmaster of Lucerne Valley's first Boy Scout Troop 71 from 1928 to 1933. Polly Snyder was also a postmaster at this location from 1937 to 1938. According to the June/July edition of the *Desert Grapevine,* The U.S. Post Office in Lucerne Valley was moved from the Koehly home on Rabbit Springs Road on Jan 15, 1935 to the front part of the building on Box S Ranch. The room was 12'x16'. Four feet served as the lobby and the mail handling room was 12'x12'. At first all mail was handled by general delivery with Ed Smith as acting postmaster.

1938 Post Office. Photo courtesy of J.S. Gobar Foundation. A 1-4

Flora Anne Clark took over as postmaster in 1938 and held the position until 1952. During her tenure, the post office was moved to the Clark Building with John Hutson's and Irving Seeberg's Hardware Store, now the China House.

Dorothy F. Moe held the postmaster position in 1952 and 1953, and it is believed, during this time that the post office was moved once again into a small building located between and behind what is now the China House and the Lucerne Valley Chamber of Commerce. Ray Verne Ely became postmaster in 1953, and was still there when the post office was moved to "the triangle" on Verdugo Road at Oracle Road. Ray Bonin and David Phillips were also postmasters at that location. According to the inscription on the back of this picture, the lady is Anna Casser.

Post Office Building behind China House. A 7-12

Dedication of New Post Office, 1958. A 7-13

On March 1, 1958, Lucerne Valley dedicated a new post office building located on the corner of Verdugo and Oracle Roads, where the Sheriff Substation is currently located. According to the *Lucerne Valley Leader* newspaper, "Hundreds of Valleyites turned out for the gala affair that proved to be a milestone in the progress of Lucerne Valley." The new building was built and owned by contractor Arnold Morrison. The corner stone of the building was constructed from the first bag of cement produced by the newly operational Kaiser Permanente Cement Plant, which had been donated to the Lucerne Valley Chamber of Commerce. This new post office had 1,584 square feet, more than doubling the size of the previous building.

Pictured inside the post office on Verdugo Road in 1971 are Del Gates who delivered mail to those on the "Star Route" for 11 1/2 years. Ray Bonin, who was the postmaster at that time, had been in postal service since 1959. Ed Wojcik had begun work in the Lucerne Valley Post Office in 1965. Standing on the right are Linda Davis, who had recently begun delivering the mail

Postal Employees.

from Victorville, Linda Reed, with 2½ years of service and, Jean LaChance, who had also been there since 1965. Not pictured was postal employee Ann Bantz who had started work in the post office in 1954.

The post office was moved to its current location on Highland Road in September, 1987. This picture was taken at its location on the Corner of Verdugo and Oracle Roads just before the move.

Post Office before it moved in 1987. A 7-13

Modern Post Office, 2018. Photo courtesy of Millie Rader. A 7-14

Ray Bonin, Postmaster

Compiled by Jan Lembright July 30, 2017, from the November 15, 1973 Leader Newspaper and from Ray's daughter, Carol Tevis. Photo courtesy of Lucerne Valley Leader Newspaper

Ray Bonin and wife Lois.

Ray and his wife, Lois left their home state of Minnesota in 1954 and settled in Torrance, California. He was employed as an airplane mechanic at Douglas Aircraft. Shortly thereafter, he became employed with the postal service, Terminal Annex in Wilmington, Calif.

In 1962, Ray and Lois moved to Lucerne Valley to take over the post office's star route mail delivery duties. He shared this responsibility with Lois, while working at the Naval Tracking Site near Norco. At that time the Lucerne Valley Post Office was located on Verdugo Road, where the San Bernardino County Sheriff's office is currently located.

Being the good sport that he was, Ray laughingly commented that his appointment as Postmaster came on "April Fool's day 1966, which he felt might have some significance. His most refreshing comment came in answer to the question of what position he enjoyed the most. He immediately answered "serving people well."

Ray served in the army air force during World War II and claimed great luck and fortune, in that he survived a B-29 Bomber crash at Tucson, Arizona, and the fact that the war ended one day after his squadron arrived on Saipan in the Pacific.

In Lucerne Valley he had been involved with Little League, was Chairman of the Church Council at St. Paul's Church, served as secretary of the Lions Club, chaired the Cemetery District Board of Commissioners and sat on the Elementary School Board of Trustees. He was a Boy Scout leader and umpire, and a member of the Lucerne Valley Sheriff's Posse.

Ray was a man of character as illustrated in this story. One Sunday morning, Ray drove to Victorville to pick up eight geese that were waiting for a local customer. He was afraid they would perish in their box so he delivered them to the resident's home. He was also known to deliver late packages that he knew were Christmas gifts to homes while he was dressed as Santa Claus. Now that's service!

Lois was also very active in the community, she not only carried the mail, but was very dedicated to St. Paul's Catholic Church. She took care of the linen for the priest and was in charge of many social

Citizen of the Year, 1974.

gatherings. She was PTA president for the Lucerne Valley Elementary School until their youngest daughter moved on to the school in Apple Valley, where she also became PTA president. Lois was also involved with the Lucerne Valley Lions Club for many years.

Their children are Nancy Higgins, Charles Bonin, Carol Tevis and Joan Medici. They have nine grandchildren and 13 great-grandchildren. Ray passed away in 2002, and Lois in 2007.

A Market with a Mission – Lucerne Valley Market & Hardware

By Linda Gommel. Photos courtesy of Linda Gommel.

Ernest Gommel, 1976.

The story of Lucerne Valley Market & Hardware cannot be told apart from the story of its entrepreneur and founder, Ernie Gommel.

From construction and carpentry with his contractor father, to a civil engineering degree from UC Berkeley, to climbing the corporate ladder at U.S. Steel, to President of Alberta Phoenix Tube and Pipe Co. Ltd. (Edmonton, Alberta, Canada), to a degree from Christian Theological Seminary in Indianapolis, Indiana, to minister of a suburban church, to leader of a house church and at the same time entrepreneur of two grocery stores – that in brief is the story of Ernie Gommel's pilgrimage through this world, ending on November 10, 2012 at age 91.

Why the radical changes in his life, you may wonder? Because Gommel, as he was known, gave his life to God in about 1957 while in Canada, and then spent several months soul-searching, trying to decide what God wanted him to do with the rest of his life. He decided God wanted his whole life, fulltime, and so he enrolled in seminary to become a minister.

Within a few years, God led him to realize that churchianity is a trap, and that fulltime service to Him meant following God's calling, whatever it might be. By this time, Gommel was leading a house church, and he and the members felt led to buy the Hitchin Post Market in Reche Canyon, Colton, California, beginning on July 7, 1967. Starting with a small box building that was sitting in the middle of a bare lot, Gommel and crew learned the grocery business from scratch. In addition, Gommel used his construction and engineering skills to add to the building, made a rolling feed store on a truck chassis, installed some of the earliest self-serve gas pumps and a mini car wash, and even did auto repair for a growing clientele.

Gommel and his wife, Barb, took days off in Big Bear Lake where they had a travel trailer parked near Fawnskin. Often they would come down the back road through Lucerne Valley, having loved the desert all their lives. (On a personal note: they also had taken a vacation at Sky High Ranch (aka RW Ranch on High Rd.) in about October, 1948, and I, their daughter, was born 9 months later in June, 1949, so I can probably claim to have very deep roots here in Lucerne Valley. Hee, hee, hee.)

The group running the Hitchin Post, began to feel a tug to buy a store in Lucerne Valley. There were two markets in town at the time, and after deciding that the smaller of the two, one more like the Hitchin Post, was not what God wanted, the Gommels decided to find out if the larger one, Leo's Market, was for sale. They stopped at local real estate offices as they passed through, stating each time, "We want to buy Leo's Market, and we don't have any money."

Barbara Gommel, 1976.

Lucerne Valley Market & Hardware Groundbreaking, 1983.
L to R: Bill Lembright, John Schmolle, Barb Gommel, Ernie
Gommel, Construction Worker, Linda Gommel, Jan Lembright.

The real estate people thought this was a joke until one day one of them decided to ask the current owners if they wanted to sell. To everyone's great surprise, yes, they were eager to sell the store.

Within a short time, financing was arranged, and the operators of the Hitchin Post Market were now also operators of the renamed Lucerne Valley Market. The first day of operation was March 10, 1975, and once again, Gommel used his skills to rearrange, update, and bring new things into the store. Old cases and shelves were updated with newer ones. Computers were still in Bill Gates' and Steve Jobs' garages, but electronic cash registers were now available. (Oh, if things had just stayed that simple, clean, and easy!! – LG)

The Gommels and some others split their time between the two stores, travelling down the hill twice a week. But in 1981, tiring of the travel, the smog in the basin, the separation, and most importantly, bugged once again by God, the Hitchin Post was sold to a local Reche Canyon resident and the group turned all of its attention to Lucerne Valley Market.

In order to protect the assets of the business and keep them in God's hands, the business was incorporated into a for-profit corporation wholly owned by Church of Our Lord and Savior, so that all of the assets would be legally bound to remain with the Church or another non-profit the church might designate.

Since the business had outgrown the old building on Old Woman Springs Road, Gommel bought a 13 acre piece of property that fronted on Highways 247, Barstow Road, and Highway 18. Once again, his construction, engineering, and executive skills were put to use as a new store was planned and built through one of the coldest, wettest winters in Lucerne Valley. A groundbreaking ceremony took place in November 1982, and by March 1983, the new store was ready to go. Opening day was March 10, 1983.

The store was half its present size, about 15000 square feet. New departments were added in order to create a variety of merchandise for customers shopping at home and give the store the greatest stability and chance for survival in a tough business climate. A hardware, a deli, and variety merchandise were some of the new departments.

In 1991 Gommel expanded the store to its full size, 33000 square feet, involving himself again in the design and construction of the second "half." This was done without closing the store even for a day, using huge tarps to close off the construction area from the sales floor. As always, the convenience of the customers came first, and closing the store was not an option.

As of this writing in April, 2017 the store is still the same size and still serving customers with the same passion for God and for our customer/neighbors that has been the driving force over the years. We like to think of it as a lighthouse in a darkening world, a place with a special warmth and spirit (Spirit) that even those who come in for the first time can sense.

"But thanks be to God, who always leads us in triumphal procession in Christ and through us spreads everywhere the fragrance of the knowledge of Him." (2 Cor. 2:14) We pray that the store in its mission fulfills that calling.

Old Store, 1976. Photo by L.V. Leader Newspaper. A 7-9

New Store, 2016. Photo by Linda Gommel. A 7-15

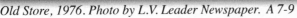

United Farm Agency Real Estate –
Gates, Veales, Regensberg, and Reddens

Compiled by Millie Rader. Photos courtesy of Lucerne Valley Leader Newspaper.

Del Gates. A 7-16

In August 1971 Darrell "Del" Gates opened a United Farm Agency Real Estate office in the little building on the north side of Old Woman Springs Road, just west of Café 247. He had just been appointed as the exclusive High Desert representative for the company.

By 1976 Real Estate was a booming business in Lucerne Valley and Gates added two more brokers to the office, Allen Redden and George Veale Jr. and salesman, soon to be a broker, Danny Regensberg. By 1978 Gates had retired, and Redden had moved on to another company. Veale and Regensberg then built a second office on Bear Valley Road near the I-15 freeway. Real Estate was still on the upswing.

George's wife, Barbara, had her real estate license by the time they opened the Victorville office and she took over the management there.

United Farm Agency, now United Country Real Estate had been publishing a free real estate catalog since 1928 that listed, with pictures, its rural properties for sale. This catalog brought people to Lucerne Valley from all over the US and even from other countries. Veale's daughter, Emmalena, after graduating high school, also had her real estate license and worked in the local office. She said people would come through the door with their catalog in hand and be ready to buy a piece of property based solely on the picture and description they saw there.

Many other salespeople sold real estate in that office including Ray Clark, who was 95 years old the year this book was first published, but has since passed.

After the passing of both Danny Regensberg and George Veale in 1989, Barbara Veale closed both Real Estate offices. Many pieces of property had changed hands in the 18 years United was in town.

George Veale. A 7-16

Burger Depot – Dave and Laura Mount

Compiled by Millie Rader.

Laura, Dave and David Mount, ground breaking. Photo courtesy of David and Laura Mount.

David and Laura Mount are two very hard working people. When I met with them at 8:00 am in the dining area of their little restaurant, Burger Depot, they were already prepping food for the day. Laura was cooking bacon and the place smelled amazing. As Laura hugged me, she apologized for smelling like bacon and I said, "no problem, that it is the best perfume ever." David reached for her and said he agreed.

In preparation for my visit, David had written out a summary of how their little enterprise came to be. He invited me to sit down but never really sat down himself. Laura also was constantly on the move, stopping here and there to help David answer a question.

He said that when this famous little eatery opened in 1979, their customers automatically associated "depot" with trains and soon began bringing them train décor. Every train in the place was a gift from various customers. David and Laura have enjoyed having their customers do their decorating for 40 years.

So how did this little place, known far and wide for its amazing cheeseburgers, come to be?

David and Laura both moved to Lucerne Valley with their families in the mid-sixties as young teens. It wasn't long before they met and became friends, and then married in 1972.

As a young married couple, they lived in the little house behind where their business is now. David worked seven years fighting fires for the US Department of Forestry. David, their son was still quite small, when his dad came home one day from an 18-day stint driving fire trucks. Dad was all black with soot, he had a beard and his little guy did not recognize him, and though he enjoyed his job, David and Laura realized they needed to make a change.

It was Laura's idea to build a small restaurant in the front yard. Their property fronted Highway 18, but was zoned residential. It took two years to jump through the many governmental hoops before they finally had all of the permits needed to build.

After high school David had attended Los Angeles Trade Tech to study Restaurant Management, so he had the training and with that, and a lot of hard work, they developed a fine establishment with an extremely loyal fan base.

Laura and Dave Mount in 2018.

Tonya Judkins, a Lucerne Valley resident, who works in Apple Valley and passes by numerous restaurants to get home, would rather call ahead on the nights she does not feel like cooking and have a hot and ready meal from Burger Depot because, "They have been faithfully feeding me since I was a child," she said, and their food is amazing."

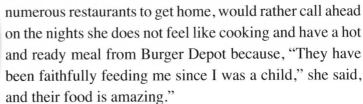

Burger Depot Serving Window.

For the first 26 years they were open eight hours a day, seven days a week, and the first five years they hired employees to help. At one time, they had eight local teens working for them. David said they soon realized that too many employees caused the place to lose its mom and pop flavor. As the hired help grew up and moved on, David and Laura began to take on more of the operation themselves, until they were the only employees.

They said it took awhile to build up the stamina needed to run the business by themselves. David, who had worked as a rancher, horse trainer, wrangler, lumber jack and firefighter, said this is the hardest job he has ever had. Laura said for the first couple of years, they used Absorbine Jr. every night on their legs and backs before they built up their strength.

In 1996 they began to take Sundays off, and in 2005 decided to close shop on the weekends. David said they still catch a lot of flak for not always being there when someone is hankering for Burger Depot nourishment.

According to David, they thought about selling a couple of years ago and actually put it on the market for awhile. They had prayed about it first, and asked God to show them, that if it was His will for them to sell, it would sell quickly. It did not, so they took it off the market and will continue to serve Lucerne Valley until God has other plans.

David said that they love, not only working together, but the great camaraderie of their terrific customers, who they consider friends.

Burger Depot Exterior. Photos on this page are courtesy of Millie Rader. B 7-17

Van Norman – Well Driller

*By Barbara LaGrange, 1987.
Photos courtesy of Sandi Partin*

*Left to right: Mike Partin, Larry Lindley, Van,
Jim Hoggatt, and Sandi Partin*

Even though most of us knew that Van Norman Well Drilling had been around a long time, few probably remember "Van" settling in the valley back in 1946.

When F.M. "Van" Van Norman came to the valley with his new wife, Vera, he was a service station attendant and car repairman. He had trained a few years in Victorville, working for several stations; one being the J. Clay Garrison Garage on 7th and Forrest Streets.

It wasn't long before Van was itching to run his own station and he took over the old Shell Station, where most of us remember Lucerne Valley Auto Parts in operation. "We even had the glass bowl gas pumps, two of them," said Van. "We were a big outfit."

He eventually took over the Chevron Station at the "Y" next to Johnny's Café, until the whole corner literally burned down in 1953. That's about the time the Y Café was built in its place. He recalled that it was purchased by a family named Pangburn.

Van and Vera were an enterprising couple. They next invested their efforts into Baker's Café (which in 2018 is Adelita's Mexican Restaurant). "It was a busy little place then," said Van. "Vera ran it pretty good and we had a couple of employees, but then a new job opportunity came along."

He was referring to a logging truck operation. He cut and transported lumber down the hill to Carruthers Company, which in turn provided finished wood to Winter's Cabinet Shop in San Bernardino. "It was another of those big outfits that kept us busy," said Van. "Vera was even driving the second truck, hauling logs down from the north slope of the San Gorgonio. I was working alongside Albert Swarthout, who used to have Heart Bar Ranch. It was good hard work until we went broke."

Van explained that the wood had to be of excellent quality, but you couldn't tell the quality until the log was on the ground. Too many felled trees and not enough good wood forced Van and Vera to look elsewhere for work.

Well drilling was just on the horizon. Another old driller, Cliff Steele, saw what hard workers the Van Norman's were and offered to teach Van the well business. It was 1952 and Steele wanted to establish a ranch of his own. After six months of training, Steele turned the drilling business over to the Van Normans.

Work was steady, they drilled domestic wells

Van Norman Well Rig. B 7-18

Service Station at the "Y" A 7-19

and a few irrigation wells. Cliff had dug the Ace Motel's well and Van kept the pumps working. "Joe Uhlencott built the Muffin Motel now known as the Ace Motel," Van said adding a tidbit of history. (The motel was later owned for many years by Don and Pat Judkins).

In 1955 they bought their first rotary rig, a proud addition to any drilling outfit, but by 1957 they had to sell it due to a collapse in the economy. "I call it Eisenhower's fall," said Van. "There wasn't any money to buy wells. That nearly broke me. We kept things going by doing pump and machine repair."

Before things got better, Van was working graveyard shifts at Kaiser Cement and trying to keep his well drilling business alive. In late 1987 (the time this article was first written) Van decided to invest in the rotary rig again.

"It's quite a jump into the future for us," said Van at that time. "This new rig averages 4-5 days on a job site, where the cable rig can take 3-4 weeks." With a grin he added, "We've completed 11 wells since the rotary rig went into service in April."

The company had incorporated in 1978, and in 1987 Van, age 74, was President, daughter Sandi Partin was Secretary/Treasurer, son-in-law Mike Partin Vice President, grandson Jim Hoggatt, who worked for his grandpa since high school, was Vice President and they had recently hired Larry Lindley.

"I am slowing down some; taking service orders, estimating contracts and doing light pump work, and such."

Y Intersection.

According to Van's daughter, Sandi, her mom, Vera, passed away in 1983, which was a huge loss to both the family and the business. After they purchased the rotary rig they dug 100 more wells before they lost Van in early 1991. With a sluggish economy, and their business icons gone, they closed the business in 1996.

"My dad was never happier than when we were working 10-12 hours a day, 7 days a week. Even in

Van Norman and daughter Sandi.

his last few years, when he was ill, he still went to every job site to make sure all the work was going smoothly."

Sandi, who was born at home here in Lucerne Valley, worked for Bank of America at the same time she was taking care of the books for the well business. When Bank of America closed in Lucerne Valley she was transferred to the Apple Valley branch. After working for Bank of America for 10 years she went to work back in Lucerne Valley for First Mountain Bank now known as First Foundation Bank, where she still worked in 2018.

Bank of America

LUCERNE VALLEY LEADER

A WEEKLY NEWSPAPER SERVING THE CROSSROADS OF THE HIGH DESERT.

VOL. 18 NO. 28 LUCERNE VALLEY, CALIFORNIA 92356 TEN CENTS JULY 11, 1974

BANKMOBILE — Bank of America's new "Bankmobile" modular facility will house planned Bank of America office at Highway 18 and Old Woman Springs Road in Lucerne Valley. The unit, scheduled to open in November, will serve as interim office until a permanent structure is built. It was developed to replace the bus-like mobile units the bank has used for such interim facilities in the past.

Bank of America To Arrive In November

Plans for a Bank of America office in Lucerne Valley were announced today by Regional Vice President William H. Baughn.

Baughn said the new office, tentatively scheduled to open in November, will be located on a 50,000 square foot site recently acquired by the bank on the south side of Highway 18 just east of Old Woman Springs Road.

Initially, the office will be housed in one of Bank of America's newly-developed "Bankmobile" interim units. Eventually, said Baughn, a permanent structure will be built on the site.

The pre-engineered "Bankmobile" features a modernistic exterior, somewhat resembling a large rapid transit car, assembled over a 600 square foot modular foundation. It will contain a three-station teller line, a lending officers' section, an outside walk-up deposit window for extended hours service and will provide all normal banking services except safe deposit facilities.

In the past, B of A has often used a specially-equipped mobile van to provide immediate banking service to an area pending completion of a permanent structure. The much larger and more fully-outfitted "Bankmobile" was developed to provide more convenient and complete interim services, explained Baughn.

A 7-20

Hutson Hardware / Post Office / Malt Shop / Country Kitchen / China House

Compiled by Millie Rader. Photos courtesy of Lucerne Valley Leader Newspaper.

The pretty red and white building that sits square in the center of this little town and now houses the China House Restaurant owned by the Wu family is probably one of the oldest commercial buildings in town, and has to be the oldest still in use.

Piecing together information from Ethel Owen's Quick History and the memories of Allen Stanfield, Geninne (Gross) Walker, Sam Clark, Ellie Filippi and her son, John, and Felix Wu we have what we hope to be a complete history of this wonderful old monument to the past.

Post Office, Hardware Store

The building was constructed by Roy and Flora Ann Clark in 1947. Flora Ann was the postmaster at the time in a little building just back of the current China House location. After the new building was built, the Post Office was moved into it along with a Hardware store owned by John Hutson and Irving Seeberg. In the June, 1947 *Desert Grapevine* there is a small article titled "A New Store." It reads, "John Hutson and Capt. I.L. Seeberg opened the Lucerne Valley Supply Store on June 1st. It is located in the recently completed building next to the post office. The space behind the store is utilized for lumber and cement. The village needed such a business as this. Everything necessary for the rancher can be had there."

Malt Shop

In 1950, Dick Grobaty leased a portion of the building and ran a malt shop there until 1959, when he purchased Rene Belbenoit's Ranch Store located just east of the Lucerne Valley Chamber of Commerce Office.

Coon's Country Kitchen

Probably soon after, Reverend and Lucille Coon purchased the building and it became the Country Kitchen. In 1962, the Coons sold it to Jimmy Nasif who owned Tall Trees Hotel and Trailer Park at the time. Nasif's sister, Ellie, and her husband, Al Filippi, lived in Rhode Island where Al ran nightclubs and Ellie waited tables. Soon after Nasif made his purchase, he needed money and asked Al and Ellie to come in as partners in the restaurant.

"We mailed him $1500 sight unseen. That was a lot of money in 1962," said Ellie. She said they mailed the money and then drove across the United States and into a strange and wonderful place that was to be their home for the rest of their lives.

"It was love at first sight," said Ellie. "Al was entranced with this valley between the snow topped mountains."

After their initial investment, Ellie said they paid $102 a month for the tables and chairs and everything else that went with the restaurant business. It wasn't long before they became the full owners and the business was renamed "Filippi's Country Kitchen."

Ellie said that when they first came to town, nobody would trust them. They thought that since they were from the East Coast and Al was Italian, that they must be mafia, and nobody would cash their checks.

"One day Beryl McDougall (Bob's mom) came in and I asked her why people wouldn't trust us? She said that we had to prove ourselves, and the trick was to never talk about people, just the weather. So that is what I did. I only talked about the weather," she said with a laugh.

When they first started up, they were low on funds and could not afford to pay waitresses, so Ellie's sisters Gladys Halleck and Jen Russell worked for tips until the business began making money. Then they hired their first paid waitress, Jane Chase.

"She was the apple of our eye," said Ellie. "She was irreplaceable, she could work the front and the back dining rooms all by herself, all the while selling pies as fast as Al and I made them." Jane worked for the Filippis the entire time they were in business there.

Ellie said that they did get off to a rocky start. The first year they were in business, Al got a letter from a guy who wrote, 'Mr. Filippi, if you want that restaurant to be a success you better learn how to cook.'

"He kept that letter," said Ellie. "He had never cooked in his life. He came from a nightclub family and all he knew was how to serve drinks. So Al bought cookbooks and taught himself to cook. He became the best cook around."

All their children worked in the family restaurant. Son, John, started working there while in high school and stayed for 16 years before going into construction. Their son, Ray, also worked there along with both daughter-in-laws, Pam and Jennie.

"We also employed most of the high school boys around town," said Ellie. "If they wanted to work, we put them to work bussing tables and doing dishes."

David Rader was one of those boys whose first real job was working at Filippi's Country Kitchen. He remembers that they always ate well while employed there. They could stop in

Country Kitchen, Gladys Halleck, Ellie Filippi, little Sally Filippi, 1965. A 7-21

any time for a meal. He said that while he and his brothers, Bob and Richard, all worked there at the same time, Al decided they could have sodas but no milk. The Rader boys loved milk and were going through their supplies too quickly.

Al and Ellie lost their daughter, Sally, to epilepsy in 1985, and according to their son, John, they just didn't have the heart for the business after that. The Filippis sold the restaurant to Mr. and Mrs. Wu in 1986.

China House

People will drive many miles to eat at the China House. In 2001 they had a fire in the kitchen that caused enough damage to shut them down for a few months. This writer was the office manager at the Chamber of Commerce office next door at that time and many people would stop in at the Chamber to ask in dismay about the closed restaurant. Some had driven from as far as Ridgecrest just to eat here. We have heard from residents of Hinkley and Temecula that the China House is a day trip destination.

Mrs. Wu is Ho Li Chu Wu and Mr. Wu is Chyk Yuan Wu. This well loved couple immigrated to the US from Taiwan in 1979. According to their son, Felix, his dad learned to cook while working in China Town, Los Angeles.

In 1985 they rented a building in Apple Valley near the AM/PM on Highway 18 near Navajo Road. They were very successful that first year which caused the landlord to raise their rent. The Wus then drove out to Lucerne Valley and talked to Al and Ellie Filippi about buying their restaurant. The Filippis were ready for a change so the agreement was made for them to sell to Mr. and Mrs. Wu and the Filippi's carried the loan paper.

"I didn't think a Chinese Restaurant would make it in Lucerne Valley and that we would soon be back in the restaurant business," said John Filippi. "But the China House did succeed and each payment was made on time until the Wus owned it in full.

Current Owners, the Wu Family, China House.
Photo courtesy of Felix Wu.

Felix said that it has never been easy to run a restaurant in Lucerne Valley. But by running it mainly with family they have made it work. With his mom and dad, he and his sister I-chin and her husband Chuan-Jen Chen and two other employees they run a tight ship. Their other two sisters, I-Jung Wu and I-Hsua Wu, were also involved in the business for many years but now live in San Francisco and Minnesota. Felix also mentioned his two nieces, Pei-hua and Meng-hua, who were a big help before graduating high school here and going off to Berkley University. He said they were very hard workers and he is very proud that one is now a pharmaceutical researcher and the other is an eye doctor.

Mr. and Mrs. Wu are older now and Felix said that with the minimum wage hikes and increasing California taxes that they may not be able to stay in business for much longer. He hopes for five more years.

China House, 2015. A 7-21

Jack Rabbit Cafe

Compiled by Millie Rader

We have a picture of the interior of one of our old restaurants but did not know which one. Today Allen Stanfield was able to identify it as the Jack Rabbit Cafe. His mother worked there and he spent a lot of time there after school waiting for her to get off work. Here is an article written by Leader Editor Jack Hutson after the Cafe burned on October 21, 1956.

Jack Rabbit Cafe. Photo courtesy of Lucerne Valley Phone Book. A 7-22

Midnight Fire Destroys Cafe

A famous old landmark of Lucerne Valley, the Jack Rabbit Cafe, located at the Y intersection of Highway 18 and Old Woman Springs Road, (now Hwy 18) owned and operated by Lew and Bess Cowan since December 2, 1946, was completely destroyed by fire of undetermined origin Sunday at midnight, Oct. 21, 1956.

One of the first to observe the flames was Bob Corbin, who stated that he was awakened by what seemed to have been an explosion. From his home he saw an increasing glow in the sky toward Jack Rabbit Corners. He hurried to the pay telephone booth at Union Service Station, across the street from the cafe, to call out the Volunteer Fire Department crew. There he found Dick Grobaty, of Center Variety Store, already sending out the call. Those responding were Jack Pittman, Jim Goulding, Jim and Ed Hayes, Dale Wilson, Mac McDougall, Cliff Inslee, Ed Havlik, and Chuck Webb.

Deputy Sheriff Bob Woods rushed to the scene in his patrol car and radioed an emergency call to the Electric Power Company to divert danger from the loosening of heavy voltage wires. During the 20 minutes before they arrived, a threatening butane explosion was averted due to courageous efforts of the firemen to disconnect and remove a large butane tank.

A surprise threat of injury to the men came when rifle and shotgun shells, part of additional merchandise sold in the cafe, began exploding, sending slugs wildly in every direction.

Hesperia Forestry Service Fire Department arrived at 1:30 a.m. and remained with Lucerne Valley Volunteers until 4:30 am when it was determined there was no longer danger of sparks from the cooling ashes. Hesperia Fire Chief praised the successful efforts of the Lucerne Valley Volunteers for the manner in which they controlled what, otherwise, could have been a complete loss of several adjacent wooden structures.

As the crowd gathered to watch the burning of the popular cafe, the Rev. Charles Coon of the Lucerne Valley Community First Baptist Church, drove up in his car with his wife, Lucille. They parked as near as safety would permit, opened the rear compartment of the car from which they served hot coffee and home-made pie throughout the early morning hours.

Many calls were made to the home of Lew and Bess Cowan with no success. Then it was learned that the Cowans were out of town attending a convention in San Francisco. They returned to their home at approximately 6 a.m. Monday to hear the news.

In speaking of his loss Lew became

Charred ruins. Photo courtesy of Lucerne Valley Leader Newspaper. A 7-22

reminiscent. He said: "Nellie Goulding, whose father and the family built the Box S Ranch, now out of circulation as a ranch, built the original Jack Rabbit Cafe in 1921. She operated the one room cafe, since enlarged and also owned and operated a gas station next door at that time. Then there was Mildred and Orlando Jacobs who took over the cafe, along with their operation of the old Homestead Market. Dale and Marge Wilson, now operators of the Jack Rabbit Corners Union Service Station, worked at the cafe for the Jacobs, from whom they later purchased it. In turn they sold to Frank and Lois Baker and

Cafe Interior before fire. Photo courtesy of Lucerne Valley Museum Association.

it was from them that Bess and I bought the historical eating place. There will be many former travelers, hunters and sightseers who will miss stopping in at the Jack Rabbit.

When asked if he planned to rebuild, Mr. Cowan said that while it remains a probability in the future, he has no immediate plans.

The Little Known History of Nelson Studios

Compiled by Bill Lembright with help from Bob Riddle, Max McNeely, and Millie Rader. Photos courtesy of Bill Lembright.

North of Highway 18 between Tradepost and Oxbow, behind Keep Warm Firewood and across the street from General Feed, stands a unique water tower adorned with the name Nelson Studios. Farther north on the same property is a living museum of structures which memorialize the artistic industry of Robert (Bob) Nelson, the Howard Hughes of Lucerne Valley.

Before we get into the Nelson portion of this story, we need to include local researcher and history buff, Sam Clark's personal memories of this property and of the previous owner.

When Sam was a boy, in the 1950s, a Mr. Alexander had developed that place. He built the exceptional tank tower with water tank that is still standing there.

"I don't know that I ever did see a nicer or more substantial and well engineered water tank and tower anywhere else in our valley," writes Sam.

He had quite a large chicken operation on the west side

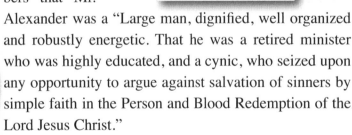

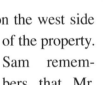
Water tower. A 7-23

of the property. Sam remembers that Mr. Alexander was a "Large man, dignified, well organized and robustly energetic. That he was a retired minister who was highly educated, and a cynic, who seized upon any opportunity to argue against salvation of sinners by simple faith in the Person and Blood Redemption of the Lord Jesus Christ."

Now, fast forward to the 1970s through the mid-1990s, when Bob Nelson made good use of the place. He used the well-made chicken barn that still exists today, along with buildings that he and others constructed to house his sculpture-making factory, storage facilities, and personal living space. He created a good sized reservoir with a bridge, two rowboats, trees, a fountain, and colonnades. He purchased his raw materials locally, buying cement from Delperdang's Valley Hardware, lightweight vol-

Jan Lembright in front of decorative mantel.

Statue and mantel factory in chicken barn. A 7-23

canic cinder from the cinder mine, and thin-wall conduit for lightweight reinforcement from Lucerne Valley Market and Hardware.

He crafted urns, statues, and columns for the movie industry and elaborate fireplace hearths, mantels, and statues for mansions in Hollywood, where he operated a storefront for years.

In the 1970s he offered shelter to Vietnamese immigrants. My guess is that Bob offered the immigrants an opportunity to work for wages in his factory. Bob also hired many locals who had difficulty finding jobs elsewhere.

When Bob would call me at Lucerne Valley Market and Hardware, he would ask for the total of an order to the penny so he could send a worker to buy it and not have to worry about getting change back. When Bob would pick up bags of cement at Valley Hardware, he would jump right in and speed up the yard clerks by loading the bags alongside them, according to Bob Riddle who worked there at the time.

Bob tended to be reclusive. I only met him in person a couple of times. He was tall, had long hair, and only one eye. He was a pleasant character and kept his creations secret as if he wanted to be sure no one copied his art.

In the ruins today, there still exist the remains of his factory set up in a 300 foot long poultry barn (possibly built by the Delperdangs), cluttered with many fiberglass molds and many mostly broken remains of his sculptures. What an ideal industry for our small town. It was situated near the cement plant and the cinder mine, purchased hardware and grocery needs locally, and hired locals, who might otherwise have been unemployed. In addition, it was landscaped to enhance local beauty. The ruins are massive and testimony of the industriousness of this artistic businessman. There were no records found to indicate where or when he spent the last years of his life. No one here knows much about him except that he was a hard worker, he had quite a sense of humor, according to Bob Riddle, and he had a soft spot for those less fortunate. Lucerne Valley is truly a town of character(s)!

Bull Sculpture.

*Medical Building, 1970s. Photo courtesy of
Lucerne Valley Leader Newspaper. A 7-24*

Medical Center

*Compiled by Millie Rader with help from
Sam Clark and Martha Rader*

The Medical Center in Lucerne Valley was first constructed and operated by Dr. Smith in the 1950s as remembered by local history buff, Sam Clark. Sam and several other local residents remember being treated in that facility.

Sam remembers being treated once for "Pink Eye" and at other times for ear and throat ailments when he was in early grammar school. He said what still features large in his small boy memory, were the strips of cellophane encased, tear-off, multicolored candy suckers that hung on a wall near the examining table. He remembers receiving a sucker after his "Pink Eye" treatment. He also remembers longing for, but not receiving one on other occasions.

After Dr. Smith moved on, Dr. Novak took over the practice and ran it for some time before moving his practice to Apple Valley about the time St. Mary Hospital was built.

Before Dr. Smith moved on, he delivered three babies in row in February of 1957. Martha Rader could still remember that occasion as her first born son, Bobby, was born February 16, that year. She remembers that when she and husband Chuck (Snarky) finally decided she really was in labor, they could not find the doctor. Finally, their friend and neighbor Bert Jensen remembered hearing that the Doctor was supposed to have dinner at the Block's house on Rabbit Springs Road that evening, and she drove there and brought him back to the Rader's home. The Doctor had not had time to eat dinner before he was fetched, so he had a bowl of stew at the Rader's before he decided they had better get Martha down to the Medical Center. Martha said they got to the Center at 7:00 pm and Bobby was born at 7:19 pm in the northeast corner of what is now the kitchen at Café 247. She said she spent the night at the Center with Nurse Coleman looking after her and the baby, before she went to her mother's house the next day.

*Cafe 247, 2016.
Photo courtesy of Millie Rader. A 7-24*

The building was a business center for awhile after Dr. Novak left. David Rader remembers that there was a doctor again in that building sometime between 1982 and 1989. When he got something in his eye and the doctor there pulled it out. Shirley Althide opened Café 247 there in the early 1990s which is under the new ownership of Alan and Kathy Nielsen as of April 2015.

Pueblo Property
Compiled by Millie Rader.

As with most of the historical places in Lucerne Valley; the property and Pueblo building that currently house the Cadillac Antique Shop, has a long list of past owners and uses. Piecing together the entire story from memories and newspaper ads took a bit of doing.

The first piece of the puzzle came in the form of an A&W Restaurant Grand Opening announcement in the October 23, 1958, issue of the *Lucerne Valley Leader* newspaper. Then two other articles highlighting the new ownership by the La Scalas and then the Herts were found and the pieces began adding up.

In the A&W story, we know that the newly built restaurant was located on the Triple L Ranch. But what was the Triple L Ranch? After calls and texts to several longtime residents, Sam Clark recalled that Juanita Stack, formerly Juanita LeBeuf and her first husband had a dairy at that location in the early years. They bought the 13.5 acre property in 1945; and according to Michelle (Gist) Boren, built four small cabins just east of where the big pueblo house sits today. One for themselves and the others for the plumbers, framers and electricians who came and stayed while helping the LeBeufs build the Pueblo. Michelle is the granddaughter of Don and Louise Herweh, who later obtained the property from Juanita. She also shared that the LeBeufs imported all of the construction oak from the state of Virginia.

The A&W Drive-In story states the Grand Opening was celebrated Saturday, October 25, 1958. The owner/managers Juanita and Wayne Stack had in-

A WEEKLY NEWSPAPER SERVING LUCERNE VALLEY, CROSSROAD OF THE HIGH DESERT
VOL. III, NO. 47   Lucerne Valley, Calif., Thursday, Oct. 23, 1958   Return Postage Guaranteed   10¢

JUANITA AND WAYNE STACK, owner-managers, toast each other on the completion of their A & W Drive-In. The grand opening will be celebrated this Saturday, October 25.
Leaderfoto

Grand Opening For Drive - In Saturday

Grand Opening of the A & W Drive-In will be celebrated Saturday, October 25, starting at 2 p.m. announces Mr. and Mrs. Wayne Stack, owner-managers. Juanita and Wayne cordially extend an invitation to everyone to join them at this time in helping to celebrate.

The Drive-In is located on one corner of the 13½ acres of the Triple L Ranch, also owned and operated by Mr. and Mrs. Stack and is across from Marty's Trading Post on Highway 18.

Juanita and Wayne conceived the idea of a drive-in some three years ago but plans were not actually started until this year. Building began August 1 and completion date was October 7. Wayne, a graduate of Oklahoma University, spent 1 year at Hills Business College and was a captain in the medical corps in the U.S. Army during World War II. He has been a resident of the valley for the past 4 years. Mrs. Stack has been in Lucerne Valley for the past 13 years.

The A & W Drive In is open daily from 11 a.m. to 11 p.m. and is serving fried chicken, shrimp, fish sticks, bar-b-qued sandwiches, hamburgers, cheeseburgers, hot dogs, french fries and coffee, orange juice, pop-cycles and of course, A & W Root Beer.

Mr. and Mrs. Stack would like to take this opportunity to thank everybody for their support and patience in the past two weeks, while they prepared for their Grand Opening. With your continued loyal support they hope to keep the drive-in paced to the fast growing Lucerne Valley.

General contractors for the building were Russell Brothers of Lucerne Valley.

A&W Root Beer article. A 7-7

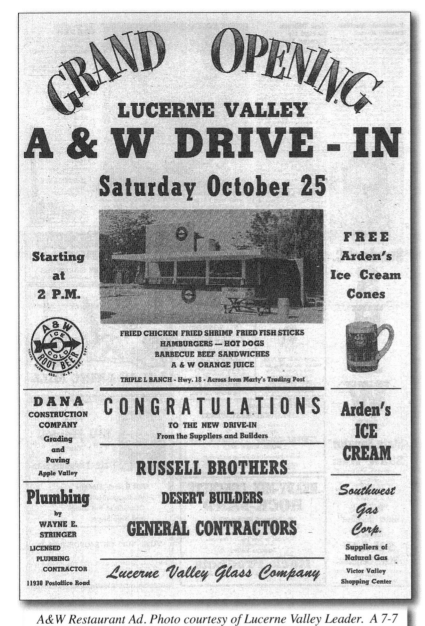

A&W Restaurant Ad. Photo courtesy of Lucerne Valley Leader. A 7-7

vited everyone to come help them celebrate. The Drive-In was located on one corner of the Triple L Ranch, also owned and operated by Mr. and Mrs. Stack and was located across from Marty's Trading Post on Highway 18. Juanita and Wayne had conceived the idea of a drive-in in 1955, and construction of the building was begun August 1, 1958 by the Russell Brothers. Wayne, a graduate of Oklahoma University, spent one year at Hills Business College and was a captain in the U.S. Army Medical Corps during World War II. He had been a resident of the valley four years. Juanita had been in Lucerne Valley for 13 years.

David Rader and his mother, Martha, remember that each Sunday afternoon; they would go to the A&W Drive-In after church for a gallon of root beer and ice-cream to make root beer floats. David remembers the drive-in had its own still for making the root beer, and it cost less if they brought in the glass gallon jug from the previous visit.

Not long after the couple built the restaurant, the marriage dissolved and Juanita then tried to run it alone, but soon had to close the restaurant. In 1974 she traded the property including the "Pueblo" and the restaurant to the Herwehs for property they owned in San Bernardino.

We know from Scott and Kathy Hert, that Kathy's parents, Joe and Mae LaScala, reopened the restaurant in 1975. Many people still remember Papa Joe's. Michelle recalled she had just come to live with her grandparents and remembers the LaScala's paying her a nickel apiece for each outdoor table she cleaned. She was seven-years-old at the time.

One year later, Scott and Kathy Hert took over the management of Papa Joe's and according to the ad in the *Leader* Newspaper it was still Papa Joe's in 1977. The Herts ran it until the insurance became too expensive.

There may have been others who managed the place after the Herts but the next operator of record is Donna (Gist) Smith, Don Herweh's daughter. She opened the Sunshine Place in 1979. This writer was just months away from graduating high school at that time, and Donna gave me my first real job. She had to teach this immature teenager how to cook and handle money. I am thankful for her patience. Donna ran the business for a couple of years before turning it over to Gayle Little in 1981, who re-named it the Hungry Tummy. Gayle ran it until late 1986, when Tony and Pam Spagnuolo took it over, renaming it Pop's and Pam's. In 1993, Hal Hampton and his sister, Shirley Althide, took it over for a short while before moving the business to the corner of Highway 247, where they renamed it Café 247.

During this time, the Herwehs sold and re-purposed the property a couple of times before selling it to Tom and Arla Daugherty sometime in the late 1990s. Arla had a western clothing store in the Lu-cerne Valley Shopping Center at the time called Country Styles which she then moved into the Pueblo building and renamed the property Pueblo Plaza.

After Hampton and Althide moved their business, Herweh was forced to demolish the little restaurant building due to the many Health Code regulations. The building and parking lot once stood just north of where the east driveway is today.

The current owner/operators of the Cadillac Antique Store, Ralph and Patty Muldoon, purchased the property from the Daugherty Trust in May of 2014, and opened the store on July 4, that year.

Ralph had owned a Hot Rod Shop called Muldoon's Customs in Los Angeles for 40 years. After selling the shop they purchased acreage east of Lucerne Valley and the Pueblo property. Patty said the antique store was not planned, it just happened when they gathered their collection in one place. Patty said there are more collectables than antiques and they are thinning their inventory as they plan to transition to a western-themed wedding venue. At the time of this writing they still have an amazing collection of bikes and trains and many western collectables.

Cadillac Antiques. Photo courtesy of Lucerne Millie Rader. A 7-7

CHAPTER 8

What The Hicks Do For Kicks

Compiled by Millie Rader

Organizations

Not long after James "Dad" Goulding moved onto the Box S Ranch and began to organize this little town, groups of people came together for the purpose of bettering this community. Here are listed just a few of those organizations. It is not a complete list, as our historical documents and the memories of those who were around then are not perfect. If you have information or pictures to add to what is recorded here, please contact the Lucerne Valley Museum Association. There will be others who come after us who will want to continue the saga of this little town.

Baseball / Little League / Pony League / Bobby Sox

Sam Clark remembers playing in little league in the late 1950s. He recalled that Bernice Ellis, an older woman who built the house he grew up in on Strawberry Lane, also built the three cottages on Cody Road just south of Highway 18. In the early 1950s she, along with Mildred Jacobs, wanted to build the park. Mrs. Ellis was the major spark plug in initiating and establishing the parks and was instumental in getting Midway School and Pioneer Park into the County Parks District.

A June 1965 article in the *Lucerne Valley Leader* mentions Mr. Pat Arendt as manager of the pony league baseball for boys ages 13-15 and announces that Rick Marty was captain and Percy Pride co-captain. Those interested in playing were urged to contact Mr. Arendt at practice or at his home. Directions were given to his Desert Dawn home off Custer Road.

According to David Rader, Phil LaCroix was coach when he was in Little League in the

Proud 1970 Lucerne Valley Junior Youth Baseball League champs, the Cardinals managed by Art Sherman. (l-r) front row, Jonny Francis, Calvin Sisk, Gordon Leftwich, Walter Leftwich, James Allen, Larry Freed, (back row l to r) Tim Larson, Keith Sullivan, Joe DeGuire, Manager Art Sherman, Richard Reynolds, Steve Freed, Rodney Neiss, and Robin Rickett. Photo courtesy of Lucerne Valley Leader Newspaper.

Little League in Pioneer Park before grass. Photo courtesy of Lucerne Valley Leader Newspaper.

1960s. He tells of the time they practiced on the dry lake bed because the park only had one diamond and another team was using it on that day. The park didn't have many trees at first, only the Arizona Cypress trees and there was no grass in the park or on the ball field.

At practice, to help the kids warm up and to clear the field, they had the team start in a line at home base and pick up rocks and throw them toward the outfield, then they would move to outfield and throw them again and again until they threw them over the homerun fence.

When the park district was finally able to put in grass, Pfizer donated limestone for the infield, although Chuck Rader, who worked with limestone at Kaiser Cement, recommended against using it, the park district did anyway. By the second year, it was packed so hard, the players didn't want to slide on it.

Many years later, crushed brick and grass were put in the infield. Sometime in the 1980s, the fence was removed and a second diamond was put in. The first lights were floodlights on top of five poles. The pole at center field had a short and would flicker out during the games; a hit with a bat would get it to come back on. If someone in the stands caught a foul ball, they could trade it in at the concession stand for a free soda. Art Bristol and Ray Bonin would umpire, along with Joe and Josie Reyes, who would both coach and umpire. Dick Grobaty would call the games on the PA system. The west field is named after Dick Grobaty, and the east field is named for Josie Reyes; both had contributed much time to the field and the local athletes. From 1965-1972 Claire and Gerald Decker were very involved in Little League and Pony League, Claire and Martha Rader kept stats, and Chuck Rader and many of the dads helped to rake the field each week to get it ready. These are only a few who have helped maintain it over the years.

Boy Scouts

No one can remember when the first Boy Scout troop was formed, but we do have record of Theodore Powell Owen being the first Scoutmaster in Lucerne Valley, starting Troop 71 sometime after he and his family moved back to Lucerne Valley in 1928. There are also records of Theo's son, Dick Owen, belonging to a troop in the 1940s, and then later leading that same troop as seen in the photo.

Sam Clark, who still lives in Lucerne Valley, was in Troop 150 with Jim and Louie Pinard in the early 1960s. His Scout Master, Chris Gibbs, took them on

This 1957 photo shows Troop 150 receiving badges at the Court of Awards held in the First Baptist Church, (Now Crossroads Chapel). Those receiving badges were Bobby Delperdang, Richard Myrick, Kit Carson, DeWayne Carson, Barry Strunk, Edson Connal, Harry Francis, Paul Shehorn, Henry Wilson, Lee Wayne Truluck, Jim Barrow and Skippy Pinard. Also pictured here are Scoutmaster Dick Owen, Assistant Scoutmaster Frank Kashmer, David Russo of Johnson Valley and three new members, Peter Anderson, Dennis Francis, and Rusty Orr. Photo courtesy of Lucerne Valley Leader Newspaper.

several campouts. He remembers camping where Silverwood Lake is now, before the dam was built. They also camped in Grapevine Canyon. Sam said that Harold Reed may also have been a Scout Leader.

David Rader was in the Cub Scouts and Boy Scouts in the 1970s. He remembers Alice Bristol and his mom, Martha Rader, helping with Cub Scouts. One of his Boy Scout leaders was John Martin Sr, and they held meetings at Midway Park. John Martin was a gunsmith, so they were able to

Left to right front Forestry Fire Fighters Noel Lockwood and Joe Reyes, (Reyes later became the first resident Fire Chief.) scouts Mark Strehle, Jay Cornett, Jim Bowne, Dennis Bristol, Steve Strehle and Larry Garrett. Back Row, Jann Maxwell, Bob Ledesma, Jim Russell, Bernard Smith, Assistant Scoutmaster Ray Bonin and Scout David Walker. Photo courtesy of Lucerne Valley Leader.

Leader Newspaper photo shows a 1960s version of Troop 150 visiting the local California Division of Forestry Department. First the scouts are shown checking out the dash of the fire truck. Left to right Jim Russsell, Steve Streble, Dennis Bristol and Jim Bowne. Photo courtesy of Lucerne Valley Leader

learn gun safety and shoot many different kinds of guns. He remembers that he and his brothers Bob, Richard and Ed and three other families, the Schuegers, Beckers, Deckers and John Martin helped his dad, Chuck Rader, build a pinewood derby track. They also raised money for the supplies to build a canoe, which they gave back to the Boy Scout Council when his troop disbanded.

Scouts cooking breakfast, 1973. Photo by Chuck Rader.

Boy Scout Troop 150 campout March 1973. Picture on left standing Casey Jones, David Rader, Tommy Turner. Front, Roland Reyes, Richard Rader, John Pebworth, Mike Gentner, Tim Larson. Photo courtesy of Chuck Rader.

Photo sketched by Virginia Hemphill.

First Scoutmaster – Theodore Owen
Compiled by Millie Rader from Desert Grapevine and Lucerne Valley Leader newspapers

Theodore Owen was very active in this valley in the early 1900s. He started Troop 71, the very first Boy Scout Troop in Lucerne Valley. He was involved in scouting here for 20 years, with a troop that turned out nine Eagle Scouts. His son, Dick, later took over for him and was also involved with the scouts for many years. Dick's story can be found in the *Characters Chapter*.

According to Virginia Hemphill, without knowing it, Theo and Stella Owen were preparing a haven, that they would need in a hurry later, when they came to Lucerne Valley in 1911. They came looking for government land and purchased a claim of 160 acres, with a 50-foot domestic well that had been drilled with a post-hole digger.

When Theo's health failed five years later, three doctors told him he didn't have long to live. He was diagnosed with bronchial catarrh and Stella was sure that their property in Lucerne Valley had just the dry climate he needed. It took them two days to make the trip from Los Angeles because he was in such critical condition. There was a shack on the claim, but it was so poorly built that the weather came right in. It was December and it rained and snowed. They had only a cranky old wood burning stove, their only fuel being sagebrush roots they had to grub out themselves. Stella said that within two weeks Theo had gained back seven and a half pounds and by week six he was cured. Hemphill wrote, "This statement is going to tax your credulity if you don't know this Mojave Desert climate."

Hemphill continued: In 1917 they bought a homestead relinquishment of 320 acres with a 294 foot, 12 inch well. They installed a turbine distillate engine that pumped 1460 gallons per minute as government records show. This was ample water for 20 acres of alfalfa.

The rest of the information here was found in Theo's, January 23, 1975 obituary, published in the *Lucerne Valley Leader* newspaper. Before his illness, Theodore had been the superintendent of the Vernon Refinery for Union Oil. In 1918 he moved his family to Fillmore, California to help his half-brother supervise an oil refinery there. During the ten years he was away, Theo continued to develop his Lucerne Valley alfalfa and turkey ranch, returning in 1928 to take personal charge of it. He developed the "Desert Gold" strain of turkeys, which became known all over the United States. He had the world's largest, exclusive turkey hatchery at that time. Theo was also one of the early trustees of Midway School and helped in the building of it. He also helped build the Women's Club building, where the Kingdom Hall is now.

He and Stella are known to have started the first Sunday school in Lucerne Valley; and Theo was awarded an Honorary Life Membership in the Lucerne Valley PTA in recognition of his interest in and devotion to youth.

Theodore Owen's 1920 Car. Photo courtesy Lucerne Valley Leader.

Girl Scouts

Photo courtesy of Lucerne Valley Leader Newspaper.

Girl Scouts selling cookies in front of Leo's Market. Millie Veale, Leader, Mrs. Barbara Veale, Carrie Findley, Terri Reed, Angie Reed.

The earliest record of Girl Scout activity in Lucerne Valley is from an April 1929 article in the *Lucerne Valley News*. This article was re-printed in an issue of the *Desert Grapevine*. It was written by Nina Baumgardner and Lorraine Koehly. It stated that the six girls had passed the Tenderfoot Test on March 16 and more were ex-pected to do so at the next meeting. That anyone wishing to acquaint themselves with the intri-cacies of knot-tying would do well to consult one of the Tenderfoot Girl Scouts, who are well-versed in the square knot, clove hitch, bop-line, sheep-shank and sheep-bend. The local Girl Scout troop is also mentioned in the June 1946 *Desert Grapevine,* which states, "The Girl Scouts are be-ing sponsored by the Women's Club. Flora Ann Clark and Mae Nolan are in charge for the present. Mae replaces Jean Rodda who resigned."

Though that is all the info we have on the early troops, we still have girls in the valley who fond-ly remember Barbara Veale as Girl Scout Leader for Troop 680. Barbara led the troop from 1970 through 1976, and Amy Scobey, was the cadet lead-er in 1976.

Millie Rad-er, who was a scout, re-members her

This photo taken of the first camp out in Pioneer Park features in no particular order, Scout Leader Barbara Veale. Teresa Miller, Sharon Miller, Kim Robertson, Millie Veale, Ilene Veale, Renate Becker, Lisa Miranda, Marcia Bron, Tamera Martini, Sandra Hoggatt, Jacque Kuehn, Mary Egan, and Penne LaRue.

mom, Barbara, who had never been camping, taking the girls on many camping trips. They camped in Pioneer Park the first time to figure out how to set up the tents and start the campfire while still close to home. After they learned to set up tents and cook their own meals, they camped at Calico and Jellystone Park in Yucca Valley. They also sold many Girl Scout cookies. Sherry (Yetto) Vaughn remembers Mrs. Veale teaching her to sew, so that she could earn her sewing badge.

Back Row, Cadet Scouts Jill Marshall, Jackie Reyes, and Julie DeWitt, front row, Scout Leader Amy Scobey, her daughter Rachael and Karen Byrne.

Teen Club

Fran (McDougall) Jones tells a fun story of how she and a handful of teens used to hang out at the park and the fire station. One day in 1969, they were trying to figure out something positive to do; the town had no ambulance so the kids decided to do fundraisers to purchase what was called a "Rescue Wagon."

Teen Club washing cars to raise money for the town's first ambulance. Photo courtesy of Lucerne Valley Leader Newspaper.

On August 18, 1970 Fire Captain Jerry Holloway drove the new Rescue Wagon to Lucerne Valley from the factory in Springfield, Ohio. Lucerne Valley has had its own ambulance ever since.

The group that called themselves, "Teens to the Rescue," included Fran, her cousins Patty, Chris and Teresa Hoffman, Ray and Diane Marty, Mike DeAuria, and Laura Mount. They held bake sales and car washes, but their biggest fundraiser, which turned out to be fun for the whole town, was a talent show patterned after the television show, "Laugh-In." Though the group raised a good chunk of money during the six months they worked at it, they soon went on to other things and others picked up the reins to gather in the final amount of money needed to purchase Lucerne Valley's first ambulance.

4-H Club
Millie Rader

We know there was a 4-H Club in Lucerne Valley as early as 1948 because Janine Gross Walker, who is still alive and kicking, remembers being a member. Somewhere along the way that early charter was dropped.

The earliest picture, found to date, of the local 4-H Club, was on the front page of the August 29, 1963 *Leader* newspaper. The headline reads, "Lucerne Valley Dudes 4-H Club receives charter." The three leaders pictured were Mrs. Eth-

New 1963 4-H Charter for the Lucerne Valley Dudes. Photo courtesy of Lucerne Valley Leader Newspaper.

In this 1963 photo Frank and Lloyd Francis practice their sheep judging skills at a recent agricultural judging school at Pacific High in San Bernardino.

el Owen, Mrs. Evelyn Kumley and Mrs. Joyce Raschke. The members were Judy Raschke, Jimmy Steingall, Janet Thrush, CarolMcDougall, Sharon McDougall, Vickie Raschke, Lilli Ann Owen, Bobby Kumley and Nancy Kumley. Not pictured were members Elizabeth Craig and Danny Curtis. They met with five other High Desert 4-H Clubs at the Apple Valley Junior High School for an awards night. The Lucerne Valley club was the newest to receive a charter.

On the same page was an article titled "Fair Winners." It lists Lilli Ann Owen, Nancy Kumley and Carole McDougall as winning firsts in the 4-H clothing-textiles division for their ABC's of clothing. They had each made an apron. The club was off to a fast start. In June 1965 Lucerne Valley 4-H Club hosted a "Round Robin" gymkhana at Midway Park with competition between Apple Valley, Hesperia and Lucerne Valley clubs. Mrs. Arnhart and Mrs. Cherry supervised the food booth. The local judge was Vern Smith. Other local officials were Mac McQuown and Dean Maxwell, Mrs. Curtis and Mrs. Garton were scorekeepers, Hattie Gibson was master of ceremonies and Bill Barnett, Russ Cherry and Ed Arnhart were advisors. The charter was sponsored by the Lucerne Valley Sheriff's Posse.

The 4-H charter was still quite active in the 1970s, with this writer participating in dog training and bike riding. Hector and Pat Lugo were leaders with help from Ginger Regensberg. They had guide dogs, a bike club, animal husbandry and many of the members exhibited lambs and cows at the San Bernardino County Fair. Members also entered jams, jellies, pies and cakes and handmade items, which brought home many a blue ribbon. They also participated in the Lucerne Valley Independence Day Parade and park activities every year.

The 4-H Club provided Lucerne Valley children opportunities they would not have had before the high school was built in 1992. With the opening of the new school, Future Farmers of America (FFA) became available and though our local 4-H club did continue for awhile, it is not active at this time.

This photo was taken May 4, 1972. Left is "Scamp" and his trainer Sandi Lugo, right is Cherry LaRue with her 4-H Guide Dog trainee, three-month old "Kovak." Scamp had spent most of the year with Sandi undergoing basic obedience training under the supervision of County Liaison Officer for Guide Dogs, Myra McGinnis. Little Kovak was to begin his training with Cherry June at the Canine Courtesy Club.

Photos courtesy of Lucerne Valley Leader Newspaper.

Joshua Riders / ETI

Article in the Desert Grapevine by Lorraine Knowlton written sometime between 1948 and 1950.

That October, about 65 Lucerne Valley people formed the nucleus of the Lucerne Valley Joshua Riders, an organization for the education and pleasure of the family unit through their interest in horses.

Under the leadership of Bill Beardsley and Vernon Smith, the club was organized and activated when Vernon Smith was installed as President, Bill Barnett as Vice-President, Betty Hamel as Secretary, and Lena Barnett as Treasurer. Dues were set at $3 per year, per family.

They had riding instructions for the teenagers taught by Bill Barnett, and square dance instruction for the small fry under the direction of Bill Beardsley. There were also special get-together activities and rides as weather permits.

November 12, 1970 Little Danny Ray Regensberg captured High Point trophy and eight first places in Junior Division with the Lucerne Valley ETI Corral 25 at an Apple Valley High School gymkhana. Photo courtesy of Lucerne Valley Leader Newspaper.

The initiators of this club wanted this group to be one, in which, the entire family can be together and enjoy activities that will help to bring back that "homey" feeling of the days when settlers were few and far between, and everyone knew everyone else.

(According to Lorraine's son, George Knowlton, this article was written sometime between 1948 and 1950.)

This organization does not exist today, but was a forerunner for today's, Equestrian Trails Incorporated (ETI). In 1972, the Lucerne Valley ETI was Corral 25. Now it is Corral 70 and is combined with Apple Valley but the Midway Park Harold Keesee Sr. Arena is used as their main venue.

Rodeo Queen Janie Moretz garners high point trophy in senior division proving her riding talents that goes along with beauty. Photo by Ginger Regensberg.

Challenge Trophy winner is Judy Raschke, who snared high point honors among adults, and gains overall title at meet, in which Lucerne Valley riders score clean sweep! Photo by GingerRegensberg.

Lucerne Springs Pool / LVPAC / Russell Park

Swimming lessons and summer fun are the memories that many still have for what is now known as Russell Park. This park was created in 1959 by those who homesteaded what is now known as the Russell Tract, so named for the two brothers who attracted investors to "homestead" that area. The brothers, Bill and John Russell's parents, had homesteaded 160 acres there in 1911. (See the rest of their story in the *Characters Chapter*). The family donated the land to build a

Artist rendering of proposed Lucerne Springs Pool. Photo courtesy of Lucerne Valley Leader Newspaper. B 8-1

1970s swim lessons. Photo courtesy of Lucerne Valley Leader Newspaper.

place for their little community to gather.

The original name, shown in the *Leader* newspaper clipping was Lucerne Springs Club Recreational Center. (The name came from the springs left behind by military practice bombs dropped when the area was used as a target practice range during World War II) They had originally planned a 26 x 60 foot pool with barbecues and picnic pavilion, playground, tennis and volleyball courts and clubhouse. All came to fruition except the clubhouse.

For many years this facility served those with neighboring properties, who could afford to pay the

$200 annual membership. Those who lived outside of the Russell tract were invited to enjoy the pool in the 1970s, when Marie Russell started a swimming lesson program. Harold Keesee Jr. and Marie's daughter, Patti LaRue Smith taught the lessons that were enjoyed by many a kid, including the writer of this chapter.

In a 2004 *Leader* Newspaper article, Bryn Risler wrote:

"The Lucerne Springs Club, Inc has been closed and all assets

Full pool. Photo courtesy of Lucerne Valley Leader Newspaper. B 8-1

(the pool and property) have been donated to the recently organized Lucerne Valley Pool and Activities Center (LVPAC). This has long been a dream for many community ac-

Basketball Court. Photo courtesy of Millie Rader. B 8-1

tivists including Bill and Carolyn Russell, Helen Beikman, Harriet Pritchard and Janice Horst. This is a community project built upon the goals and dreams of the Lucerne Valley pioneers, who wanted a community pool available to all Lucerne Valley residents.

There have been numerous challenges over the years. Because of the design of the club and the bylaws, there was very little flexibility for the club to function. When the Lucerne Springs Club was built in the 1960s, the facility use was limited to

Playground. Photo courtesy of Millie Rader. B 8-1

residents of the Lucerne Springs housing tract. In the 1980s, the club invited all Lucerne Valley residents to join for a yearly membership fee. In 2000, Bill Russell, Helen Beikman, Fran and Jeff Muller, Bryn Risler, Jon and Becky Bush and others decided it was time to change the corporation to better meet the needs of the community. Thus

Modern Sign. Photo courtesy of Millie Rader. B 8-1

the Lucerne Valley Pool and Activities Center was created as a 501C-3 corporation.

LVPAC operated as long as it could with donations from the local mines and community, but eventually found that insurance and maintenance costs were too much. The property sat idle for a time before CSA Park Manager Reese Troublefield and Municipal Advisory Council President Richard Selby worked to have the property accepted into the CSA 29 County Park system.

The San Bernardino County Supervisors led by Third District Supervisor James Ramos allocated nearly $90,000 to renovate the park.

The new park grand opening was held April 8, 2016, with the Lucerne Valley Elementary School third grade classes bussed over to enjoy the new playground equipment.

On April 21, 2016, the Lucerne Valley and Johnson Valley Municipal Advisory Council(MAC) passed a resolution to name the new park, The Russell Park, after its original benefactors. The MAC board and others raised $1,400 to purchase a plaque honoring the Russell Family, which was placed in the park at a ceremony led by Third District Supervisor James Ramos.

Parent Teacher Association (PTA) / Booster Club

Photos courtesy of Lucerne Valley Leader.

The start-up date for the Lucerne Valley PTA is unknown, but we do know that Pam Pinard Turner was very involved. According to Martha Rader, Pam gathered the information to put together the history of the schools. That history is featured in this book. She was also instrumental in creating the Irish Stew and

Past Presidents honored in 1978. Right to left, Francis Hanken 44-46, Marjorie Reed 47-48, Dorothy Moore 56 and 58, Martha Rader 67-68, Jo Terry 58-59, Alice Bristol 72-73, Pamela Turner 73-74, Rosemary French 76-77.

talent shows to raise money for the Halloween Carnival, and other student activities. Rader said Pam came up with ideas, like Lifetime Membership Awards, and had the original school bell moved to the elementary school, where it is displayed on the front lawn to this day. (See *School Chapter*). The local schools no longer belong to PTA. In 2011 at the request of Danielle Weir, Keri Gasper researched both PTA and Booster Club rules and found that there would be more freedom with a Booster Club. Keri, her parents Pat and Lou Gasper, along with Joe Miller and Kim Evans, Britta Smith, Larry Kennedy helped to form the club. Within two years,

Pam Turner and Harriet Yetto decorate tea cups for each of the women who attended the 1975 Mother-Daughter-Tea.

Newly installed Executive Board of the LVPTA. From left to right: Katie Reeves, Pres. Pamela Turner, 1st Vice Ann Brewer, 2nd Vice Sara Delperdang, Secretary Martha Rader, Auditor Liz Southern, Historian Alice Bristol, Parliamentarian absent due to illness, Judy Ruttledge, Treasurer.

The PTA Mother-Daughter-Tea also provided a fashion show. In this bridal scene the bride and her attendants were portrayed by (left to right) Sherry Yetto, Melanie Yetto, CaSandra Hoggatt and Shawna Martin. All the dresses were made by Harriet Yetto.

the club was an official 501c3 non-profit. Keri said this year Sarah Courtney is on board as well.

The booster club handles all the school fundraising. Students are given the option to participate in all fundraisers, with chances to earn prizes and each year the Booster Club puts on a "DJ" party for all of the students who participated.

Two large student events are also planned and funded by the Booster Club each year: a Fall Festival and a Year-End Carnival. Gasper said the Booster Club was able to give each grade level $1,000 for field trips this year.

1975 Mother-Daughter-Tea, Jo Terry (right) was the happy winner of the bride cake decorated by Pam Turner (left). Little Miss Firecracker Leslie Delperdang drew the winning ticket.

Photo courtesy of Millie Rader. A 8-2

Chamber of Commerce (C of C)

According to incorporation papers found in the Chamber records by current Office Manager, Maureen Jordan, the Lucerne Valley Chamber of Commerce was incorporated May 21, 1956.

First there was the Lucerne Valley Improvement Association and then the Booster's Club in the 1940s, as the group worked to attract residents and businesses to our lovely valley. The Chamber of Commerce came next. An article in a February, 1964 *San Bernardino County Sun* reported the LV C of C launched a campaign to bring State

Highway 138 from Pear Blossom through Lucerne Valley to Yucca Valley and ultimately to Parker and the Colorado River. After six years, the work of the chamber and others was rewarded when a State Route (Highway 247) was designated in 1969 to connect State Route 62 in Yucca Valley to Interstate 15 in Barstow. It wasn't quite what the chamber had envisioned but it still brings people traveling across California to view our little town.

The chamber puts on the Annual Independence Day Parade and runs the contest for

1963 first separate office for the Lucerne Valley Chamber of Commerce, located at 31391 Highway 18. Photo courtesy of Lucerne Valley Leader Newspaper. A 8-2

The Chamber's Board of Directors includes: Seated from left to right, Bette Murie, Carol Turner, Ralph Chamney, Ray Clark. Standing, Warren Ritter, Bob Clark, Ernie Gommel, Russ Jones; Not shown, Elain Fielder, Joe Visosky, Sr., F.M. Van Norman and Lorene Cone. Photo courtesy of Lucerne Valley Leader Newspaper.

Honorary Mayor each year. Beryl McDougall was our very first Honorary Mayor.

The chamber office now sits on the north side of the "Y" intersection where State Route Highway 18 heads toward Big Bear. The women's division of the chamber later became, as what we now know as the Roadrunners.

This group, though birthed within the C of C, later became an independent non-profit group whose focus was to raise money for the children of Lucerne Valley.

Roadrunners

This active group of local women began as the "Women's Division of the Chamber in 1976 for the purpose of keeping the chamber office open and raising funds to further the mission of the organization.. As they slowly began focusing more and more on providing the local children with events, they renamed themselves The Roadrunners and in 2000 applied and received 501c3 non-profit status as the Lucerne Valley Roadrunners, Inc.

According to Shirley Clemmons, who joined the group in 1986, The Roadrunners put on the Biker Toy Run, Christmas Party, Easter Egg Hunt, Halloween Tailgate and many other functions throughout the year. They produced the first Roadrunner Cook Book in 1976, using recipes contributed by townspeople and have since produced a total of 5 cookbooks. This group also provides college scholarships each year to graduating Lucerne Valley High School seniors.

Clarice Peterson told us that some of the charter members were Barbara Gommel, Carol Turner, Janice Horst, Darlene Johnson, Dori Killman. Jo Richards found the Roadrunner scrapbook at the Senior Center, which contains a picture of the first Roadrunner Board Members who were installed on February 27, 1976. They were: Millie

Photo from Roadrunner Scrap Book.

Edwards, Dori Harbert, Flo Johnson, Yvonne Martin, Ellie Filippi, Rita Channey and Ida May Chamberlin. We cannot be sure if we have a complete list of the original Roadrunners, but between Clarice's memory and Jo's research, we have quite a few of them.

According to current member, Jo Richards, the second wave of Roadrunners who are active today are Clarice Peterson, who came on in 1977, then Diane Holland, Shirley Clemmons (deceased 2018), and Jo Richards who all came a few years later.

Getting in the Spirit of '76 and smiling in anticipation of the three day celebration coming up in July are the ladies of the new board of directors of the Chamber of Commerce Women's Division. Seated from left are Secretary Dori Harbert, Vice President Millie Edwards, president Carol Turner, and Treasurer Flo Johnson. Standing are elected directors Yvonne Martin, Ellie Fillipi and Rita Chamney, parliamentarian Darlene Johnson, and immediate past President Ida May Chamberlin.

LVEDA

Lucerne Valley Economic Development Association (LVEDA) is a non-profit organization serving the unincorporated community of Lucerne Valley, CA and surrounding areas.

According to Linda Gommel, who took the minutes for the first meeting, LVEDA was started in 1996, when Ernie Gommel addressed the Lucerne Valley Chamber of Commerce about the terrible economy of Lucerne Valley following

Meeting at the Lucerne Valley Senior Center.
Photo courtesy of Lucerne Valley Leader Newspaper.

the extended recession in the High Desert. Real estate had collapsed, George AFB had closed, and it wasn't looking good for the High Desert as a whole.

His message was that something had to be done as a community to keep business at home and to attract more businesses. The Chamber of Commerce (C of C) agreed and a task force of the Chamber, with the name LVEDA, was born. It was modeled after High Desert REDA (Regional Economic Development Association), in which Gommel had participated and had appreciated its approach to working on the economy for the area as a whole.

In attendance at the first meeting on April 22, 1996, were: Steve Cox representing VEDA and REDA, Chuck Bell local farmer and a member of the MAC and San Bernardino County Planning Commission, Marie Brashear local resident, Jan Morosco manager of First Mountain Bank, Joann Tylick-Lawson resident, Ernest Gommel manager of Lucerne Valley Market civil engineer, Linda Gommel drafted to take first minutes of LVEDA, Sergeant Errol Bechtel deputy sheriff, Norm Nichols member of Translator and Park and Rec Committees, Barbara Veale long time resident President of People for the West,

Chuck Rader giving a report at LVEDA 2003. Photo courtesy of Lucerne Valley Leader Newspaper.

Doug Shumway environmental manager of Mitsubishi Cement Corp., Ron Peavy Superintendent of Schools and member of the Chamber of Commerce.

After a few years, LVEDA became the independent nonprofit organization it is now, with its purpose to provide a forum for people to come hear or express issues of importance. It also provides a focal point for outsiders – politicians, county staffers,

LVEDA Tour - CSA 29 office-Dan Flores, Josie Gonzales, Jean Magee, James Ramos, Bev Lowry, Chuck Bell, Linda Gommel, Roger Peterson, Richard Selby. Photo courtesy of Lucerne Valley Leader Newspaper.

etc, to come to speak to concerned citizens about whatever issue they have. This alone has been the biggest contribution.

Currently, LVEDA has been active in the many fights to keep our desert protected from efforts at all levels to install industrial size "renewable energy" projects all over the valley. Chuck Bell also writes letters of support/opposition on these issues, with the weight of the community behind him.

LVEDA has also been involved in trying to initiate a senior living community on the donated 109 acres east of the Lucerne Valley Market.

Lions Club

According to the late Art Bristol, the Lucerne Valley Lions Club was formed in 1947. Art, who was 94 at the time, joined the club in 1958. Bob McDougall, who is age 98 now, is the only charter member who is still active today. An early slogan of Lucerne Valley was "Live here, live longer," that seems to apply, especially, to Lions Club members.

In 1960, the Leader Newspaper announced the installation of new officers: President Barney Tennis a plumbing contractor, Vice-President John Russell Contractor, Tail Twister "Doc" Ferguson an electrician, Lion Tamer Percy Kortkamp retired, Secretary-Treasurer Harley Van Zee a poultryman, Public Relations Bill Donaldson guest ranch owner, Bulletin Editor Jack Pinard editor, Director Red Stillwell Deputy Sheriff, and Director Bob Kumley contractor. Outgoing President was John Hudson, *Leader* Newspaper founder and editor. During that year they provided for five underprivileged children and started the Cemetery Fund, providing many man hours to fence the Cemetery. They also helped to develop Pioneer Park.

In 1960 the Lions raised the money and the volunteer labor force to erect over 1200 feet of 5 foot fencing around what is now the east side of the cemetery. Photo courtesy of Lucerne Valley Leader Newspaper.

A July 2, 1970, article reported that Lion Bob McDougall, a veteran well driller, had struck water at 45 feet on the Lion's Gun Range property. The well was to be 150 feet deep when completed and would provide more than enough water to meet the needs of the Gun Range. They had also completed the fence that year.

The goals for the following year were restroom facilities, shaded play area for children, trees, shrubs and perhaps a building to be used as combination Range house and storehouse. Their future plans also included rifle lanes and skeet range. The Lion President that year was Don Chase, who announced the Lions Summer Sweepstakes, in which one lucky person, who

Lions hit water. Photo courtesy of Lucerne Valley Leader Newspaper.

purchased sweepstake tickets, would win a 1/3 acre lot in the Lucerne Vista Estates or an all expense paid overnight trip to Disneyland for the entire family. The drawing would be held at the Lion's third annual Buffalo-Beef Barbecue.

The Lucerne Valley Lions Club operates a shooting range, as the primary fundraiser, to support their various charities. Lion's Pride Park is open to the public only on specific days, so please check the schedule and hours of operation when planning a visit.

The Lucerne Valley Lions Club is one of the largest

This 1963 photo has first Resident Sheriff's Deputy and Lion's Club President Red Stillwell confirming that the first Lion's Gun Club sign was pointing in the right direction. Photo courtesy of Lucerne Valley Leader.

Lions gun Range Double Bar Regulators. Photo courtesy of Lucerne Valley Leader Newspaper. B 8-3

Lions organizations in the High Desert due, in part, to the high tech gun range, as well as the archery range and monthly shooting programs, such as "Women on Target" and NRA shooting classes.

The club also hosts a Cowboy Action Shooting Club called the Double R Bar Regulators. This group meets monthly and the public is invited to come relive the old west by dressing like those from the 1800s. You can relive a shooting, in the town of Chimney Rock, with era six shooters, lever action rifles and shotguns used by cowboys to protect their family and property from the bad guys. For a schedule of events go to lvlionsclub.com.

Museum
Photos courtesy of Lucerne Valley Museum Association.

The Lucerne Valley Museum was originally a satellite of the San Bernardino County Museum Society. To quote an April 28, 1960 article in the *Leader* newspaper written by Francis Hanken, "Permission has been given by the directors of the county society to establish a branch of their (museum) organization to function under their guidance and with their help."

According to the current Lucerne Valley Museum brochure, Lucerne Valley received its museum charter on May 8, 1965, under the leadership of President Francis Hankin. It was sponsored by the Women's Division of the Chamber of Commerce and meetings were first held in the multipurpose room of the Lucerne

Valley Elementary School.

There were probably many Museum presidents over the years, but we have record of Orville Green being elected president on June 15, 1983, and of the meetings being moved to the LV Community Center that November. During Orville's tenure, the Lucerne Valley Museum separated from San Bernardino County Museum and became a separate entity in April of 1985. He acquired showcases and displays, and established the current Outdoor Display, located just

Local artifacts displayed in outdoor museum. A 5-5

west of the Community Center and east of the Janice Horst Library. Green was able to bring in more members with presentations, field trips, and potluck dinners and membership grew to over 250 by December of 1989.

The Museum Association is currently raising funds to construct a building east of the Lucerne Valley Library to house local artifacts currently in storage. Any money raised from the sales of this book will be added to this fund.

Many local people have been instrumental in keeping the Museum moving forward including; Barbara LaGrainge, past-president Chuck Rader, Martha Rader, Bernadette Gudgins, Ida Mae Chamberlin, Ethel Watson, Gilbert Sr and Gilbert Jr Tegelberg, Francis

Past museum President Chuck Rader organizing the "Green" room.

Left, current museum President Barbara (Rusty) LaGrange giving a tour. Right, museum members Martha Rader and Chelsea LaGrange sifting through the treasures.

Tegelberg, Francis Hanken, Joe and Florence Elnicky, Irene Welbrand, Joe and Janice Horst, Al Sliger, Elaine Leatherman, Scott Lasley, Barbara Jo Jones, past president Louis Kannenberg, and current president Chelsea LaGrange, to name only a few.

Pioneer Park

Compiled by Millie Rader. Photo courtesy of
Lucerne Valley Leader Newspaper.

Pioneer Park Veterans Memorial. A 8-4

According to Ethel Owen's *Quick History*, Orlando (Jake) and Mildred Jacobs moved to the valley in 1928. There were about 250 people in Lucerne Valley then, and Mildred and Jake jumped right in to help provide for this community. At the Jacobs home in North Valley, Jake baked 60 or 70 loaves of bread, sweet rolls, cakes and pies on Saturdays and sold them through Max Lewis' grocery store. Later he rented from Goulding the building that still sits on Highway 18 at the end of Highland Road, and established Homestead Bakery and Grocery. At the same

Restrooms built by Lions still standing. A 8-4

time Mildred ran the Jackrabbit Cafe, located on land now occupied by the Valero Gas Station and Mini-Mart. In 1936 Jake and Mildred moved their house onto land they bought from the Southern Pacific Railroad on the corner of Barstow Rd. and Old Woman Springs Rd, where the Lucerne Valley Market sign sits today. The Jacobs later donated 10 acres of their land to the community for what is now called Pioneer Park. As Jake's health failed, Mildred gave up the cafe and ran the Homestead Bakery. She still found time to clear and plant for the Park along with other citizens.

Ethel does not mention the date of when the land was donated or the park begun, but we do know that the Lions Club built the block restroom building that still stands today, and we know that the Lions Club was formed in 1947 so it must have been shortly after that. Clifford Reed remembers that the park was created around the time that he started going

Pioneer Park Placque – Orlando Jacobs.

Pioneer Park plaque, John Koehly.

Pioneer Park Monument. A 8-4

to junior high school in Victorville and that would be 1952. In the middle of the sidewalk, about 20 feet from the park's front gate, is a stone monument drinking fountain, that according to Floyd Thomason was built by his grandfather. On the north side of the monument a plaque is built into the rock work. It is in memory of John Koehly, husband of our first Postmistress Rosa Koehly. Below John's name it says "A Valley Pioneer," with the date 1864-1952. This plaque is built into the monument. On the South side of the monument is another plaque that is not built into the rock work but was attached later. It reads "In Memory of Orlando Jacobs Donor of this Park, 1897-1957." According to Mrs. Owen' writings above, Mildred found time to help plant the park as Jake's health was failing. Between Cliff's memory and Mr. Koehly's plaque we are taking a wild guess that the park was begun

Circa 1967 original play equipment. Celebrating his second birthday was Philip Dean Pederson. The helpers with him at his celebration were: Danny Ray & Jon Mark Regensberg, Leslie & Linda Sue Delperdang and the little one is Mrs. Mildred Jacobs' great grandson Eric.

Pioneer Park Playground 2018. A 8-4

sometime in 1952.

In the early years, the park was planted and maintained by the local citizenry. It was probably around 1962 when the county took it into the CSA 29 Park District.

Today the park has a modern playground,

Pioneer Park tables, 1967. A 8-4

Grobaty Field sign. A 8-4

picnic area with barbeques, tennis courts, basketball court, a Veteran's Memorial, two ball fields, one dedicated to Dick Grobaty and one dedicated to Josie Reyes and a Skate Park.

In this chapter titled *What the Hicks do for Kicks*, you will find memories of grown Little Leaguers who played baseball in Pioneer Park on a dirt field in the 1960s and early 1970s. Now, the lawns are lush, and the trees, of which many have been there since the park's inception, are reaching for the sky, creating a cool grassy place for kids to throw a ball or play tag. We hear many an outsider comment in amazement, that a small desert town would have such a beautiful oasis, Pioneer Park.

Pioneer Park Ball Backstop. A 8-4

Root Diggers

The Root Diggers, Lucerne Valley Genealogy Association, was established in 1992 when, according to Martha Rader, Dottie Kerns who was associated with the Hi-Desert Genealogical Society twisted her arm to help her start a Lucerne Valley Association. Martha was part of the Friends of the Library and with those connections, the association was able to hold its meetings in the county Library. The group which consists of members from all over the High Desert and beyond, now meet at the Community Center.

Some of the original Root Diggers. Seated (L to R): Martha Rader, Cam Classen, Dottie Kern. Standing (L to R): Freda Robinson, Florence Pettigrew, Elizabeth Sadler, Elizabeth Peters, Bernadette Gudgins, Jill Forrest, Karen Payne and Noreva Shar. Photo courtesy of Lucerne Valley Leader Newspaper.

James Goulding's daughter, Minnie Barrow, came to the Root Diggers and asked why there was nothing in the town named for her father, James Goulding. Martha and Dottie went to the school board and received permission to name the Elementary School Multi-purpose room after Goulding. Local artists including Bette Murie, June Fuller, Jim Bell, Martha and Chuck Rader painted pictures of all of the different school buildings and created a display that still hangs in Goulding Hall. An official Goulding Hall dedication was held at the site on May 15, 1993.

Moose Lodge

The December 12, 1974 issue of the *Lucerne Valley Leader* features a picture and story of the Moose members breaking ground at their current site on Foothill Road. The 5-acre parcel was donated by Mr. and Mrs. Frank Russell. The plan was to erect a 60 by 100 foot prefabricated metal building built by Armco.

Mr. Russell and Moose Governor Dale Burkes did the groundbreaking, using the same chrome shovel as was used for the elementary school, the school garage and the Bank of America ceremonies.

Ground Breaking. Photo courtesy of Lucerne Valley Leader Newspaper.

Present for the ceremony were Chamber of Commerce President Joe Visosky and wife, Terry, *Leader* correspondent Jack O'Malley, *Daily Press* columnist Doris Lattin, manager of the Lucerne Valley Branch Bank of America Dorcas Gross, Honorary Mayor candidates Edie Roscon and Vernon Hayes. Gladys Nelson, the current Honorary Mayor was unable to attend. Speakers were Dale Burkes and Bill Preddy. Dori Harbert and Jack Sutton provided the dance music. The Moose had occupied the Dome building on Highway 18/Trade

Grand Opening. Photo courtesy of Lucerne Valley Leader Newspaper. B 8-5

Post Road for 5 1/2 years , but set no date for the move to their new location.

A June 2, 1977 article features the Grand Opening, with a picture of the building and a group of local members including a few not mentioned above such as Deane Norris, Roy Malone cutting the ribbon. Al Lynch, Ken Towner, Dick Clement, F.M. Van Norman, Lee Risler, Bud Miller, Roger Brann, Bernie and Bessie Eringdale, Bula Johnson, and Mr. and Mrs. Lyle Brazil.

An electrical problem sparked a two-alarm fire at the Moose Lodge at 2:05 the morning of July 27, 2012, causing an estimated $400,000 damage. County firefighters faced challenges in battling the blaze because there were no fire hydrants in the area. They fought the fire for 2 1/2 hours, keeping the flames from spreading beyond the restaurant portion of the building. The business had been closed at the time of the fire and there were no injuries.

The building was completely renovated in less than a year.

VFW

VFW hosted their charter dinner in August 1971. (At the time of this edit, no further info has been found.)

Photo courtesy of Millie Rader.
B 8-6

Library

Ethel Owen wrote, in 1988, that the Lucerne Valley Library history began in 1912, with 140 books in the front room of the Box S Ranch house. Most of the books were for school use, but some could be borrowed by local residents.

In 1915 the library was at Midway School and was officially recognized as a branch of the San Bernardino County Library.

In 1916 a storm damaged some of the books and the Library was moved to the Boom Ranch, on Wilshire, northeast of Midway.

After being closed during World War I, both Mid-

Lucerne Valley Library 1956. Ruthie Shaw, Harold Reed, and Eva Shaw. Photo courtesy of Lucerne Valley Museum Association. A 7-12

way School and the library re-opened in September 1918. The library continued as a combination school/public library until March, 1928 when it became a Community Branch of the San Bernardino County Library System.

When the Lucerne school building was condemned for school use, the Library moved in. Then the church bought the building and the library stayed, but was moved into a smaller room. Later it was moved into a small, trailer behind the

New Library building in 1988. Photo taken by Fran Jones, courtesy of Lucerne Valley Museum Association. A 8-7

present China House Restaurant. Ethel Windschanz Clafton, the librarian, said that looking out the little, porthole-shaped windows during a strong wind made her feel like she was on a sinking ship.

The library moved again to the building that, in 1988, was occupied by the Sheriff's office (probably at the corner of State Highway 247 where the feed store is now). Mrs. Vera Russell (John Russell's mother) was one of the librarians at that location. In 1968 the library moved into the south-facing building in the Lucerne Val-

Lucerne Valley Janice Horst Branch Library with addition, 2017. Photo courtesy of Millie Rader. A 8-7

ley Shopping Center. This building had generously been built and provided by John Russell, at very low rent, for the purpose of housing the library.

The books stayed at that location until March 1988 when they were moved into their beautiful, new 3,000 square foot, permanent library home on Highway 247 and Allen Way; groundbreaking was on March 17, 1988.

The building was expanded by 1,000 feet in 2004 by local Contractor, Bob Riddle. The expansion was made possible through the tireless dedication of Janice Horst, who pushed the San Bernardino County Library System, the county Supervisors, and the local community and mines to raise the funds, to make this expansion possible. The library is now called the Lucerne Valley Janice Horst Branch Library.

Janice Horst
Library Champion

This article was written By Emily Berg, *Daily Press* Staff Writer, May 4, 2004.

Janice Horst was tenacious, detailed and had a passion to see the best library in her community. The 94-year-old Lucerne Valley woman died in November after 49 years in the rural community, but not without knowing that the library, which now bears her name, would have a long-awaited expansion. The 1,000-square-foot expansion of a community room to house adult and children's programs opened Monday at the Janice Horst Lucerne Valley Branch Library. About 100 people attended the library's reopening, and many remembered Janice Horst and her tireless efforts for the library. "She did it really so she could help people," said Dick Horst, her son. Dick Horst said his mother appreciated the recognition, but that wasn't what made her push for a library in the community and then the expansion. He hopes her work

Janice Horst Memorial plaque that hangs on the west wall of the main room of the Lucerne Valley Janice Horst Branch Library.

inspires others to do all they can for their community. The Friends of the Library, San Bernardino County Supervisors, and local mining companies helped pay for the addition.

"Mitsubishi Cement donated $50,000, Specialty Minerals donated $25,000 and Omya donated $10,000," said local Branch Librarian Myra Andrest. "First District Supervisor Bill Postmus contributed $175,000 of First District funding to the project, and the Friends of the Library raised $25,000. This was really a joint effort," said Andrest.

"This is a good example of your tax dollars being put to good use," Postmus said. "The project was finished on time by local contractor, Bob Riddle, and did not exceed its budget," he said.

Friends of the Library

This organization has been active in Lucerne Valley since at least 1975, when the December issue of the *Lucerne Valley Leader* published a picture of the group hosting a book sale in front the Library then located in the Lucerne Valley Shopping Center. The caption stated that the "Friends" brought in over $200 that was to be used to purchase a glass display case. The librarian at the time was Lorraine Sherman.

According to longtime member Martha Rader, the organization started when the Library was in the Green Oval Building that was located behind, what is now, the China House Restaurant. Mrs. Hollenbeck was librarian at that time, and was instrumental in getting the Friends started.

1975 Friends of the Library book sale in front of a past location of the Lucerne Valley Leader office. (Currently the location of the Center Water Company office. The Library was located at that time in the space to the right of the Leader office in what was then the north end of the Lucerne Valley Shopping Center. At the time of this writing, 2018, the current occupant is "Quality Treasures." Photo courtesy of the Leader. A 7-9

Current Friends are Martha Rader, Fran Muller, Shirley Clemmons (deceased 2018), Sharon Ravenstein, Pam Hart, Diane Krenek, and the current librarian, Robin Hawley.

Burro Races

All the action in the Burrow Race doesn't take place with the wranglers on the road. This picture was taken in Pioneertown, before the race started for the day, as the burros were being caught and numbered. Packs were then attempted to be put in place. Along with unidentified ropers and spectators, Captain Leon Ellis, Commander of the Victorville Sher-

Photo courtesy of Lucerne Valley Leader Newspaper August 1965

Burro sponsored by Lucerne Valley's Dale Wilson. Photo courtesy Lucerne Valley Museum Association.

iff's Substation is working down the lariat preparing to bulldog the unwilling burro. Making a loop at the far right is Lucerne Valley Rancher, Ralph Miller.

Moviemaking in Lucerne Valley

Compiled by Bill Lembright

In his book *Raising The Dust*, Junie Gobar tells how in the 1920s, Max Lewis, a newcomer to Lucerne Valley, convinced some film-making companies to film here. The first to respond was likely the Fox Film Co., who released John Ford's 1926 silent, classic western, *3 Bad Men*. This was during the Depression and local residents were paid $5 per day serving as extras. This boosted the local economy.

In that film, three outlaws spot the covered wagon of a father and his daughter, separated from the wagon train due to a broken

Photo courtesy of Lucerne Valley Museum Association.

wagon wheel. The outlaws attack the unfortunates and steal their horses; but as they approach

Photo courtesy of Lucerne Valley Museum Association.

the duo, a group of thugs get to the wagon first, also intent on stealing the horses. A gunfight ensues and the 3 bad men drive off the other bad men. During the gunfight, however, the girl's father is killed. As the 3 outlaws approach, the grieving daughter runs to one of them, and weeping, she buries her head on one of their shoulders, softening the outlaws' hearts. The remainder of the movie shows these former bad men helping the daughter and fighting evil on many fronts… becoming champions of right, truth, and justice.

The next film produced here was *Sundown Slim*, a silent western distributed by the Universal Film Distributing Company, produced by, and star-

Stagecoach jump to horse. Photo courtesy of Lucerne Valley Museum. B 8-8

ring Harry Carey. This production was more self-contained and contributed less to the local economy, but was very entertaining to locals.

In 1928 *The Pioneer Scout* starring Fred Thomson was produced. Once again locals were paid $5 per day and fed a big lunch. "Gobar Ranch sold hay to the company, rented the ground for tent houses, furnished water, and rented equipment," used in the production. Junie's eight year old son, Kenny, was paid $10 a day to play a miniature cowboy. Big money in those days, especially for a little tyke.

Rifling through the Leader is TV star Chuck Connors. Chuck and the crew from Four Star Films were on location in Lucerne Valley for several days.

In the film, Fred Thomson is the scout of a wagon train heading to California; encountering numerous dangers upon the way. His famous horse, Silver King, wins a big race and saves his life from an evil saloon keeper's henchmen.

From the *Daily Press*, we learned that in 1939 John Ford returned to Lucerne Valley to direct the filming of *Stagecoach*, starring John Wayne, Claire Trevor, and Andy Devine. This is one of the most famous westerns of all time. One of the most death-defying stunts in film history, at that time, was performed on Rabbit Dry Lake by Yakima Canutt. He jumped from his galloping horse onto the stage coach's galloping lead horses, lowered himself between them to disconnect their harnesses, and then let the horses and racing stagecoach pass over his vulnerable body at full speed.

In 1955, Universal Pictures filmed portions of the science fiction monster film, *Tarantula* at Dead Man's Point. Sixteen year old Barbara Veale was among the locals who watched it being filmed. A monster spider, bigger than the rock pile, is not hurt by the gunfire of the sheriff and his deputies. The sheriff also tries to dynamite the monster on Bear Valley Road, but to no avail. Finally, the air force is called in and

*James Garner filming in 1971. Photo courtesy
of Lucerne Valley Museum Association.*

kills the tarantula with a napalm attack. This was pretty entertaining stuff for Lucerne Valley.

In 1977, Ron Howard directed the production of the film, *Grand Theft Auto*, partly filmed in Lucerne Valley and other High Desert towns. In the film, two young people played by Ron Howard and Nancy Morgan elope, against their parent's wishes, in Nancy's parent's Rolls-Royce. This featured one of our most abundant resources, bouncy dirt roads. Many cars are destroyed, as in a giant demolition derby, but the two lovers escaped and were married.

From the *Daily Press*, we also found that in 2008 parts of the movie *Valkyrie* were filmed in Lucerne Valley. In WWII, the British Royal Air Force bombed a group of Nazi soldiers which resulted in the disfiguring wounds sustained by Colonel Claus (played by Tom Cruise). Two vintage P-40 Warhawks expertly navigated the rock formations of Cougar Buttes, in Lucerne Valley, for the scene.

These are only a few of the movies filmed in and around our valley. The remote beauty of Lucerne Valley has attracted many characters over the years, and likely will continue to do so in the future.

*Filming "Tarantula" at Dead Man's Point. Photo
courtesy of Lucerne Valley Museum Association. B-8-9*

*Filming "Grand Theft Auto." Photo courtesy
of Lucerne Valley Museum Association.*

*Filming of "On Any Sunday." Photo courtesy
of Lucerne Valley Museum Association.*

Motorcycle Races - Rescue 3

Photos courtesy of Chuck and Martha Rader.

Hare and Hound Race Chuck Rader, circa 1950s.

When motorcycle racers come to challenge themselves in the Lucerne Valley/Johnson Valley desert, they are supported by a group known as Rescue 3. Made up of experienced desert explorers, many who have personally raced these courses themselves, this dependable group is there to assist lost or hurt riders. They are based out of Barstow, but

Big Bear run in the snow, 1955.

have members from Lucerne Valley as well. Chuck and Martha Rader joined the group in the mid-1970s after Chuck decided to give up desert racing, but still wanted to be involved. He and Martha not only got their first aid and CPR certifications, they went back to college to earn their EMT certifications. They served motorcyclists for over 20 years.

The Rescue 3 team arrives early to each race event and sets up a command post near the pit area where they coordinate with B.L.M. and the Med-Event Ambulance Service. With powerful communications equipment, they put 3-4 vehicles out on the courses and call in for ground or air support as needed. They

Hare and Hound motorcycle in air, 1958.

Chuck and Martha Rader.

haul in broken bikes and broken riders, provide first aid and search and rescue as needed.

Rescue 3 is a non-profit organization which has provided first aid to generations of District 37 members. Founded in 1966, this team of individuals attends approximately thirty or more District 37 events each year. When out on the course look for their red shirts and smiling faces. The group is not large but they are enthusiastic about their work.

Frenchy Jensen and Chuck Rader.

First 4th of July Celebration

by Pat Judkins, Leader Correspondent

Over the years Independence Day has been observed in Lucerne Valley in various ways. Regardless of the heat, which has often been well over 100 degrees on the July 4th holiday, the time honored tradition has prevailed here.

One story we enjoy hearing repeatedly, and one that is detailed in Gobar's *Raising the Dust*, is the account of the celebration Lucerne Valley pioneers enjoyed in 1912.

On July 4, 1912, the population of this community, then known simply as the Box S, was approximately 105 residents. Box S folks were preparing for their first Fourth of July celebration, and it was so successful that those attending a meeting held at the home of Lucerne Valley's first postmaster Rosa Koehly on July 21 agreed to hold these festivities annually. They also agreed to not always hold them during that hot summer month; some years they would celebrate in the fall.

First Lucerne Valley Day Celebration, 1914 vintage, under trees at the old Box S Ranch. Photo from Lucerne Valley Phone Book.

In 1912 the Gobar family had the only car in the valley; a California Tourist. It was needed for a trip to Victor (now Victorville) on July 3 to pick up ice for the celebration. On the morning of the third of July, Harold and Junie Gobar left early to pick up Mr. Goulding. En route they learned the car would run only in low gear, so they took it to the blacksmith shop at Box S, removed the body and realigned the clutch. By that time it was noon and Goulding invited them to eat.

After "dinner" Harold and Goulding headed for Victor, and that was the last anyone here saw of them for three days. Normally, in Gobar's "Tourist" the 22 mile jaunt to Victor would have been made in two hours. However, they soon learned the car still would not go into high gear. Upon finally reaching Victor, they took the car apart and shipped the transmission to Junie Gobar's father, Frank Gobar, in Fullerton.

A 300 pound block of ice had been shipped by express from Colton to the J.C. Turner Grocery Store in Victor. The original plans called for Harold Gobar and "Dad" Goulding to load the ice, on a very hot day, and take it back to Box S within two hours. Under the circumstances, they were lucky to find two valley homesteaders, Howd and Gamby, picking up supplies in Victor. The two young men were from Los Angeles, and were homesteading an area adjacent to what would later be known as the Russell tract. They had a team of four burros hitched to a light wagon, and decided to leave at dark to take the ice home. They, and the ice, arrived back at the Box S at 4a.m. with plenty of time for the patriotic festivities, and the ice was of sufficient amount for ice cream and lemonade.

The entry in Junie Gobar's diary that day summed up this first July 4 at Box S thus:

'We played croquet, horseshoes and entered into all the meet events. The men swam in the nude in the reservoir back near the alfalfa field. We froze ice cream, ate roast turkey, fried chicken, pie, cake, cookies, jam, sandwiches, cherries, peaches, various salads and drank lemonade. After the swim we ate more ice cream till that was gone; then we froze more."

If that seems like a lot of good food to be had in 1912, remember that the Gouldings were then milking thirteen cows. They made all the butter used at the ranch, and they often made cheese. They furnished all the eggs, cream, and milk for the ice cream, which was frozen in six-quart freezers that folks brought to Box S. Then, the women opened up the washtubs and picnic baskets and there was more food than could be eaten.

Harold and Goulding missed out on a lot of Box S fun, but Goulding knew everybody on the high desert and was made welcome wherever he went. They joined in the Victor celebration until the car was back together again and they could return home.

At the July 21st meeting at Koehly's, the subject of the next July 4th celebration was the first item on the agenda.

This meeting prompted another one a week later; held at Goulding's Box S Ranch. Here the Lucerne Valley Improvement Organization was formed. But, that's another story.

Now only a lone chimney stands near Highway 18 and Highland, as an almost ghostly symbol of yesterdays' July Fourth and other Box S festivities. This charred chimney may be the only physical monument to our past, but the Box S legacy will live on in present and future Independence Day celebrations.

Early Off-Road Club

John Hawkins, marked with an "X", early ancestor of the Barnett, Veale, Rader clan. Back then (early 1900s) in the desert with only cow trails for travel, every vehicle was considered an off road vehicle.

Photo courtesy of the Veale Family Trust.

King of the Hammers

(Contributing to this article were Wikipedia, Chuck Shaner of the Victor Valley 4 Wheelers, Jeff La-Grange, and Kathryn Anema). Compiled by Bill Lembright. Photos courtesy of Bill Lembright.

Years ago the Bureau of Land Management asked off-road clubs if the open public lands in Johnson Valley could become a viable public off-road destination. In 1986 several club members from Victor Valley 4-Wheelers scouted the area and said, that with permission to create 4x4 trails, it would be a good proving ground for racers, a great challenge for 4x4 jeep clubs, and a good place for campers and rock hound enthusiasts to enjoy.

They met in work parties to concentrate on challenging courses. In 1992 the Victor Valley 4 Wheelers, whose president was then

KOH Car in first place approaching the finish line. B 8-10

Jeff LaGrange of Lucerne Valley, began constructing a set of challenging world-class off-road trails between Means Dry Lake, the Hartwell Hills, and Emerson Dry Lake. Using over 1100 volunteer hours and heavy equipment, they created their first rock crawler challenge and named it Sledgehammer. In the years that followed, they created Wrecking Ball, Outer Limits, Aftershock, Jackhammer, Back Door, and Chocolate Thunder.

In 2007 Jeff Knoll and Dave Cole, designed the now world famous *King of the Hammers* race on the back of a napkin. Their dream began by inviting 12 desert racing teams to a non-spectator chal-

Sledge Hammer. B 8-11

lenge race which incorporated the trails constructed by the Victor Valley 4 Wheelers. The racers were so enthusiastic that in 2008 the first official King of the Hammers race was held, to which were invited approximately 50 drivers. The start of the race originated at Means Dry Lake and car starts were staggered at 30 second intervals. Cars raced for 50-60 miles across open desert and then navigated through the various rock crawling challenges.

Jumbotron at Hammertown. B 8-10

The race was a resounding success and has been open to the public since. Now tens of thousands of spectators descend upon Means Dry Lake for nine days at the beginning of February, centered at a huge gathering of structures and RVs named Hammertown. For nine days more than 400 teams and more than 40,000 spectators gather. On different days there are races for dirt bikes, quads, UTVs, any 4WD vehicle, and main Ultra4 vehicle race on the last Friday of the event.

Crowds gather to watch the race. B 8-10

Crowd at Chocolate Thunder. B 8-11

Hammertown, 2017. B 8-10

Rodeos

Compiled by Millie Rader. Photo courtesy of Lucerne Valley Museum Association.

Jim Spain astride Brahma bull.

Lucerne Valley Days started in 1914 is still going today (1950). It is smaller now with so many other things to distract, the community does not seem to need to gather as it once did. The 1950 event had a 43 page program to list all of its many sponsors. James Goulding was the president emeritus and still handled the publicity. Ed K. Smith was the president who wrote his thoughts at the end of the program:

"Dear God – it's been a success once more.
Valley people have come by the score.
The helpers I needed to put it across
Gave all they had, even though I was boss.
The neighboring towns gave their ads with a grin,
And made a lot possible, we couldn't begin.
It's such cooperation that make us all blest,
For progress is bound to result from the test.
We thank everyone, their part large or small,
Who helped in any sort of way at all.
We thank those who came from far or near
To help us celebrate our 32 year.
But mostly, after these happy hours,
We thank Thee God for this Valley of ours.
Thanks a million everyone!"
-Ed K. Smith

Bill Barnett riding a bull at Box X Frontier Days 1950. Photo from Lucerne Valley Phone Book.

The photo below was clipped from the October 26, 1970 *Daily Press* newspaper with the following caption: Believe it or not, this is called recreation, entertainment and fun as well as an exciting challenge to the rodeo cowboys. Scenes like this were frequent during the International Rodeo Association's Lucerne Valley rodeo over the weekend. Thrills and spills abounded, much to the delight of the crowds congregated at the old Box S Ranch. Events calmed down during the Saturday evening dance as couples enjoyed the music of the Sundowners band. All in all, Wells Fargo Days in Lucerne Valley proved a success and the organizers plan to make it an annual affair.

This is fun!

Dancing

Ewings Ballroom, Bobby Delperdang.

This is a clipping from an old *Lucerne Valley Leader* newspaper with following caption: Master Bobby Delperdang and partner Miss Pat McCall, "tripping the light fantastic" at the weekly Saturday night dance in the Desert Dome Ballroom, sponsored by the Lucerne Valley Joshua Riders. Circa early 1950s.

Photo courtesy of Lucerne Valley Leader Newspaper.

Fishing

The February 2, 1978 *Lucerne Valley Leader* newspaper ran this picture. The caption read: Good Fishing – Anglers on Rabbit Dry Lake bring in a catch of rainbow trout. Left to right are Les Stanfield, David Nyberg, Janice Shelton, Daniela Wells, and Patty Wells. Leader of the fishing expedition was Allen Stanfield.

According to the article, Allen Stanfield fulfilled a boyhood dream when

Photo courtesy of Lucerne Valley Leader Newspaper.

he took his church youth group fishing for rainbow trout on Rabbit Dry Lake just west of Lucerne Valley.

The time was right; as recent rains had filled the normally dry lake bed. Armed with boat, oars and fishing poles the group shoved off. Strange enough, the fish they caught were already cleaned and ready for the frying pan. This might have something to do with the fact they had been purchased earlier in the day from Safeway.

The spoof paid off later when several people, with campers, were seen casting their line in the "wet" dry lake. They were less successful, probably because they didn't know to bring their own fish.

A few days later Allen's wife, Roberta, a kindergarten teacher at Lucerne Valley Elementary was eating at the Country Kitchen and noticed a special on "Rainbow Trout caught daily on the dry lake."

CHAPTER 9

Let's Go To Church

Compiled by Millie Rader

Assembly of God

Reverend Bill Oliver had just come home from Bolivia with his wife, Peggy, and their sons Billy and Victor, where they planted churches and ran an orphanage for nine years, when they were asked by the Big Bear Assembly of God Church to help plant a church in Lucerne Valley. The Olivers began holding church services in their home with five others on July 1, 1979. The congregation soon outgrew their home and they approached the local Seventh Day Adventist Church members for use of their building on Sundays. After meeting in that church building for two years, the congregation purchased land on Crystal Creek Road to build a church large enough to accommodate the growing membership.

Oliver Family while still in Bolivia, 1974. Photo courtesy of Peggy Oliver.

Church building. Photo courtesy of Millie Rader. A 9-1

The church broke ground at its current location on Crystal Creek Road in 1981, and held the first service in 1983, with the entire Seventh Day Adventist Church membership in attendance for support. After 35 years of service, the Olivers retired on May 26, 2013, due to Bill's poor health. Pastor Oliver passed away September 10, 2014. In September 2013, the Lucerne Valley Assembly of God Church became a satellite campus of the Victorville Assembly of God, and the church membership voted to hire Pastor Kevin Bryant as their full-time pastor in February, 2014.

Calvary Bible Church

December 6, 1942 Calvary Bible Church began with the name United Methodist Church of Lucerne Valley. The Sparks, Millers, Conrads and Hettick families met in homes until December 27, 1942, when they began meeting in the Ewing's Desert Dome Ballroom. Two years later the church started a building fund with $6.30. On July 3, 1944, the members were able to purchase, from Vern Chutes, two 50x200 foot lots on Highway 18, just west of what is now Crossroads Chapel for $200.

Original building. Photo courtesy of Grapevine J.S. Gobar Foundation. A 9-2

In May 1944, the congregation dropped the word Methodist from their name and formally became known as the United Church of Lucerne Valley with an elected board of four trustees. Their first church building was completed in May, 1945. The 20x24 foot building is still intact at the time of this writing. Pastor Sloan is seen standing in the doorway holding his youngest daughter. The young lady in the white hat is Barbara (Barnett) Veale who began attending that church at age 3, and was a member of the church until her passing in 2016.

United Church. Photo courtesy of the Sloan Family. A 9-2

In the beginning, Reverend Arthur J. Armstrong drove out from Victorville every other Sunday to minister to the church from 1942 to 1947, followed by Hubert Stewart along with several student volunteers from Biola. In July 1955, the church called and ordained its first full-time minister, Pastor Russell Sloan. He is pictured here with his wife; Dorothy, and children, Mark, Marilyn, and Marjorie. Pastor Sloan helped bring the church to its present location on Crystal Creek Road. Pastor Sloan was followed by Pastor Kenneth Chadbourn and his wife, Maxine (1965-1969), Pastor David Ivins and his wife, Sharon (1969-2005), Pastor Stephen Colangelo and his wife, Beth (2006-2007), Pastor Jim Reinebach and his wife, Anita (2008-2011), and the present Pastor James Souza Jr. and his wife, Marsha, who were called to the church March 29, 2014.

Sloan Family 1958. Photo courtesy of the Sloan Family.

Calvary Bible building dedication. Photo courtesy of the Sloan Family. A 9-2

This church purchased the five-acre lot on Crystal Creek Road November 4, 1956, and broke ground for the current sanctuary in March, 1960. Dedication services were held in the newly constructed building on April 29, 1962. The congregation voted to change the church name to Calvary Bible Church in April, 1959.

Local artist Verdun LaChance created this drawing of the new church building to decorate the front of the dedication day program. LaChance was a resident of Lucerne Valley for over 25 years and contributed artwork to various community organizations.

Church building drawing, Verdun LaChance. Photo courtesy of Coleen (LaChance) Trocke.

Fellowship Hall construction. Photo courtesy of the Sloan Family.

Four years later, the church was growing and in need of a Fellowship Hall and more classrooms. On December 2, 1966, the church minutes reflect a motion to accept a loan of $8,000 from Bank of America to build the Fellowship Hall. The interest rate was 7.5% with payments of $94.97 per month. The church dedicated the new building addition on May 3, 1968. Four more classrooms were added in the 1990s.

The Hetticks were one of four families present at the first meeting of this church. Donna (Hettick) Chandler is pictured here with her sister Carol (Hettick) Shields and mother Edna Hettick in front of the new church building in March, 1963. Donna was four years old when she attended that first church meeting and continues to be an active member of this congregation today.

Donna (Hettick) Chandler, sister and mother. Photo courtesy of the Sloan Family.

Ivins welcome, 1969. Photo courtesy of the Sloan Family.

Pastor longevity seems to be a trait of the early churches of Lucerne Valley. Reverend David Ivins was called to the church in October, 1969, and served the church for 36 years until he retired in April, 2005. He is pictured here with his wife, Sharon, and their daughters, Debbie and Mary, at the welcome party given by the church to celebrate their arrival. Son Joel was born later.

Church of Christ

A *Lucerne Valley Leader* newspaper article stated that the Church of Christ met for the first time in the Nolan home on Highway 18 near Strawberry Peak on March 16, 1958. A later article tells of a new church building completed in March, 1978. The caption beneath the picture here stated that Don Berset, Joe Morello and O.D. Walker put the finishing touches on the sign of the completed Church of Christ in Lucerne Valley. The building still stands on Foothill Road between Mesa and Tradepost Roads; Albert Carlyle is the last known pastor.

Church of Christ, new building, March 1978. Photo courtesy of Lucerne Valley Leader Newspaper. B 9-3

Church of the Latter Day Saints

The Church of Jesus Christ of Latter Day Saints in Lucerne Valley became a dependent Branch of the Victorville Ward of the Church in February, 1953 with the building fund being started in May. In November that same year, the church purchased five acres of land on Post Office Road. Groundbreaking ceremonies were held on December 4, 1965. Pictured here is Sterling Johnson, president of the Mojave Stake of the "Mormon" church with the golden shovel. With him are Kaarman McBride, William Bartlett, Andrew Gneck, President of the Lucerne Valley Chamber of Commerce, Bob McDougall, San Bernardino County Supervisor; Ross Dana, John Lester, Al Washburn, and Paul Smith.

Church of Jesus Christ of Latter Day Saints groundbreaking. Photo courtesy of Lucerne Valley Leader Newspaper.

The building was built in two phases with the first phase pictured here. The first phase consisted of a temporary chapel which was planned to eventually be the Junior Sunday School quarters. This room had accordion pull-outs to form four rooms and consisted of several classrooms, kitchen, restrooms, offices, and baptismal font. The foundation was poured January, 1966 with cement donated by Kaiser and Southwest Portland Cement. The first services were held Sunday July 16, 1967.

Church of Jesus Christ of Latter Day Saints. Photo courtesy of Lucerne Valley Leader Newspaper. B 9-4

Crossroads Chapel Foursquare Church

The only recorded history for the Crossroads Chapel Foursquare Church was found in the archives of the *Lucerne Valley Leader* newspaper. This early picture of the church was in the December 20, 1956 edition with the title, "Where to worship this Christmas." The announcement also included pictures of the United Church, the First Baptist Church, and the Seventh Day Adventist Church.

First building. Photo courtesy of Leader Newspaper.

A 1975 newspaper photo shows the Four-square Church building as remembered by the longest standing members of that congregation today. It is not known if the building pictured in 1956 is the same one pictured here, or if the buildings are completely different. In a 1970 article the church added new services: a Tuesday night Bible study, and a Family Night on Thursday along with a Sunday evening Youth Service under the direction of Mr. and Mrs. Howard Hunt. In 1975 there was a notice of a new group called the Foursquare Crusaders being formed for ages 14-35 and all

Second building. Photo courtesy of the Leader. A 9-5

young people were invited to attend. An Easter Sunrise service was held at the "Green" house on the corner of Barstow and Old Woman Springs Roads in 1977.

Current building. Photo courtesy of Millie Rader. A 9-6

In 2000, the congregation of the First Baptist Church disbanded and offered its building to the Crossroads Chapel Foursquare Church congregation for $1.00. The Foursquare Church accepted this offer and moved its congregation less than a mile down the street to the larger campus it occupies today.

Schlenz Family. Photo courtesy of Ruth McLoy.

Pastor Gary Schlenz was appointed to replace Pastor Ron Fraker at Crossroads Chapel Foursquare Church in 1991. Pastor Schlenz, his wife, Linda, and their children, Christy and Nathanial moved to Lucerne Valley and continue to minister in that church. At the time, the church moved onto the bigger campus, expanded with two Sunday morning services: Women's Bible Study and a Youth Center in what was previously the church parsonage. Other pastors on record for this church are Pastor Kruse, Pastor W.A. Russell, Pastor Lyman Hewitt, Interim Pastor Esther Fry, Pastor Schizler, and Pastor Dan Simpson.

First Baptist Church

First Baptist Church in 1956. Photo courtesy of L. V. Museum Assoc. A 9-6

The First Baptist Church is the first church found in the recorded history of Lucerne Valley. Though the congregation no longer exists, before disbanding, the membership donated the church building located on Highway 18, just west of Highland Road, to Crossroads Chapel Foursquare Church. The building is still in use today. This is a picture of that church building taken in 1956.

First building smoldering. Photo courtesy of L. V. Museum Assoc. A 9-6

Sometime after 1939 when the Lucerne Valley School District was formed and the three early schools had combined, the students were all attending the Midway School. At this time the early Baptist Church membership purchased the original Lucerne Valley School building and property across from James Goulding's Box S Ranch. In November 1953 the congregation paid off their mortgage and remodeled the old school building. Less than three weeks after the remodel was completed, the building was destroyed by fire. This picture was taken shortly after the flames were extinguished; smoke can still be seen rising from the ashes, and a volunteer firefighter stands in the doorway with a hose over his shoulder.

This church was originally called Lucerne Valley Community Church, but was renamed First Baptist Church in 1951 when it formed an association with the Southern California Baptist Convention. After losing the building to fire, the congregation rallied their resources and

New church building groundbreaking. Photo courtesy of Lucerne Valley Museum Association.

broke ground for a new building in the spring, 1954. "Dad" Goulding is at the far left in this photo taken at the groundbreaking.

This new, modern building was completed and dedicated in December, 1955. During the dedication service, Reverend Charles Coon stated that "the church had come a long, long way since the first offering of $1.12 was collected in 1938 in a borrowed hat, by the twelve people meeting under the trees at the Clark Ranch." The new church seated 330 people with a sliding wall that could be opened to accommodate 220 more.

First Baptist Church interior, at dedication. Photo courtesy of Allen Stanfield.

According to the October 24, 1963 *Lucerne Valley Leader* newspaper, Charles Barnett, son of Bill and Lena Barnett, accepted an assignment as the Assistant Pastor of the First Baptist Church. He assisted Head Pastor Dr. Irvin E. Cole in church work and with the youth. Barnett who had been with the church since moving to the valley with his

parents in 1942, had been working in leadership with the church youth since his early teens. In recognition of his service to the church, the congregation voted to accept responsibility for his college education. He was attending California Baptist College at that time. He married his sweetheart Patricia Rutledge in the church on June 25, 1966. Barnett worked as the assistant pastor in Lucerne Valley until he was called to a full-time pastor position at Menifee Baptist Church in 1968. He served again at the Lucerne Valley Church as an interim pastor from 1979 to 1981. Photo courtesy of *Lucerne Valley Leader* Newspaper.

Lucerne Valley Community Church

A group of 35 people headed up by Reverend Charles Coons met in the home of Cecil Miller on October 31, 1965, to create a non-denomina-

Commnity Church. Photo courtesy of Lucerne Valley Leader Newspaper. A 9-7

tional, international church. One year later they had 100 members, had performed three marriage ceremonies and four funeral services. The congregation was meeting at Midway Park. This was the start of what is now the very active and growing Lucerne Valley Community Church.

Community Banquet. Photo courtesy of Lucerne Valley Leader Newspaper.

In January 1969 with Pastor Dr. Robert "Bob" Shuler, the church held a community banquet in the old Grange Hall, what is now the Lucerne Valley Community Center. Those gathered had come to see the building and construction plans of what would soon be their new church building on Ladera Road, just east of Pioneer Park. This dinner united local contractors who pledged their support for the project.

The church plans called for a 3,558 square foot structure that would include a sanctuary, vestibule and three classrooms. January 15, 1970, church moderator, and construction supervisor, Al Ludlow, announced to the *Lucerne Valley Leader*

Church walls rise. Photo courtesy of Lucerne Valley Leader Newspaper.

newspaper that more than a score of skilled craftsmen turned out to build and raise the wall sections of the church that Saturday morning. With all local builders pitching in, the crew must have set a speed record. Four walls, complete with studding, joists and window frames were up and secured by 3:30 p.m.

Trusses added. Photo courtesy of Lucerne Valley Leader Newspaper.

January 29, 1970, roof trusses were hoisted on ceiling joists by the expert crew of Phil Pederson, Joe Vugrinec, and Bob Delperdang Jr. On the ground were Ray Chamberlin, Bob Kumley, Art Bristol, Reverend Bob Shuler, Arlie Beam and Joe Reyes, while Jon Carter operated the crane.

On Father's Day, June 20, 1971, the church held the first service within its new walls. Pastor Shuler gave tribute to Al Ludlow, church moderator and "Guiding Light," in the construction of the church. To open the services, Dick Grobaty, accompanied by Dori Harbert on piano, used his fine tenor voice to the singing of "Bless this House." In 1989 the church constructed a Fellowship Hall, and is currently planning another building expansion.

First Service. Photo courtesy of Lucerne Valley Leader.

Pastor Richard Wood and his wife, Gloria have served the church since 1982, dedicating many years to the community of Lucerne Valley. This picture, taken in 1987, includes their boys Gabriel, Gilbert, Timothy and baby Richie.

Wood Family, Photo courtesy of Lucerne Valley Community Church.

Art Bristol, groundbreaking. Photo courtesy of Lucerne Valley Community Church.

Art Bristol, who passed in 2017, was a member of the church when the services were still being held at Midway Park. He and his late wife, Alice, were always active members. Art is seen here breaking ground for the addition of the Fellowship Hall. He was a valued member of Lucerne Valley Community Church.

The distinctive cross and rock work that grace the west side of the sanctuary today, was added in April, 1977 by local stonemason and church member Hank Adams in memory of his late wife, Helen Adams. Helen was a long time church member and church pianist.

Helen Adams Memorial. Photo courtesy of Lucerne Valley Community Church. A 9-7

Church of the Living Word

Kenneth and Esther Fry founded the Church of the Living Word in their home in 1985. The couple replaced their furniture with benches and lived on their porch for a year to provide a meeting place for a congregation of 85 people. In 1986 they purchased a mobile home just off Highway 247, east of Moss's Mobile Manor to use as their church building.

Esther provided the preaching and Kenneth handled the administration for Church of the Living Word until he passed

Esther and Ken Fry. Photo courtesy of Esther Fry.

away in 2000. Esther continued to hold services for a year, but soon found that it was more than she could handle on her own and had to close the doors. Pastor Fry said they were privileged, in those 16 years, to see many people set free to live productive and healthy lives.

Church Building. Photo courtesy of Esther Fry. A 9-8

Jehovah Witness Kingdom Hall. Photo courtesy of Lucerne Valley Leader Newspaper. B 9-9

Kingdom Hall of Jehovah's Witnesses

Jehovah's Witnesses Kingdom Hall is located on Highway 247 (Barstow Road) just south of Rabbit Springs Road. It was originally the Federated Women's Clubhouse located on land formerly owned by James Goulding. The congregation renovated the building by taking down all but one wall and rebuilding the rest. First open house was held on Saturday, November 30, 1974. According to Donna Bytheway, on June 1, 2018 the Lucerne Valley Jehovah's Witness congregation merged with the Cheyenna Kingdom Hall in Apple Valley, but have kept Lucerne Valley as their "Missionary Territory." Pictured here are three congregation elders, Joe Meade, Joe Chaney and Robert Littleton.

Old Paths Assembly

Allen Stanfield was the associate pastor of The First Baptist Church of Lucerne Valley in 1991 when he was realized that the church should be keeping the Saturday Sabbath. He was the senior pastor in 1999 when the church voted to become Sabbath Keepers. In 2000 the congregation realized their building and property on Highway 18 was too large for their needs and sold it to Crossroads Chapel Foursquare Church for $1.00. The congregation then moved into the Lucerne Valley Christian School building on Laramie Road, just east of Mesa Road, renaming themselves, Old Paths Assembly.

Stanfields Beside Old Path Sign. Photo courtesy of Valerie (Stanfield) Rice.

According to Allen's daughter, Valerie Rice, Old Paths Assembly is a Torah pursuant group of Messainic Israelites, searching for the lost sheep of the whole house of Israel. According to President of the Board, Bill English, they study the whole Bible cover to cover. Allen was the shepherd of this church for many years, but he and his late wife, Roberta, stepped down in 2013 and now he enjoys raising many different kinds of farm animals on their small ranch in Lucerne Valley. Current Pastor is David Gipson.

Seventh Day Adventist Church

According to Dennis Medici, his grandfather Leslie Friend built the Seventh Day Adventist Church building in 1948. It is still in use today. The *Lucerne Valley Leader* announced the new officers for 1956 as Pastor Clarence Schram, the Elders were Doyle Dyer, and Woody Cowart, and the deacons were Wayne Stringer, Vernon Rowe and Walter Richards. Deaconesses included Lillian Wheeler, Florence Voris and Stella Favors. Other officers were Rebecca Dyer, treasurer/receptionist, Rachel Morse and Mrs. W. Richards are listed as assistant secretaries, and Esther Holler as pianist. Eddie Stringer and Lonnie Cowart were listed as young people's missionaries.

Photo courtesy of Lucerne Valley Leader. A 9-11

Seventh Day Adventist School. Photo courtesy of Lucerne Valley Leader Newspaper.

The church hosted a K-8th grade school from about 1951 to 1957. Several students who attended the Seventh Day Adventist School still live in the valley today. According to long-time local business owner, Carol (Richards) LaCroix, there were 13 students in attendance when she and her family moved here in 1955. The students pictured here in May 1956 are: James Rowe, Merle Morse, Chuckie Medici, Alise Schram, Bonnie Rowe, Penny Medici, Hal Curtis, along with teacher Myrtle Gallion, and youth director Harry Garlick.

St. Paul's Catholic Church

The Catholic Church in Lucerne Valley began as a mission church. Services were held in the Women's Clubhouse on Barstow Road, where the Jehovah's Witnesses Kingdom Hall was for many years after. On October 9, 1960, Father Joseph Brennan, assistant at St. Joan of Arc Parish in Victorville, California, ministered to the spiritual needs of the 114 parishioners who attended the first mass.

Social Hall. Photo courtesy of Pat Lugo. B 9-12

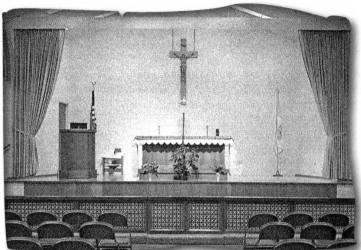

Church interior. Photo courtesy of Pat Lugo.

On Easter Sunday, April, 1963 the Catholic Church was officially named St. Paul's Parish. Father Patrick J. Scanlon announced the name and explained that it is customary in every country to have Catholic Churches of higher standing, such as cathedrals, named after the great apostle St. Paul. The Lucerne Valley Catholic Church was the first one in the vast San Diego Diocese to be named St Paul's. He remarked that the Bishop must have great expectations for this church.

April 11, 1965, Monsignor Van Garsse blessed the ground and Father Patrick Scanlon conducted groundbreaking ceremonies at the Mesa Road Church site that would soon house a social hall. The 50 by 125 foot hall was designed to be used for both church services and youth recreation; it included a basketball court, and seating for 700. Frank Rial donated the five acres of land for the hall. Jonathon Carter built the social hall using local subcontractors. Mc-Dougall Well Drilling installed the water pipes. The first service was held November 21, 1965.

Groundbreaking. Photo courtesy of Lucerne Valley Leader Newspaper.

Weiser Hall. Photo courtesy of Lucerne Valley Leader Newspaper. B 9-12

The Most Reverend Leo T. Maher, Bishop of the Diocese of San Diego, administered the sacrament of Confirmation at St Paul's Catholic Church on March 1, 1973. It was followed by the groundbreaking ceremonies for the new smaller sanctuary called Weiser Hall, to be constructed just north of the Social Hall. The first services were held March 18, 1974 in the new sanctuary that seated 120 people. In less than 20 years the congregation outgrew Weiser Hall and the Social Hall was remodeled in 1990, dividing it in two sections with one half serving as the recreation hall and the other half once again in use as the Sanctuary.

CHAPTER 10

Last Thoughts

Desert Treasure

by Millie Rader, January 5, 2018

The old saying "All that glitters is not gold," tends to get reversed here in the desert in that "All that is gold may not always glitter." Most desert dwellers are not interested in monetary riches. We live here for treasures that are far greater than money can buy.

Treasure hunting for some of us, is the hunt for history or historical places and people. In late 2013, a small group of Lucerne Valley residents met to discuss the possibility of compiling a history book about this valley. Chuck Rader, Chuck Bell and myself originally began working with a small publishing company that puts out small picture books on the history of rural towns. But we soon realized that the book we were compiling would be much bigger than originally envisioned. We then brought in more people with experience in both local history and in writing and publishing; Bill and Jan Lembright and myself did the bulk of the present day writing, Gary Lister brought in publishing experience, Cyndie Granados helped with the early native information and Lorraine Cross was our main copyeditor from the start. Together this team decided to self-publish.

This has been quite a long process, and a bigger project than any of us ever anticipated. But as one of the writers, I was quite excited to see the end result. It has been a huge learning experience for all of us. We took a group of volunteers, some we knew, some we didn't and formed a team that worked together well. We also became good friends along the way. We experienced many ups and downs. Many times we thought we were almost done and then either realized we had left out a big chunk of history, or somebody would bring us information that was too good to pass up. This required many more hours of research to fill in all of the missing facts.

When we first started to research for the book I read *Raising the Dust*, and *Range One East*, written 1969 and 1972 respectfully, by Virginia Hemphill-Gobar. Then I went to the Lucerne Valley Museum Association. They had all the copies of the first newspaper called *The Desert Grapevine*, also written and published by Virginia Hemphill-Gobar and her first husband, William Hemphill, in the years 1946-1952. These early newspapers are full of colorful descriptions of the people, places and events that made up the early town, but the photos having been taken on early film and reproduced on a home printing press were grainy at best. So I went looking further and thanks to the editor of the *Lucerne Valley Leader* newspaper, I was given access to the Leader archives 1955-1972. I stopped at 1972 because our first publisher did not want any history past that date.

Thankfully the Leader has always been a weekly paper, usually not having more than 8 pages per issue. I went through 17 years' worth, meaning I flipped through the pages of 884 week's worth of papers.

Fun, interesting and time-consuming are all words to describe that journey. As I would find a picture or article that I thought we might use, I scanned and saved it to my computer. I then went through the Lucerne Valley Museum files and photographed any material I thought might be helpful. I also ended up with four file boxes and a shelf full of material donated by local residents to help us in our research. These I have donated to our Museum.

We also interviewed many of the old-timers who were still with us. Some of those interviewed have since passed on and we are grateful for the information they willingly shared with us before heading off to greener pastures.

I want to share here just one fact finding treasure hunt that illustrates one of my exciting moments while working on this book. Early on, I went online and plugged our town name into the search engine and a couple of stories popped up from an old publication titled *Desert Magazine*, published by Randall Henderson and Wilson McKenny, 1937-1960.

In the October 1965 issue of the *Desert Magazine*, they ran a story written by Charles Allen called the *Eggheaded Caveman*. He described himself as a college professor who bought five acres from the US Government for $270.00, to get away now and then from students, colleagues and family and to read non-academic books and think non-academic thoughts.

What caught my eye in this story was that he said that on his way out to his cave he would stop in the small village of Lucerne Valley for a few groceries and ice. Then he would drive the final 10 miles to his cave. Once there he would unload a few necessities from his car like a cot, sleeping bag, water and food and spend 2-3 days a month enjoying the solitude of the desert.

After reading the story, I was pretty sure I could find the Egghead Cave. I pulled up Google Earth and using old "Charlie's" description of what he saw around him, I pinpointed all of the small granite outcroppings around a volcanic butte that might be big enough to contain the Egghead Cave. My husband printed up the picture he had provided of his cave.

Charlie's description contained these clues: Southern base of a dark butte, granite run, a finger of fracturing stone, 600 feet long, 50 feet wide, five to 30 feet high. Rough and tumbled, with crevices and recesses, sunny and shady nooks, wind-breaks and wind-blows. Cave itself is not large, about 15 square feet, high enough to stand in, towards the front. The entrance is sheltered from the prevailing wind.

He said that he parked among several flat-topped boulders. He then carted his supplies "up" to the den. He said his grotto entrance faces south toward San Bernardino Range. In the foreground dry washes twist toward the small dry lake bed a mile and a half to two miles below. He looked down on the Blackhawk Landslide. He was four miles from Old Woman Springs. A larger dry lake lay about three miles to the east, the Rodman Mountains were to the east, to the north, the Ord Mountains, the highway was three miles to the south.

It was 2014, a cloudy New Year's day, my husband and I loaded the Jeep and headed east on Highway 247 until we lined up south of what we thought could be his dark butte. We started driving through the desert with me holding up the picture as we drew near to each granite outcropping. We then came upon a road headed directly toward the dark butte. We drove another quarter mile and were within about 100 yards of the butte when I held my picture up to a pile of rocks just east of us and cried out in victory. The pile matched my picture exactly and we drove across the soft sand until we reached the flat topped boulders. We parked on them were the Eggheaded Caveman did all those years ago. We then jumped from the jeep to examine our treasure. We walked to the left a bit and found the correct angle for a perfect

Eggheaded Caveman

match to the picture, and then up we climbed and into the cave entrance. It was more of a hollow than a cave, but big enough to serve the professor's needs of shelter from sun and wind. We could see where he must have put his cot and also the cool area where he described storing his food and water. Then we sat for awhile and looked out the entrance to the view he had enjoyed each morning when he awoke.

We then hiked through the creosote over to the butte, an old dorment volcano, and climbed to the top finding his description of the view to be completely accurate, it was "magnificent."

Later as we pulled away from our treasure, we wondered about old Charlie. Was he still alive? If not, does his family still own the land and do they appreciate it and the cave as much as he did?

I hope that those of you reading this book will do some exploring of your own. Go find the Egghead Cave, or the old guzzlers provided by past cattle ranchers. The only thing we ask is that you honor the memories of those who put their blood, sweat and tears into this land. Enjoy, and then leave these historical places as you find them.

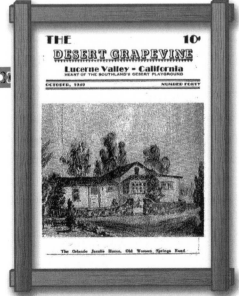

Millie Rader

This book, *Lucerne Valley, A Wild West Town of Character(s)*, has truly been a hard labor of love. I really did not understand what I was getting myself into when I told a group of very active community leaders that I would take on this project. I think my desire as a writer, to actually publish a book, and my pride caused me to say yes before I had even had a chance to think about it, much less go home and ask my husband, David, what he thought. I certainly did not ask God if this was something that He wanted me to do or if it even had any relevance in His big picture. I did not ask for His help until a week later when I realized how deep I had gotten myself.

Thankfully God already knew that I was going to leap without looking, but He let me thrash around on my own for two years until I was ready to humble myself and ask others for help. Immediately after I publicly asked for help at a Lucerne Valley Economic Development Association meeting, God provided that help in the form of a team of people with the various skills to get this job done.

I am so thankful for Cyndie Granados who has connections with local Native Americans to help gather info on our earliest citizens, Chuck Bell who has many contacts and intimate knowledge of the early ranches in the area and he hooked us up with Gary Lister a man who worked in the publishing industry for many years and provided direction. Lorraine Cross also jumped on board and has since been the first to read and copy-edit each story with Barbara (Rusty) LaGrange and Donna Bytheway doing a second and third proofing. Debbie Schultz came on board late in the process but just in time to put her graphic artist skills into play by pulling all of our words and pictures into an actual book format. But Bill and Jan Lembright were the first to jump when I cried "help!" They came alongside me to share the job of researching and writing the bulk of the stories. With their daily contact of Lucerne Valley residents at the Lucerne Valley Market, they were able to corral and coerce many of the old-timers into sharing their stories. These two are my fellow writers and supporters without whom this book would not have made it into print. Along with this "team" were the trusted few that I have known all of my life, longtime residents who had many of the answers when none could be found in written accounts. Allen Stanfield, Sam Clark, and my amazing Mother-in-Law, Martha Rader, who are still with us in 2020 and have been such a help. My Father-in-Law, Chuck Rader, and my mother, Barbara Veale, who both passed before we were able to complete this book, and they too were always ready early on to search their memories when a question arose.

I also have personal reasons for wanting to bring this book to print. My family has lived in this valley since 1942 producing five generations of Lucerne Valleyites. I come from a long line of active community members, interested in the well-being of this little town and its inhabitants. One was the first principals of the Lucerne Valley School District-my Great Aunt Alice Barnett; my Grandfather Bill Barnett who operated the heavy equipment that created the roads of the Gem-Tract where I live today. Many in my family were involved in local mining-my dad and mom, both grandfathers, my uncles, my great uncle, my father-in-law and my husband. They were all involved in the local churches, LVEDA-my mom and father-in-law, Girl Scouts-Mom, and the Joshua Riders-my grandparents Bill and Lena Barnett. They sat on the Chamber board, and the MAC board and pretty much had their fingers in most of the local action. I want the fifth generation of my family to follow in their ancestors footsteps and not just take what this valley has to offer, but to give back in return for the many blessings this town has provided.

But this book is more than a family history. It is the history of a little town with many interesting and colorful characters who gladly shared their time and diverse talents to make this community what it is today.

I am thankful for the historians that came before us and shared in writing their memories and the memories of others. I also thank God that He allowed me to grow up and raise my children in a place where people still care about each other, this town of characters; Lucerne Valley, California.

TRUCKS OUST HORSES ON DESERT
MOTOR TO AID DEVELOPING VALLEY

Moreland Truck Loaded For Twenty-seven Mile Runs Across the Mojave

LUCERNE VALLEY TRANSFER CO.

THE GOLDBRANDSEN COLLECTION

Jan Lembright

Doing this book has been a learning process and many people have graciously allowed me to interview them, asking many questions, and ask them to repeat so I can get the details correct.

I borrowed research from my friend and desert historian, Carolyn Clark who would be proud to be a part of this book. Many thanks to the book committee: Chuck Bell, Cyndi Granados, Gary Lister, Lorraine Cross, Debbie Schultz, Millie Rader, Bill Lembright. Many thanks to Lorraine Cross for her hours of editing; she did so much to help us.

When Millie asked at a LVEDA (Lucerne Valley Economic Development) meeting for volunteers she looked at Bill and me, I shook my head no, since I knew nothing about writing. I must have had that deer in the head lights' look and Millie said "You can do it, I know you can." Thanks to Millie for putting many hours into this book, it was a pleasure working with her.

Thanks to Carol Tevis for all the information she gave me on her father, Ray Bonin, Postmaster in 1966. Thanks to Greg Carpenter, Gene Hedly and Kathryn Anema for information on the Miller Ranch. Lynn Dee Hilton wrote out her family story on Cushenbury Ranch many years ago when Bill and I were working with Bill Mann on his book of Lucerne Valley. She gave me a lot on insight I never knew about the area and our history. Lynn will never know how much she helped me, as she passed away a few years ago. I know she wouldn't mind, she loved this desert and appreciated all the pioneers who went before us. Thanks to Joni (Mortez) Ross for her contribution to Old Woman Springs Ranch, and Don Stuart for his input on his grandmother, Frances Hanken. Robert Penn was a delight to interview; he too loved this valley and the people who influenced him. He is now 80 years old and still loves this desert. He no longer lives here but he fondly spoke of those he grew up with and had an influence in his life. The Donaldson family story, written by Sally Emerson gives us a peek into her pioneer family and how life was when they were growing up here in Lucerne Valley.

Sam Clark has given us invaluable information and he has been a pleasure to work with, also giving us an interview on his own family history. Talented artist Evelyn Carpenter was informative and helpful, and is still painting. Bob Halleck was also helpful. His father, George, was quite a character. Cliff Reed gave his family history and his sister, Linda, backed up what he told me , put in her own two cents worth, she said she didn't know anything, but then went on to tell me lots. Allen Stanfield was also a pleasure to interview; he was very helpful giving a look into his past and the influence his family had on this community. Lee Risler was one of the first people I interviewed; he showed me a lot of pictures and spent quite a lot of time with me. Last but not least, thanks to Bob & Gert McDougall for their patience and all the time they took with me. It was a pleasure listening to them both for hours. Most of all, my deepest thanks to God for his help, and for all his guidance to help us accomplish this task.

Bill Lembright

As a teenager I had lofty goals of meeting agricultural needs of the world by conquering diseases such as Verticillium Wilt which cripple food crops and cotton production. My goal was to help the poor, become famous, and become wealthy. Then God got my attention and said my life would either be dedicated to service for HIM or to self service. I opted for HIS service.

Yucca ring preserve southeast of Anderson Dry Lake. Photo courtesy of Bill Lembright.

A group of us built and operate Lucerne Valley Market and Hardware as the mission outpost to which we believe God has assigned us. This mission involves providing grocery, health, general merchandise, hardware supplies at affordable prices. It also has been heavy with the need to provide political and spiritual assistance.

Politically, Lucerne Valley is in danger of being transformed into an industrial renewable energy wasteland, overrun with huge cannabis farms and drug labs, or a solid waste dumping ground for large cities down the hill. Many San Bernardino County reps seem more concerned with pleasing outside special interests than they are with protecting us county residents against the collateral damage that results from those outside interests. The Market and Hardware is heavily involved in these fights.

Spiritually, we are involved in helping distraught neighbors whose lives have been adversely affected by the corruption of the modern culture in which we live. We sit outside the fold of modern churchy Christianity and try to carry out God's marching orders for us with the guidance and assistance of His Holy Spirit. It's a challenging life which I do not wish to trade for another.

BUT, what has that got to do with helping write this book on the history of Lucerne Valley? If I said I was positive that God wanted us to invest so many hours in something this discretionary, I would be lying. The answer probably lies somewhere between it being a good idea, to letting myself get sucked into it, to hopefully God approves of the effort and it is just one of many varied projects He has assigned us. If He is NOT pleased with this investment of time, I hope he will forgive us.

For those hoping to preserve the history and lessons of the past, this book can serve as a reminder of the challenges overcome by our predecessors and hopefully a reminder of missteps to avoid in our future. At the same time it can serve as a call to commitment to preserve the hard work put into making Lucerne Valley the desirable home that it has become for us current residents.

It has been 47 years since the last comprehensive history of Lucerne Valley was written by Virginia Hemphill-Gobar in the two books *Raising the Dust* and *Range One East*. Please save all the additional history and photos you can. Maybe in another 50 years someone will update where we have left off. Good luck with that!

King Clone east of Bessemer Mine Rd - Oldest living organism in Lucerne Valley. Photo courtesy of Bill Lembright.

INDEX

Just one more story that you won't see in the first Edition!

The Homestead Shack at Willow Wells Road

Written by Pam Turner and Millie Rader

Like "Love for your native land," I've said.
Or "Stars and Stripes waving overhead."
Or "love of dear ones," or "Daily Bread,"
Is the family's love for this old homestead.
-Pamela Turner 1972

Willow Well

There is a road on Highway 18, just west of Rabbit Dry Lake bed called Willow Wells. I must admit that though I have noticed this road many times over a lifetime of driving to "town," I have never given the name a thought until recently when my friend David Turner shared the history of his family and the actual Willow Well. This old homestead and the shack built shortly after World War One has witnessed some interesting early pioneer struggles in its lifetime.

David's late mother Pam was one of Lucerne Valley's early historians, and the first to compile the complete history of our Lucerne Valley Schools. You will find the results of her extensive school research located in chapter four of this book, and most of the information found within this story is also due to her family research on the old homesteaded property where she and her husband Bill raised their two children.

It was 1973 when she wrote to her father-in-law Al Turner, who lived in Oregon, to pick his memory of the homestead and the little shack located there. She preserved his original letter and the photos he sent in a photo album that David kindly shared with me, asking that it eventually be turned over to the Lucerne Valley Museum for safekeeping.

Al's memories jumped around a bit so I will summarize them here. He tells that his acquisition of the homestead was neither planned nor chronologically linear, but we will get to that in a bit. His information on the early history of the homestead came from many different sources, the land office told him that this particular area of the desert had been surveyed before the turn of the century, but many of those stakes were then removed and they suspected local cattlemen who would not have been keen on sharing that prime grazing land with sodbusters. He also mentions friendships with early pioneers Julian Gobar and James (Dad) Goulding who provided details on the previous owners. He was told that sometime after 1912, a man named Doherty filed on the land and built the original portion of the shack. Doherty then married James Goulding's daughter Manilla (Nellie) Goulding. But the couple only lived in the little shack for one month before he took off and never returned. Al said that nobody ever heard from him again. We know from other historical documents that Nellie lived most of her adult life in the little house across from her father's Box S ranch. This house still stands near the corner of Highland Road and Highway 18, so we surmise that she chose to let the homestead go rather than try to prove it up on her own.

Back then before a homestead grant could be obtained the homesteader had to live on the land for a certain amount of time, clear it and plant it with government provided seed to see if it would produce.

Al went on to write that after WWI, an army officer who had been gassed in France, put in a claim for the homestead with his sister and moved to the desert in hopes that the dry air would help him to recover. They were the ones who added the lean-to on the north side of the shack to park their car in. They also had a man named Cherry drill the well that would later come to be known as Willow Well. This well used a pitcher pump to raise the water to the surface. Unfortunately, the officer never recovered and after his death, his sister sold the homestead to Al's friend Albert Boden.

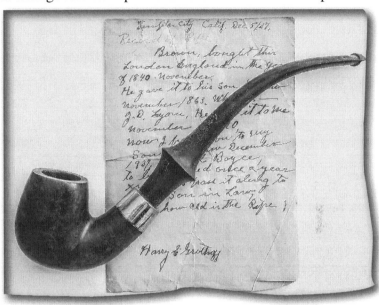

Harry E. Grothoff family outing.

Sometime after that Albert's wife needed an expensive surgery and Al Turner then purchased the homestead in November 1922 for $500 to help his friend. He realized in hindsight that he really should not have made that purchase as he did not have the time or money to prove up the homestead. When his year to start work on it was about up and he was going to lose it, he put a for sale ad in the LA Examiner, and his father-in-law Harry Grothoff (Gramp) saw it and told him he would take it over. Al then signed it over to his father-in-law. This is the non-linear part.

Gramps then lived in the old shack and worked the homestead for seven months out of each year for three years. The grant was then made out to Mr. Harry E. Grothoff. It was signed by the President of the United States, Calvin Coolidge. That original grant is included in the well-preserved artifacts collected by Pam Turner.

The property eventually ended back up in Al Turner's possession, and he then sold it to his son Bill who married local gal Pam Pinard. They built a home and raised their two children David and Sharon within a hundred yards of that old homestead shack and well. Though David moved away once he was grown, he remembers as a kid being very grateful to his Grandfather and Great Grandfather for providing him the opportunity to grow up in this amazing valley.

A few more tidbits included in Al's writing were the fact that Mr. Hitchcock, a well-known historical cattleman, came to Gramp in September 1926, just before Gramp came home from serving his last 7 months. Hitchcock asked him if there was enough water in the well to water the cattle he had just brought them down from the mountain for the winter. Gramp did

Dad Goulding, Goulding's 2nd wife, Mary, Harry E. Grothoff (with pipe) and his wife. July 4, 1927, probably at Box S Ranch.

not know so Mr. Hitchcock said he would have a well man sand-pump it. He had Julian (Junie) Gobar come check the well. The sand he brought up in the bailer was nearly white, which must have been a good thing because in October 1926 ,Hitchcock mailed Gramp a lease to sign, and he put up the windmill and tank. The windmill frame and the water tank are still in place, and according to David, this original well served the Turner family until the 1970s when they drilled a new well west of their house. He said that the water was at 35 feet, and the well was only 50 feet deep. David also shared that when he was growing up the old well had four willow trees growing around it, which would account for the name.

Another interesting piece of this story came from David's best-friend, Bob Riddle. In 2018 after both of David's parents had passed, Bob helped David prepare the old homestead for sale, David gave him an old pipe with a handwritten note signed by David's great-grandfather Harry. It said:
"Temple City Calif. Dec 5/37, Record of Pipe. John Brown bought this in London England in the year of 1840, November. He gave it to his son-in-law November 1863. Who was – J.D. Lyon. He gave it to me November 1890. Now I pass it on to my son-in-law December 1937, Merrill Boyce, to be smoked once a year xmas. So, pass it along to your son-in-law. Now, how old is the pipe? (signed) Harry E. Grothoff."

David also sent many well-preserved pictures with captions on the back. In one we find James (Dad) Goulding and his second wife Mary, then Harry Grothoff and wife, (no name given), the caption also says "Probably at Box S Ranch July 4, 1927." In the photo you see a pipe in Harry's hand and using a magnifying glass we find it looks very much like the pipe given to Bob Riddle. That pipe and letter, pictured here, are also slated to end up in the Lucerne Valley Museum.
(Debbie, please insert picture of Harry with pipe here.)

We appreciate David taking the time to find and share this Lucerne Valley history with those who are sure to come later.

Just four more photos that you won't see in the first Edition!

Old Miners Burro Races, 1963, from Apple Valley to Big Bear. This photo was taken in the dry lake between Apple Valley and Lucerne Valley.

Mr. & Mrs. Tegelberg and their son Gil in their Cactus Garden on Camprock Rd. in 1963. Look for more info in the Tegelberg story on page 139.

August, 1956, Claire Huck's Homestead Cabin, which is part of the Homestead story on page 62.

Claire's Homestead Cabin 1968.

Made in the USA
Monee, IL
20 June 2021